Sarbanes-Oxley

FOR

DUMMIES®

2ND EDITION

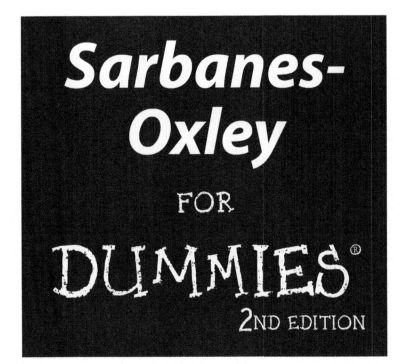

Sarbanes-Oxley

FOR

DUMMIES®

2ND EDITION

by Jill Gilbert Welytok, JD, CPA

WILEY

Wiley Publishing, Inc.

Sarbanes-Oxley For Dummies®, 2nd Edition
Published by
Wiley Publishing, Inc.
111 River St.
Hoboken, NJ 07030-5774
www.wiley.com

Copyright © 2008 by Wiley Publishing, Inc., Indianapolis, Indiana

Published by Wiley Publishing, Inc., Indianapolis, Indiana

Published simultaneously in Canada

For general information on our other products and services, please contact our Customer Care Department within the U.S. at 877-762-2974, outside the U.S. at 317-572-3993, or fax 317-572-4002.

For technical support, please visit www.wiley.com/techsupport.

Wiley also publishes its books in a variety of electronic formats. Some content that appears in print may not be available in electronic books.

Library of Congress Control Number: 2008920765

ISBN: 978-0-470-22313-0

10 9 8 7 6 5 4 3

WILEY

About the Author

Jill Gilbert Welytok, JD, CPA, LLM, practices in the areas of corporate, non-profit law, and intellectual property. She is the founder of Absolute Technology Law Group, LLC (www.abtechlaw.com). She went to law school at DePaul University in Chicago, where she was on the Law Review, and she picked up a Masters Degree in Computer Science from Marquette University in Wisconsin, where she now lives. Ms. Welytok also has an LLM in Taxation from DePaul. She was formerly a tax consultant with the predecessor firm to Ernst & Young. She frequently speaks on nonprofit, corporate governance, and taxation issues and will probably come speak to your company or organization if you invite her. You may e-mail her with questions you have about Sarbanes-Oxley or anything else in this book at jwelytok@abtechlaw.com. You can find updates to this book and ongoing information about SOX developments at the author's Web site, located at www.abtechlaw.com.

Dedication

To Dan.

Author's Acknowledgments

Several exceptional professionals (whom I call The SOX SWAT Team) contributed their time and expertise reviewing and making technical edits to this book. Feel free to e-mail or call them with questions you may have about Sarbanes-Oxley that weren't answered in this book.

Amy R. Seibel. Amy is an attorney and a CPA with Absolute Technology Law Group, LLC. Amy is an AV- rated attorney (highest rating available for lawyers) with more than 25 years of experience in legal, business, tax, and financial matters. She has practical experience as well, having previously served as CEO/CFO for two separate manufacturing businesses. More recently, she assisted several large public companies in the documentation, testing, and remediation phases of their SOX internal controls compliance initiatives. She also served as a technical editor for *Nonprofit Law & Governance For Dummies*. She is past president of the Association for Women Lawyers and past chairman of the Wisconsin and Milwaukee Bar Association Tax Sections.

Richard Kranitz, JD — Kranitz & Philipp. Rich has been an attorney in private practice since 1970, emphasizing securities, banking, and business law. He has served as venture capital consultant to, and director of, various private companies and a number of professional, civic, and charitable organizations.

Ronald Kral, CPA, CMA — Candela Solutions, LLC. Ron knows auditing and consulting well, having assisted more than 200 clients as a Principal Consultant at PricewaterhouseCoopers and Managing Director of a statewide CPA firm, where he worked extensively with Ernst & Young. Ron is a nationally recognized speaker on governance, business ethics, internal controls, and the Sarbanes-Oxley Act of 2002, including the COSO and COBIT frameworks, NYSE and NASDAQ requirements, PCAOB standards, and SEC regulations. Ron is also a Director of Financial Executives International's Milwaukee Chapter. He can be reached at rkral@candelasolutions.com.

Anna Klement. Anna has completed coursework in computer engineering at the Milwaukee School of Engineering and also has a journalism degree from the University of Wisconsin-Milwaukee. Anna also has three years of experience as an IBM applications developer at a major Milwaukee-based food manufacturing firm, along with various freelance projects including Web and graphic design and technology consulting.

Daniel S. Welytok, JD, LLM — Whyte Hirschboeck Dudek S.C. Dan is a partner in the business practice group of Whyte Hirschboeck Dudek S.C., where he concentrates in the areas of taxation and business law. Dan advises clients on strategic planning, federal and state tax issues, transactional matters, and employee benefits. He represents clients before the IRS and state taxing authorities concerning audits, tax controversies, and offers in compromise. He has served in various leadership roles in the American Bar Association and as Great Lakes Area liaison with the IRS. He can be reached at dsw@whdlaw.com.

Publisher's Acknowledgments

We're proud of this book; please send us your comments through our Dummies online registration form located at www.dummies.com/register/.

Some of the people who helped bring this book to market include the following:

Acquisitions, Editorial, and Media Development

Project Editor: Natalie Faye Harris

(Previous Edition: Tim Gallan)

Acquisitions Editor: Lindsay Lefevere

(Previous Edition: Kathy Cox)

Copy Editor: Jessica Smith

(Previous Edition: Elizabeth Rea)

Editorial Program Coordinator: Erin Calligan Mooney

Technical Editor: Amy Seibel

Editorial Manager: Christine Beck

Editorial Assistants: Leeann Harney, David Lutton, Joe Niesen

Cartoons: Rich Tennant (www.the5thwave.com)

Composition Services

Project Coordinator: Kristie Rees

Layout and Graphics: Stacie Brooks, Alissa D. Ellet, Melissa K. Jester, Christine Williams

Proofreaders: John Greenough, Todd Lothery, Toni Settle

Indexer: WordCo Indexing Services

Publishing and Editorial for Consumer Dummies

Diane Graves Steele, Vice President and Publisher, Consumer Dummies

Joyce Pepple, Acquisitions Director, Consumer Dummies

Kristin A. Cocks, Product Development Director, Consumer Dummies

Michael Spring, Vice President and Publisher, Travel

Kelly Regan, Editorial Director, Travel

Publishing for Technology Dummies

Andy Cummings, Vice President and Publisher, Dummies Technology/General User

Composition Services

Gerry Fahey, Vice President of Production Services

Debbie Stailey, Director of Composition Services

Contents at a Glance

Table of Contents

Introduction

*W*elcome to *Sarbanes-Oxley For Dummies,* 2nd Edition. Whether you're a CEO or CFO, governance officer, CPA, manager, entrepreneur, file clerk, or cleric, this book is for you. It's designed to tell you where you fit into the grand scheme of corporate compliance and why you're being asked to do what you do by your board of directors, banker, customers, and clients.

Having the big picture straight in your mind helps ensure that you won't lose track of the minutiae and details that accompany the sweeping piece of legislation that is Sarbanes-Oxley, whether you're gearing up for initial compliance or attempting to streamline in subsequent years. If you're part of a private company or not-for-profit, I offer special congratulations to you. After all, you're savvy enough to know that Sarbanes-Oxley is here to stay and that it's becoming the gold standard for fair, ethical, and efficient business practices (whether you're obligated to comply or not).

About This Book

The Sarbanes-Oxley Act, or SOX as it's affectionately called in the world of corporate governance, is a responsive piece of legislation. Like the securities laws passed in the 1930s, SOX was passed in response to a real crisis and to genuine public outrage. It sailed through Congress on a wave of bipartisan support surprisingly free of lobbying and loophole legislating. Instead, Congress left the details to the Securities and Exchange Commission (SEC) and the newly created Public Company Accounting Oversight Board (PCAOB). This book walks you through SOX's rather piecemeal rules and pronouncements and gives you a sense of how to anticipate future trends and traps in this area of the law.

The goal of *Sarbanes-Oxley For Dummies,* 2nd Edition, is to give you a helicopter view of the regulatory terrain while helping you focus a beam on the key details of the legislation. This book is intended to give you a sophisticated understanding of the purpose and structure of the legislation as it affects many disciplines and areas of the law. This book is sure to empower you with the level of insight you need for practical, cost-effective decision-making. It will assist you with the following:

✔ **Understanding why SOX was passed:** Looking at the kind of conduct SOX was intended to combat can help you create meaningful standards for the company with which you work or are affiliated.

- ✓ **Instituting cost-effective compliance with SOX:** This book's practical view of the legislation can keep you from becoming bogged down in regulatory details and allowing lawyers and accountants to go off on expensive tangents that have little to do with the essence of SOX.

- ✓ **Finding answers on specific SOX issues:** This book explains how and where to find SEC rules and pronouncements that are critical to implementation of SOX and translates those rules into plain English.

- ✓ **Avoiding lawsuits and regulatory actions:** This book, although not intended to be a substitute for a good securities lawyer or a CPA, takes a hard look at who gets sued under SOX and how you can avoid having your company or yourself added to the list of litigants.

- ✓ **Anticipating future rules and trends:** SEC rules and PCAOB pronouncements under SOX continue to be issued with regularity. But with a comprehensive understanding of what the law is designed to do, you'll be less surprised by what's ultimately issued.

Conventions Used in This Book

It's unfortunate, but understanding SOX means that you're going to run into lots of legal jargon and accounting minutiae. To give you a jump start, I define some legal and accounting terms in this book and use *italic* font to make such terms stand out a bit. I also use **boldfaced** words to highlight key words in bulleted lists and numbered steps. `Monofont` indicates Web addresses, which I refer to often.

When this book was printed, some Web addresses may have needed to break across two lines of text. If that happened, rest assured that we haven't put in any extra characters (such as hyphens) to indicate the break. So, when using one of these Web addresses, just type in exactly what you see in this book, pretending as if the line break doesn't exist.

What You're Not to Read

I occasionally wander off-topic to discuss something historical, technical, or interesting (or, at least, interesting to me!). In these instances, I set the discussions apart by placing them in sidebars, which are the gray boxes you'll see from time to time throughout the book. Because the text in sidebars is nonessential, feel free to skip it if it doesn't interest you.

Foolish Assumptions

When writing this book, I had to make a few assumptions about who my readers would be and what kind of information they'd be looking for. This section explains those assumptions. For example, I assume you want to understand the Sarbanes-Oxley Act in a way you can't achieve by suffering through the 80-some pages of the statute and 1,000 or so pages of related congressional hearings. You want to make sure you have a handle on the important aspects of the legislation, how it affects you and your company, and how companies can comply most cost-effectively.

Additionally, if you're a service provider such as a lawyer or CPA, I assume that you're looking for insight into the following tasks — insights you would glean from the legal and accounting professionals involved in writing this book (whose credentials and accomplishments are listed on the acknowledgments page):

- Recognizing and creating a legally effective, fully compliant corporate governance framework

- Determining what aspects of SOX apply to your company or should be voluntarily adopted by your company (whether it's publicly traded, privately held, or not-for-profit)

- Managing and streamlining Section 404 compliance as well as seizing opportunities and benefiting from information resulting from the unprecedented testing and documentation of business processes all across the United States

- Interpreting media accounts, court cases, and economic projections involving SOX

How This Book Is Organized

Sarbanes-Oxley is an extremely broad piece of legislation, spanning legal, accounting, and information technology disciplines, so this book is chock-full of information. But not to worry: The index and table of contents will help you find your way. The chapters in this book treat each topic independently without assuming you've read previous chapters (as a textbook might), so you can use them as references and jump around to find what you need. This book is divided into six parts, which I explain in the following sections.

Part I: The Scene Before and After SOX

This part of the book starts at the beginning, explaining why SOX was passed and taking you on a tabloid tour of the corporate scandals that inspired it — Enron, WorldCom, Adelphia, Global Crossing, and more. These chapters shock you with tales of greed and manipulation and walk you section-by-section through the legislation, explaining what each provision is intended to accomplish.

Part II: SOX in the City: Meeting New Standards

The chapters in this part spell out who's affected by which provisions. You find out why the accounting profession is no longer self-regulating, and you're introduced to the new audit ambience that SOX provides. You also get a good look at what SOX means for management, including what's expected of boards and the committees formed under their direction.

Part III: Scaling Down Section 404

SOX Section 404 is a big enough deal to warrant its own part in this book. These chapters take you by the hand and guide you through the dreaded Section 404 audit process. They tell you how to manage a Section 404 project and when and how to cut compliance costs without cutting corners.

Part IV: SOX for Techies

This part is all about software. It explains how software can help you comply with SOX and what to look for when investing in information technology to carry out SOX objectives. These chapters show you some of the more cost-effective products on the market and suggest particularly useful systems for small to mid-size companies.

Part V: To SOX-finity and Beyond

This part looks at the future of SOX and corporate governance. These chapters take you into the courtroom to see who's getting sued under SOX and what the outcomes are. This part also looks at what SOX means for outsourced services and service providers and explains when special SAS 70 reports are required (as well as when they aren't).

Part VI: The Part of Tens

The chapters in this part provide the skinny on important subjects, including what every audit committee absolutely needs to undertake, how to avoid getting sued under SOX, and even how to save money with SOX. In essence, this part of the book is about taking control and proceeding confidently under SOX.

Part VII: Appendixes

The appendixes in the book contain useful reference materials and forms you can actually put to use in your company.

Icons Used in This Book

For Dummies books use little pictures, called icons, to flag parts of the text that stand out from the rest for one reason or another. Here's what the icons in this book mean:

Time is money. When you see this icon, your attention's being directed to a compliance shortcut or timesaving tip.

This icon signals the type of advice you may get in a lawyer's office if your company were paying the exorbitant going rates. Of course, the information highlighted by this icon is no substitute for sound legal advice from your own company attorney, who actually knows the facts of your individual situation.

This icon indicates that you're getting the kind of tip your audit or CPA firm might dispense. Of course, you should actually consult a real accounting professional before acting on anything that follows this icon.

This is a heads-up warning to help you avoid compliance mistakes, legal traps, and audit imbroglios.

This icon flags particularly noteworthy information — stuff you shouldn't forget.

Where to Go from Here

Because I wrote each chapter of this book as a stand-alone treatment of the topic covered, you can start with Chapter 1 and read the whole book, or you can skip around and brush up only on the topics that interest you at the moment. If you're new to SOX, I recommend you start with Part I. If you're hip to securities law in general and SOX in particular, skip ahead to the parts in the book that address your particular needs or concerns.

Feedback, Please

I'm always interested in your comments, suggestions, or questions, so I'd love to hear from you. Send me an e-mail message at `jwelytok@abtech law.com` or visit my Web site at `www.abtechlaw.com`. On that site, you'll find contact information for all the great legal and accounting professionals who helped with this book (I've included their credentials and accomplishments on the acknowledgments page).

Part I
The Scene Before and After SOX

The 5th Wave   By Rich Tennant

"I've got to work this weekend again. There are over 200 games of Torpedo Alley, Click Ball, and Blockbreaker that haven't been tested for Sarbanes—Oxley compliancy yet."

In this part . . .

The Sarbanes-Oxley Act, or SOX, didn't pop up out of nowhere. Rather, its passage is rooted in some steamy corporate scandals. This part examines how Congress responded to events surrounding Enron, Tyco, WorldCom, Global, TelLink, and Adelphia in a bipartisan whirlwind. This part also looks at how this far-reaching legislation affects existing securities legislation, what it says, what it certainly doesn't say, and how it has spawned some mighty media myths.

Chapter 1

The SOX Saga

*I*n response to a loss of confidence among American investors that was reminiscent of the Great Depression, President George W. Bush signed the Sarbanes-Oxley Act into law on July 30, 2002. SOX, as the law was quickly dubbed, is intended to ensure the reliability of publicly reported financial information and bolster confidence in U.S. capital markets. SOX contains expansive duties and penalties for corporate boards, executives, directors, auditors, attorneys, and securities analysts.

Although most of SOX's provisions are mandatory only for public companies that file a Form 10-K with the Securities and Exchange Commission (SEC), many private and nonprofit companies are facing market pressures to conform to the SOX standards as they become the norm. Privately held companies that fail to reasonably adopt SOX-type governance and internal control structures are facing increased difficulty in raising capital. They're also facing higher insurance premiums and a loss of status among potential customers, investors, and donors. They've even been threatened with greater civil liability. In the nonprofit world, the lack of SOX internal controls may be viewed as a violation by the directors of the business judgment rule.

July 30, 2007, marked the fifth anniversary of SOX, the law deemed to be the most significant piece of corporate legislation. Now look at the last few years. What was SOX supposed to accomplish? What did it actually accomplish? Who are the winners and losers in the SOX saga? In this chapter, I take a look at the political impetus for SOX and summarize some key provisions of the SOX statute in plain English. I also dispel a few common SOX myths.

Plowing Through the Politics of SOX

SOX passed through both houses of Congress on a wave of bipartisan political support not unlike that which accompanied the passage of the U.S. Patriot Act after the terrorist attacks of 2001. Public shock greased the wheels of the political process. Congress needed to respond decisively to the Enron media fallout, a lagging stock market, and looming reelections (see Chapter 2 for details). SOX passed in the Senate 99–0 and cleared the House with only three dissenting votes.

Because political support for SOX was overwhelming, the legislation wasn't thoroughly debated. Thus, many SOX provisions weren't painstakingly vetted and have since been questioned, delayed, or slated for modification.

For the past 70 years, U.S. securities laws have required regular reporting of results of a company's financial status and operations. SOX now focuses on the accuracy of what's reported and the reliability of the information-gathering processes. Because of SOX, companies must implement internal controls and processes that ensure the accuracy of reported results.

Prior to SOX, the Securities Act of 1933 was the dominant regulatory mechanism, and it remains in force today. The 1933 Act requires that investors receive relevant financial information on securities being offered for public sale, and it prohibits deceit, misrepresentations, and other fraud in the sale of securities.

The SEC enforces the 1933 Act requiring corporations to register stock and securities that they offer to the public. The registration forms contain financial statements and other disclosures to enable investors to make informed judgments when purchasing securities. (For more about the securities registration process, flip to Chapter 3.) The SEC requires that the information companies provide be accurate and certified by independent accountants.

SEC registration statements and prospectuses become public shortly after they're filed with the SEC. Statements filed by U.S. domestic companies are available on the EDGAR database accessible at www.sec.gov.

Taking advantage of a loophole

SOX provides that publicly traded corporations of all sizes must meet its requirements. However, not all securities offerings must be registered with the SEC. Some exemptions from the registration requirement include:

- Private offerings to a limited number of persons or institutions
- Offerings of limited size

- Intrastate offerings
- Securities of municipal, state, and federal governments

The SEC exempts these offerings to help smaller companies acquire capital more easily by lowering the cost of offering securities to the public. In contrast, SOX provides that publicly traded corporations of all sizes must meet certain specific requirements depending on the size of the corporation.

Not everyone's a SOX fan

In 2002, only three Congressmen opposed the 2002 passage of SOX: GOP Representatives Ron Paul of Texas, Jeff Flake of Arizona, and Mac Collins of Georgia. Congressman Flake observed:

> *Obviously there are businesses that were acting in a fraudulent manner. We still have that today, and there are laws on the books that thankfully are being used more aggressively today to get at these businesses. But when we react so quickly, sometimes without the best knowledge of how to do this, without some of these investigations taking their course, without these enforcement agencies giving us full recommendations, then we have unintended consequences.*

Five years after the passage of SOX, many businesses and politicians are echoing the sentiments of Congressman Flake. The greatest criticism has been the financial burden imposed on small companies. The SEC received so many complaints about the disproportionately high costs of compliance for smaller public companies that it convened an Advisory Committee on Smaller Public Companies to investigate them.

In response, the SEC has voted twice to extend the compliance deadline for Section 404 smaller public companies, called *non-accelerated filers,* (Section 404 is discussed in Chapter 12.) The SEC has continued to extend the compliance deadline primarily because it has acknowledged that the costs of compliance for smaller companies greatly exceeded estimates.

The ongoing date debate

The SEC first extended the deadline for small-cap companies by one year, voting in March 2005 to push the compliance date to July 2006. When this extension failed to stop the grumbling about costs and confusion regarding compliance, the SEC decided in September 2005 that small companies (defined as those with less than $75 million of stock in the hands of public investors) wouldn't be required to comply with the Section 404 requirements until their first fiscal year ending on or after July 15, 2007. Two more extensions followed.

In December 2006, most publicly traded companies got a very special Christmas gift. This gift came in the form of an extension for compliance with financial reporting requirements set by SOX for at least one more year. This deadline extension means that smaller public companies don't have to provide a dreaded auditors report until the time the financial reports are due for fiscal years ending December 17, 2007, or later. Because the financial reports usually aren't due until six months after the close of the fiscal year, this generally means that the companies affected are looking at 2008 compliance deadlines.

The SEC reports say that 7,402 smaller public companies make up 78.5 percent of the total number of public companies nationwide. This means that the majority of companies to which SOX applies have yet to ante up.

As this book is being written, the SEC is talking about granting yet another extension, because the agency isn't sure it has enough guidelines and rules in place to help companies comply. SEC officials have publicly stated that they're considering extending the deadlines again.

Examining the perceived woes of compliance

In addition to the burden on small business, SOX is criticized for the sheer confusion it has created. SOX requires accounting firms and companies to simultaneously monitor several evolving sets of interpretive standards from the SEC and the PCAOB. Early attempts to implement SOX have been accompanied by more resignations within regulatory agencies than shake-ups in corporate boardrooms. The PCAOB is on its third chairman in as many years, as discussed in Chapter 7, and turnover at the SEC has been equally eventful since SOX.

Regulatory confusion isn't the only culprit; many companies have contributed to their own SOX woes by simply failing to plan properly. The start-up costs of any initiative are always highest in the beginning; however, many companies simply panicked, hiring teams of expensive consultants and launching overlapping and ill-conceived projects to document their controls under SOX. This initial "spare-no-expense" approach may have helped some companies meet a deadline, but it also established the framework for new internal bureaucracy.

A final, broader criticism waged against SOX is its effect on the competitiveness of U.S. businesses. Many argue that SOX is a major distraction from the core activities of businesses, making them less viable in a global marketplace. In other words, management must spend more time jumping through regulatory hoops and less time innovating. According to other folks, SOX also makes it more difficult and costly for technologically innovative companies to raise capital by selling their stock on U.S. exchanges because of the increased regulatory burden. (See Chapter 3 for an explanation of securities registration requirements and stock exchanges.)

New ammunition for aggrieved investors

SOX gives public companies specific directives as to how financial information offered to the public must be compiled. However, it stops short of giving investors a right to sue companies privately for failing to meet these standards. Rather, with the exception of SOX Section 306 (dealing with stock trading during pension fund blackout periods), investors must wait for the SEC and Justice Department to bring actions against companies for SOX violations. In other words, investors can't hire their own lawyers to initiate action on their behalf.

Although there's no "private right" to sue directly under SOX, shareholders and litigants are in a much stronger position after SOX than under the old federal and state statutes. For instance, companies are facing increased exposure when they're defending lawsuits brought by shareholders under other securities laws. Many of these lawsuits involve evidence that's uncovered during the course of complying with SOX.

Prior to SOX, federal and state laws didn't establish specific standards for corporations in *compiling* the information they fed to the public in their financial reports. If investors were damaged or defrauded, the investors themselves were responsible for persuading judges that the information they had received wasn't truthful or accurate, without reference to any specific standards. In fact, aggrieved investors had only an amorphous body of analogous facts from prior court cases to try to convince courts to apply their specific situation. Now plaintiffs may strengthen their claims and arguments by referencing the standards set forth in SOX.

Corporate America after SOX

SOX defines specific duties for employees and board members and dictates the structure of boards of directors. It even tells corporations how they have to conduct their day-to-day operations to prevent theft and misappropriation, which requires them to maintain adequate internal controls. (I talk more about internal controls in Chapter 12.) SOX also elbows out state governments in their traditional roles of governing corporations, making corporate law in the United States much more federalized.

In late 2006 and early 2007, after a great deal of haggling, both the SEC and the Public Company Accounting Oversight Board, or PCAOB, issued all new rules for companies and auditors regarding reporting and auditing on internal control of financial reporting under Section 404. These new rules were a reaction to the financial burden that implementing SOX Section 404 placed on most of the nation's companies.

For example, the SEC issued special safe harbor rules to provide companies clearer guidance so they don't incur unnecessary costs by guessing under SOX. And the PCAOB has decided to replace its much-dreaded and criticized Auditing Standard No. 2, which detailed what audit firms had to do to comply with SOX, with a new standard, Auditing Standard No. 5 (see Appendix A for more on these standards). The PCAOB is collecting public comments on its proposed standard as this book is being written. In February 2007, the agency will start reviewing the comments and drafting the new standard.

Combating Corruption under SOX: Everyone Has a Role

SOX is a multidisciplinary piece of legislation that regulates several professions simultaneously. Board members, auditors, attorneys, management, small business owners, and even rank-and-file employees all have their own statutorily scripted roles to play. The following sections explain everyone's role, and the effects that those roles have.

Assisting with internal control: The independent audit board

One of the most significant reforms introduced by SOX is the requirement that corporations create audit committees made solely of *independent* directors. Board members are considered independent as long as they receive no salary or fees from the company other than for services as directors.

The audit committee is responsible for obtaining information from management that's relevant to the audit and otherwise assisting in the audit process. This committee is viewed as an important part of a company's internal control because it provides a company presence that's entirely independent from management and interfaces with the independent auditors (from an outside firm). For more coverage of the audit committee's responsibilities, check out Chapter 8.

Ironically, one firm that would have been able to comply with SOX's director independence requirements *before* the law was passed was Enron. Eighty-six percent of Enron's board was independent. A former dean of the Stanford Business School and professor of accounting chaired its audit committee. Yet when the scandal broke, the professor claimed he didn't understand the audit documentation.

SOX presumes that boards made of independent directors will look out for shareholders' interests and ask auditors to more carefully review management policies and decisions that can affect profitability. However, in the end, an independent audit committee isn't a panacea and doesn't guarantee objectivity in the audit process. The committee, the board, and the auditors all must rely on the accuracy of the information they get from management and regarding management to recognize, anticipate, and prevent problems.

SOX regulates the membership composition of boards but doesn't specifically regulate their behavior.

Testing the accounting data: Auditors

In the wake of Sarbanes-Oxley, many corporations have reported that they can't find a sufficient number of internal auditors. Prior to SOX, Arthur Andersen was not only the world's largest public accounting firm, but it was also the largest training ground for auditors of publicly traded companies.

Auditors are the traditional arbiters of accurate information within a company. They're the accountants responsible for testing the accounting data gathered from management and from rank-and-file employees. Auditors may be either internal employees of a company or independent auditors working for an outside firm.

Both internal and independent auditors adhere to Generally Accepted Accounting Principles (GAAP). GAAP is a term that refers to the rules established by the Financial Accounting Standards Board, the American Institute of Certified Public Accountants, and the SEC, which is the standard-setting body for publicly traded U.S. companies and the exchanges that list their stock. GAAP contains a number of provisions designed to ensure auditors' independence, objectivity, and professionalism. An auditor must certify that a company's financial statements are fairly presented in accordance with GAAP and contain no material irregularities that would adversely affect reported results.

Tainting the reputation of auditors

Traditionally, auditors have been viewed as pretty trustworthy people. The Enron scandal that led to the demise of the nation's largest independent auditing firm, Arthur Andersen, changed all that. Congress and the public were shocked that one of the world's largest corporations (Enron) could collapse within five months of receiving a clean opinion from its auditors at Arthur Andersen. (I talk more about the Enron and Arthur Andersen stories in Chapters 2 and 6.)

At the Enron trials, senior managers testified that the auditors never brought material issues to the managers' attention. The managers claimed that although they had ultimate responsibility for what was included in the financial statements with the SEC, they couldn't know what the auditors didn't tell them. It also came to light that the so-called independent auditors weren't so independent. In addition to providing audit services, they provided a myriad of highly lucrative consulting, tax, and other support services to Enron, which meant that the audit firm had tremendous financial incentives to stay on good terms with Enron instead of being vocal about the company's accounting flaws.

Enron wasn't the only scandal that tainted the audit industry. During the Savings and Loan (S&L) crisis of the 1980s, auditors failed to take into account the industry's shift from home loans to riskier real estate ventures and junk bonds. As a result, many S&Ls went bankrupt just months or even weeks after getting clean opinions from their auditors.

Eliminating self-regulation

To resolve problems associated with self-regulation (which had previously been the norm for the accounting profession), SOX creates the Public Company Accounting Oversight Board (PCAOB), a regulatory oversight board. This board is charged with the enormous responsibilities of setting ethics and conflict of interest standards as well as disciplining accountants and conducting annual reviews of large accounting firms. (For more on the PCAOB, turn to Chapter 7.)

Besides losing the right to regulate itself, the accounting profession can no longer market and compete for business in the same way either. SOX makes it unlawful for a registered audit firm to provide many types of nonaudit services to its clients that were formally its bread-and-butter. For example, an audit firm can't provide bookkeeping, financial information systems design, appraisal, evaluation, actuarial, or investment services to clients that it audits. (However, audit firms can make up some, if not all, of this lost income by performing internal control audits under Section 404 of SOX; see Chapter 12.)

According to a survey by the law firm Foley & Lardner, accounting, audit, and legal fees doubled under Sarbanes-Oxley. The costs of directors' liability insurance skyrocketed in the first year after the Act was passed. These costs have since leveled off, but experts agree that they will never drop to pre-SOX levels.

Using the new noisy liability: Lawyers

Incident to its authority to make rules under SOX, the SEC has proposed a controversial *noisy withdrawal* rule for attorneys. The rule would require a lawyer who learns of a corporate client's wrongdoing to alert SEC regulators to the nature of any ongoing fraud before withdrawing from representation. Attorneys who are unable to persuade a corporate client to mend its ways would be required to notify the SEC that they're withdrawing from representation. Not surprisingly, opponents have argued that the rule violates traditional concepts of attorney-client privilege. However, the American Bar Association has taken the position that noisy withdrawal doesn't violate the privilege.

Certifying financial reports: CEOs and CFOs

SOX forces corporate chief executive officers (CEOs) and chief financial officers (CFOs) to take responsibility and possibly face criminal penalties for earnings misstatements. They're required to certify in writing that the information appearing in the company's report is a fair and accurate representation of the company's financial status and activity.

Not only do criminal penalties apply if officers and directors misstate financial information, but these individuals also can be required to give back their bonuses to compensate the company for the costs of redoing the financial statements. (For more on the consequences that officers and directors face for misstatements, check out Chapter 2.) Under SOX, each member of management is expected to certify that he or she runs a clean ship — no excuses.

Staying clean voluntarily: Small businesses and nonprofits

Although SOX was passed to deal with mega-scandals like Enron and World-Com, it's becoming a catastrophe for American small business. As of this writing, although the wording of the SOX statute technically applies only to publicly traded corporations, it's the benchmark against which every privately held company's financial and corporate governance practices are measured.

For instance, banks and insurance companies report that they routinely ask small, privately held companies about their internal controls and audit procedures. Failure to answer convincingly can result in more costly credit or higher insurance premiums.

Nonprofits, which can't afford a hint of scandal that may ruin their credibility with donors, are rushing to adopt governance and conflict-of-interest policies in line with SOX. (See Chapter 19 for more on how SOX affects the nonprofit sector.)

Start-ups and new ventures are also facing increased hurdles as they attempt to "go public" by becoming eligible to list their stock on exchanges.

Adhering to procedures: The rank-and-file employees

SOX imposes new burdens on rank-and-file employees, often requiring them to adhere more carefully to company procedures or to complete additional documentation to carry out new internal control measures. However, SOX empowers blue-collar and other nonmanagerial employees in other ways:

- ✔ Section 301(4) requires publicly traded companies to collect, retain, and resolve complaints from employees.
- ✔ Section 806 specifically protects whistle-blowers who report violations of law or company policy from suffering retaliation by the company.

Overseeing corporate policy: New high-paid governance gurus

Nearly every public company has designated specific management or legal personnel who are responsible for overseeing the corporate governance policies that help them stay in line with SOX. A 2005 survey posted on Salary.com reported compensation for many top global ethics and compliance executives to be approaching $750,000.

A Summary of SOX: Taking It One Title at a Time

The SOX statute is more or less an outline, with full details coming in the form of SEC rules for implementation as well as pronouncements from the newly created PCAOB. Most of SOX's provisions currently apply to public companies that file Form 10-K with the SEC; however, more and more companies are opting for voluntary compliance to insulate themselves from future litigation risks and unforeseen management liabilities.

This section gives you a broad view of what the new law contains and what it requires of today's companies in the United States.

Title 1: Aiming at the audit profession

SOX establishes a five-member Public Company Accounting Oversight Board (PCAOB) that tells auditors what they're supposed to be evaluating and sets rules about the relationships and ties auditors can have with the companies they audit.

The SEC oversees the PCAOB, which is funded through fees collected from issuers. The PCAOB (affectionately nicknamed "Peek-a-boo" by many auditors, attorneys, and other professionals) has the following responsibilities:

- **To oversee the audit of public companies:** The accounting profession used to regulate itself through a voluntary organization known as the Association of Independent Certified Public Accountants (AICPA), but Enron proved that the old system didn't work very well.

- **To establish audit report standards and rules:** Auditors wait avidly for the issue of these standards and rules to clear up confusion and aid them in performing their day-to-day duties after SOX.

- **To register audit firms:** The PCAOB is in charge of registering, inspecting, investigating, and enforcing compliance of public accounting firms as well as CPAs and other people in the profession. Any public accounting firm that participates in any audit for a company covered by SOX is required to register with the PCAOB.

Title I of SOX also empowers the PCAOB to impose disciplinary or remedial sanctions on audit firms. Title I of SOX provides for change in several major areas:

- **Work paper retention:** Title I contains some new administrative requirements for auditors, including a rule that audit firms retain all their work papers for seven years.

- **Two-partner requirement:** Two partners now have to sign off on every audit.

- **Evaluation of internal control:** Auditors must evaluate whether the companies they audit have internal control structures and procedures that ensure that their financial records accurately reflect transactions and disposition of assets. Auditors must also assess whether the companies appropriately authorize receipts and expenditures and verify that transactions are made only with authorization of senior management. If companies don't have adequate internal controls in place, the auditors must describe any material weaknesses in the internal control structures and document instances of material noncompliance.

- **Inspections of audit firms:** Auditors must submit to continuing inspections by the PCAOB. Firms that provide audit reports for more than 100 public companies get inspected once a year. Firms that audit fewer than 100 companies get reviewed every three years.

Title II: Ensuring auditor independence

Title II of SOX focuses on conflicts of interests arising from close relationships between audit firms and the companies they audit; namely, it prohibits auditors from performing certain nonaudit services to clients they audit. However, SOX allows *audit committees* (internal committees charged with overseeing the audit process within publicly traded companies) to approve some nonaudit services that aren't expressly forbidden by Title II of SOX (see Chapter 8 for more on audit committees and nonaudit services). Title II also requires auditors to report to the audit committee on accounting policies used in the audit and document communications with management.

To further protect against conflicts of interest, audit partners must be rotated to prevent individuals from getting too close to the companies they audit. Specifically, a partner is prevented from being the lead or reviewing auditor for more than five consecutive years. An auditor faces a one-year prohibition if the company's senior executives were employed by that audit firm during the one-year period preceding the audit initiation date.

Title III: Requiring corporate accountability

Title III of SOX focuses on the company's responsibility to ensure that the financial statements it distributes to the public are correct. Its two main provisions include:

- **Establishment of audit committees:** SOX requires each company subject to SOX to form a special audit committee. Each member of the audit committee must be a member of the board of directors but otherwise *independent* in the sense that he or she receives no other salary or fees from the company. (See Chapter 8 for more on these committees.)

- **Management certification:** Title III requires CEOs and CFOs to certify:

  - That periodic financial reports filed with the SEC don't contain untrue statements or material omissions

  - That financial statements fairly present, in all material respects, the financial conditions and results of operations

  - That the company's CEOs and CFOs are responsible for internal controls, and that the internal controls are designed to ensure that management receives material information regarding the company and any consolidated subsidiaries

  - That internal controls have been reviewed within 90 days prior to the report

- Whether any significant changes have been made to the internal controls

Title III also makes it unlawful for corporate personnel to exert improper influence on an audit for the purpose of rendering financial statements materially misleading. For example, Title III does the following:

✔ It requires a company's CEO and CFO to forfeit certain bonuses and compensation received if the company has to issue corrected financial statements (called *restatements*) due to noncompliance with SEC rules.

✔ It bans directors and executive officers from trading their public company's stock during pension fund blackout periods.

✔ It obligates attorneys appearing before the SEC to report violations of securities laws and breaches of fiduciary duty by a public company.

✔ For the benefit of victims of securities violations, it creates a special disgorgement fund that's funded by the fines companies have to pay to the SEC.

Title IV: Establishing financial disclosures, loans, and ethics codes

Title IV contains several key SOX provisions, including the following:

✔ **Disclosure of adjustments and off–balance sheet transactions:** Financial reports filed with the SEC must reflect all material corrections to the financial statements made in the course of an audit. This title also requires disclosure of all material off–balance sheet transactions and relationships that may have a material effect on the financial status of an issue.

✔ **Prohibition of personal loans extended by a corporation to its executives:** Such loans are prohibited if they're subject to the insider lending restrictions of the Federal Reserve Act.

✔ **Disclosure of changes to inside stock ownership:** Senior management, directors, and principal stockholders have to disclose changes in their ownership of corporate stock within two business days of making the transaction.

✔ **Internal control certification:** The now-famous Section 404 provides that annual reports filed with the SEC must include an internal control report stating that management is responsible for the internal control structure and procedures for financial reporting. The report should also state that management assesses the effectiveness of the internal controls for the previous fiscal year.

✔ **Code of ethics:** Companies subject to SOX must disclose whether they have adopted a code of ethics for their senior financial officers and whether their audit committees have at least one member who's a financial expert. (For more on the financial expert requirement, flip to Chapter 8.)

✔ **Regular SEC review:** Article IV requires regular SEC reviews of the disclosure documents that companies file each year with the SEC.

Title V: Protecting analyst integrity

SOX Title V is aimed at preventing several types of conflicts of interest. Among other things, it does the following:

✔ Restricts the ability of investment bankers to preapprove research reports

✔ Ensures that research analysts aren't supervised by persons involved in investment banking activities

✔ Prohibits employer retaliation against analysts who write negative reports

✔ Requires specific conflict of interest disclosures by research analysts who make information available to the public

Title VI: Doling out more money and authority

Title VI authorizes the SEC to spend at least $98 million to hire at least 200 qualified professionals to oversee auditors and audit firms. It also gives the SEC the authority to

✔ Censure persons appearing or practicing before it for unethical or improper professional conduct.

✔ Consider orders of state securities commissions when deciding whether to limit the activities, functions, or operations of brokers or dealers.

Title VI also directs federal courts to prohibit persons from participating in small (penny) stock offerings if the SEC initiates proceedings against them.

Title VII: Supporting studies and reports

Title VII of SOX funds and authorizes a number of reports and studies that do the following:

✔ Look at factors leading to the consolidation of public accounting firms and its impact on capital formation and securities markets

✔ Address the role of credit-rating agencies in the securities markets

✔ Examine whether investment banks and financial advisors assisted public companies in earnings manipulation and obfuscation of financial conditions

Title VIII: Addressing criminal fraud and whistle-blower provisions

Here are the main points of SOX's Title VIII:

✔ It imposes criminal penalties (maximum 10 years in prison) for knowingly destroying, altering, concealing, or falsifying records with intent to obstruct or influence a federal investigation or bankruptcy matter.

✔ It imposes sanctions on auditors who fail to maintain for a five-year period all audit or review work papers pertaining to securities issuers.

✔ It makes certain debts incurred in violation of securities fraud laws nondischargeable in bankruptcy.

✔ It extends the statute of limitations for private individuals to sue for securities fraud violations. Individuals can sue no later than two years after the violation is discovered or five years after the date of the violation.

✔ It provides whistle-blower protection by prohibiting a publicly traded company from retaliating against an employee who assists in a fraud investigation; executives who target whistle-blowers are subject to fines or imprisonment of up to 25 years. (For more on the whistle-blower provision, check out Chapter 18.)

Title IX: Setting penalties for white-collar crime

Title IX increases penalties for mail and wire fraud from 5 to 20 years in prison and penalties for violations of the Employee Retirement Income Security Act of 1974 to up to $500,000 and 10 years in prison.

In particular, Title IX establishes criminal liability for corporate officers who fail to certify financial reports, including maximum imprisonment of 10 years for knowing that the periodic report doesn't comply with SOX and 20 years imprisonment for willfully certifying a statement known to be noncompliant.

Title X: Signing corporate tax returns

Title X of SOX expresses that a corporation's federal income tax return "should" be signed by its chief executive officer.

Title XI: Enforcing payment freezes, blacklists, and prison terms

Title XI adds to the criminal penalties aimed at fraud that are established by SOX's other sections. Here are some of the main parts of this title:

- ✔ This section amends federal criminal law to establish a maximum 20-year prison term for tampering with a record or otherwise impeding an official proceeding.

- ✔ It authorizes the SEC to seek a temporary injunction to freeze "extraordinary payments" to corporate management or employees under investigation for possible violations of securities law. Currently, there's no specific definition as to what constitutes an "extraordinary payment." However, Chapter 18 discusses some interesting litigation in this area (particularly the Gemstar case).

- ✔ It prohibits persons who violate state or federal laws governing manipulative, deceptive devices and fraudulent interstate transactions from serving as officers or directors of publicly traded corporations.

- ✔ Title XI increases penalties for violations of the Securities Exchange Act of 1934 to up to $25 million dollars and up to 20 years in prison.

Some Things SOX Doesn't Say: SOX Myths

Although SOX costs corporations billions of dollars and diverts massive resources from production and profit-generating activities, it's not all bad. In fact, there are things it doesn't require; this section puts to rest five common SOX myths.

Myth #1: SOX put Jeff Skilling (and other Enron execs) in jail

This myth is anything but true. SOX was passed as a *response* to the Enron and WorldCom scandals. Because SOX was created in response to these events, it came too late to try the people whose names became synonymous with these scandals.

Despite the fact that most corporate executives are still tried on the basis of statutes other than Sarbanes-Oxley, SOX has shown itself to be an effective tool for convicting corporate executives who steal shareholders' money. There have been more than 600 corporate crime convictions and more than $250 million in restitution ordered by courts under SOX.

Myth#2: Auditors can't provide tax services

SOX doesn't segregate to absurd extremes the services that accountants can provide to companies. In passing SOX, Congress recognized that in many cases it's practical and cost-efficient for audit firms to prepare tax returns. So even though SOX precludes auditors from providing certain services to their clients to prevent Enron-type conflicts of interest, the legislation doesn't ban tax preparation services outright. Rather, the company's audit committee is charged with the responsibility of determining who provides tax services. However, some caveats must be considered in each case; for example, SOX's ban on software consulting may sound a death knell for audit firms that sell tax software to their audit clients and provide consulting services to support it.

Myth #3: Internal control means data security

Internal control refers to financial controls that impact financial statements — not data security. SOX doesn't specifically spell out any data security requirements for companies. Other legislation, such as the Health Insurance Portability and Accountability Act of 1996 (HIPAA), has rules about data security, but SOX is silent on things like password protection and encryption standards. This myth that internal control and data security are synonymous likely results (at least in part) from SOX's emphasis on internal control, which is a term sometimes used by information technology professionals.

There is a lot of confusion in this area. According to the SEC, SOX is directed at making sure that there is compliance with laws and regulations relating to how financial statements themselves are prepared, not with securing the data that's used to prepare them. SOX ensures that audit procedures are in place to ensure control over financial reporting and catch problems with data security. In fact, SOX has a trickle effect, causing auditors to lean hard on IT professionals so that the auditors can confidently exercise their internal control function. However, SOX doesn't directly speak to IT professionals.

Myth #4: The company isn't responsible for functions it outsources

Not true. Under SOX Section 404, it doesn't matter whether you outsource a system, process, or control or handle it internally — if it impacts the financial statements, the reporting company is on the line. This means you may have to directly test the controls used by your outside service providers. Or, in some circumstances, you may be able to get a special type of report, called an SAS 70 (type 2), from the service provider; this report documents the effectiveness of the provider's internal controls. (For more on the SAS 70 report, flip to Chapters 14 and 19.)

Myth #5: My company met the deadline for Section 404 first-year compliance. We're home free!

Sorry, Section 404 certification is an annual event. And when it comes to Section 404 compliance, a corporation is never "done." Compliance is a continual and ongoing process. Your systems must evolve as the company evolves, and so must the tests that are performed on those systems.

Chapter 2

SOX in Sixty Seconds

. . . .

. . . .

*A*merican investors lost their innocence in 2001. The public learned that numbers do in fact lie. And so do CEOs and the so-called "objective" analysts that are paid to evaluate the financial strength of companies.

Each provision of the Sarbanes-Oxley Act (SOX) was drafted in response to events that occurred at one company: Enron. Every section of the statute can be traced to a particular transgression that occurred at that single company. Congress began drafting the legislation in response to the Enron bankruptcy, when word of the even larger WorldCom bankruptcy sent shock waves throughout the nation in July 2002. WorldCom, the second largest long distance carrier in the country, had overstated its earnings by $3.8 billion dollars without anyone seeming to notice until the corporation collapsed. Congress didn't delay in passing SOX legislation that was already in the works.

On July 30, 2002, just five days after news of WorldCom's collapse, SOX, was signed into law by President Bush. It passed through Congress on a wave of bipartisan support, which meant that the provisions of the law that had been drafted in response to Enron passed without time to modify them to reflect the even bigger frauds occurring at WorldCom. So if you want to understand what Congress really intended when it passed SOX, look carefully at what happened at Enron, and you'll know exactly what Congress was thinking.

Reestablishing Control after the Scandals

SOX is intended to be a mechanism for asking the questions that must be answered in order for investors to have enough confidence to invest in U.S. companies. These important questions include the following:

- Can you rely on a company's financial statements?
- Are the companies telling the truth about their earnings?
- Does the company have big liabilities that have been kept off its balance sheet, causing investors to be unsure of whether the company is running on borrowed funds and could collapse at any time?

These are the types of questions that were raised by Enron and that Congress was trying to address when it passed the provisions of SOX dealing with "internal control over financial reporting."

If you look at the events at Enron, and what Congress was responding to at the time, it's easy to see that Congress wasn't worrying about who was authorized to order supplies or whether there were enough levels of password protection in place by the IT department. In fact, Congress wasn't even worrying whether companies were counting their inventory or aging their receivables correctly. There were already lots of accounting rules and quality control standards in place to deal with things like that.

Instead, Congress was concerned that companies were letting management take control over financial reporting and that they were circumventing all the audit and accounting procedures that were in place. Further, Congress was concerned that the auditors were failing to exercise enough control to keep companies from taking part in these fraudulent activities.

Enron events everyone initially overlooked

Unquestionably, corporate America had a major case of "the uglies" as the calendar turned on the new millennium. It was a historic time for corporate America, with an impact on the nation that was reminiscent of the great depression. Long-buried losses, financial shell games, corrupt practices, and secret self-dealings were suddenly thrust into the light of day and became front-page news. The United States was forced into a realization that international confidence in its financial markets was being jeopardized by a handful of powerful individuals who were at the helm of the nation's largest corporations.

Most frightening to Congress and the Securities and Exchange Commission (SEC) was the fact that major credit reporting agencies failed to identify the events leading up to the collapse of Enron, which was at the time the largest bankruptcy in history. Moody's Investors' Service, Standard & Poor's Corporation, and Fitch Rating Services all gave Enron good credit ratings a mere two and a half months prior to Enron filing Chapter 11. (The story of Enron's demise is discussed in detail in the sidebar "A brief chronology of the Enron collapse.")

The key omens that foreshadowed Enron's implosion, which SOX reporting standards now address, include the following:

- ✔ **Successive resignations of key management:** On August 14, 2001, CEO Jeff Skilling resigned after being in the position only six months. On October 16, 2001, coinciding with a huge restatement of third-quarter earnings, Enron announced that its CFO, Andrew Fastow, would also be replaced. SOX now requires corporations to report changes in management on Form 8-K within four days after they occur (as discussed in Chapter 3). Prior to SOX, changes in key management weren't required to be announced to the public, nor did they justify scrutiny by the SEC.

- ✔ **Inaccurate and unreliable financial statements:** On October 16, 2001, Enron announced third-quarter earnings that reflected an unexpected $544,000 earnings change and a $1.2 million change in stockholders' equity. On November 8, 2001, Enron further announced that it needed to restate its financial statements for the first and second quarters of 2001 and for the four years prior, 1997 through 2000. The grand total of overstated income was $586 million. Several sections of SOX now place responsibility on management and auditors for the accuracy of information used to prepare the financial statements. (See Chapters 5 and 10 for a discussion of these provisions.)

- ✔ **CEO stock sales during a blackout period:** During the period from October 29 to October 23, 2001, Enron employees were prohibited from selling the plummeting Enron stock in their 401(k) plans. (The average employee retirement had 63 percent invested in Enron stock.) These blackout dates were imposed to allow a chance for recovery. Nevertheless, CEO Ken Lay sold most of his company stock. SOX now prohibits preferential treatment of management during blackout periods.

- ✔ **Nondisclosure of earlier CEO stock sales:** In addition to selling his stock during a blackout period, CEO Ken Lay also reportedly sold large amounts of Enron stock earlier in 2001. At the time, SEC requirements didn't technically require the reporting of these sales. (Chapter 3 explains the new post-SOX reporting requirements for such provisions.)

✔ **Off–balance sheet transactions to hide losses:** A big factor in Enron's eventual collapse was its use of so-called *special purpose entities,* which were separate companies set up to hide Enron losses on their own financial statements. This arrangement ensured that the losses didn't see the light of day on Enron's books. (Off–balance sheet transactions are explained in Chapter 4.)

Essentially, Enron got banks to advance funds to off–balance sheet entities "non-recourse to Enron," which meant Enron couldn't be held liable for the debt, and therefore the debt didn't have to be disclosed on Enron's financial statements. Instead, the debt was collateralized by shares of appreciating Enron stock. The deal unraveled when the shares began declining in value. Then, to placate the banks, Enron began to guarantee the debt. However, because Enron hadn't reported this obligation previously, the financials were deemed fraudulent.

✔ **Document destruction:** On January 10, 2002, Enron's audit firm, Arthur Andersen, admitted to Congress that it had destroyed or shredded an undisclosed number of documents related to Enron's use of special purpose entities to hide losses and related matters. At the time, no one within the audit firm questioned or took steps to stop the shredding.

✔ **Rigging the ratings:** During the congressional hearings, it was revealed that Enron had contacted the agencies responsible for maintaining its credit rating to persuade them to alter their ratings of the company. The rapidly declining Enron retained its investment grade rating up until three weeks before it filed for Chapter 11 bankruptcy protection. SOX Section 501 now provides stronger conflict-of-interest rules that prohibit companies from retaliating if they're adversely reviewed.

A brief chronology of the Enron collapse

Prior to filing bankruptcy in late 2001, Enron had revenues of around $101 billion and was one of the world's largest energy companies, providing electricity and natural gas. The company also had branched out into financial and risk management service. *Fortune* magazine had named Enron "America's Most Innovative Company" for six previous consecutive years.

Many experts attribute the initial financial troubles of Enron to its launch of EnronOnline, which was an innovative Web-based transaction system that allowed selling and trading of commodities products (such as gas and electricity) over the Internet. However, the system was neither profitable nor attractive to customers.

During 2001, the company became tainted by corporate scandal. Enron shares fell from more than $90 per share to about 30 cents per share. The following are some key events chronicling the roles of Enron management in the energy giant's rise and fall:

✔ **1997:** Chief Financial Officer Andrew Fastow creates the first in a series of partnerships, which are established for the purpose of keeping debt from showing up on Enron's balance sheet.

✔ **August 2000:** Enron shares reach their peak price of $90.

✔ **December 2000:** Enron announces that Jeffrey Skilling is appointed CEO. Skilling resigns after six months.

✔ **August 2001:** Founder of Enron, Kenneth Lay, is named CEO of Enron (for the second time). Finance executive Sherron Watkins meets with Ken Lay after submitting an anonymous memo saying, "I am incredibly nervous that we will implode in a wave of accounting scandals." Watkins later becomes a role model for corporate whistle-blowers and ethicists.

✔ **October 2001:** Enron reports a $638 million third-quarter loss and discloses a $1.2 billion reduction in shareholder equity, mostly due to the partnerships created by Fastow to hide debt. Fastow is fired.

✔ **November 2001:** Enron files documents with the SEC revising its financial statements for the preceding five years to reflect previously undisclosed losses of $586 million.

✔ **December 2001:** Enron files for bankruptcy protection and lays off thousands of workers.

✔ **January 2002:** The Justice Department announces that it's conducting a criminal investigation of Enron. Lay resigns as chairman and CEO of Enron and several weeks later resigns from the board of directors.

✔ **March 2002:** Enron's audit firm, Arthur Andersen LLP, is indicted for destroying Enron-related documents.

✔ **June 15, 2002:** Arthur Andersen is convicted of obstruction of justice and fined the maximum amount allowed by statute, which is $500,000.

✔ **August 21, 2002:** Michael Kopper, a former top aide to Fastow, strikes a deal with prosecutors. He pleads guilty to money laundering and conspiracy and identifies a web of partnerships designed to make Enron appear profitable and to financially benefit Fastow and other Enron management.

✔ **October 2002:** Fastow is indicted for 78 charges of conspiracy, money laundering, and various types of fraud.

✔ **May 2003:** Andrew Fastow's wife, Lea, is charged with participating in some of her husband's deals.

✔ **September 2003:** Former Enron treasurer Ben Glisan Jr. strikes a deal with prosecutors. He receives a five-year sentence for one count of conspiracy to commit securities and wire fraud, and he agrees to cooperate with prosecutors.

✔ **January 2004:** Fastow pleads guilty to conspiracy, receives a ten-year sentence, and agrees to help the prosecution.

✔ **February 2004:** A 42-count indictment charges former CEO Jeffrey Skilling with 35 counts of conspiracy, fraud, and insider trading.

✔ **July 2004:** Enron CEO Kenneth Lay is indicted for participating in a conspiracy to manipulate Enron's quarterly financial results, making false statements about Enron's financial performance, and omitting facts necessary to make financial statements accurate and fair. Lay pleads innocent.

✔ **May 25, 2006:** Lay is found guilty of 10 counts against him of conspiracy and fraud. Jeff Skilling is found guilty of 17 counts involving conspiracy, insider trading, and making false statements to auditors.

✔ **October 23, 2006:** Skilling is sentenced to 24 years and 4 months in prison, and fined $45 million. The case is currently under appeal.

✔ **October 17, 2006:** Ken Lay dies while vacationing in Snow Mass, Colorado, prior to his conviction and exhausting his appeals. Pursuant to the law, "abatement" was granted, which means that the law views it as though he had never been convicted.

More tales from the corporate tabloids

When a public company's stock plummets because of a scandal, the event has a distinctly human element. After all, employees of that corporation and members of the public at large may have invested substantial retirement funds and life savings in the stock, and the betrayal of public trust fuels an outrage that transcends partisan politics. Ultimately, it's the kind of event that made possible the rapid and near unanimous passage of SOX in 2002.

This section touches on a few headline stories that came after Enron's collapse and prompted Congress and the SEC to unite in legislative and rule-making initiatives in order to calm the public.

Global Crossing

Just three months after the Enron scandal, Global Crossing, Ltd, a high-speed Internet company, filed bankruptcy in the largest filing ever by a telecommunications company. The company concealed its ailing financial condition by swapping fiber-optic network capacity with other companies and deluded the public by improperly recognizing the revenue. Also, Global Crossing Chairman Gary Winnick reportedly reaped $734 million from the sale of his company stock before it became virtually worthless.

WorldCom

On July 25, 2002, WorldCom, the second largest long-distance and Internet carrier in the country, was the next company to become the subject of an accounting scandal. An SEC investigation disclosed that WorldCom had overstated its earnings by $3.8 billion. The SEC called the revelation one of the largest cases of "false bookkeeping ever" and lamented its "unprecedented magnitude."

The House Financial Services Committee immediately called for public hearings into the matter. However, WorldCom CEO Bernard Ebbers and other key management enraged the public by invoking the Fifth Amendment protection against self-incrimination and by refusing to testify. WorldCom had loaned Ebbers more than $366 million and even issued loan guarantees to cover his potential losses in WorldCom stock!

Tyco

In 2002, Tyco International, Ltd. became embroiled in a controversy regarding millions of dollars in questionable bonuses, loans, and other payments to its CFO, CEO, and others. In one instance, Tyco paid an outside director $10 million and paid his charity an additional $10 million.

In the Tyco case, the public accounting firm PricewaterhouseCoopers was on the hot seat. As Tyco's auditors, the firm had to answer questions about whether its audit had disclosed such bonuses and why the auditors had signed off on them.

Adelphia

On March 27, 2002, Adelphia Communications Corporation, the nation's sixth-largest cable television company, disclosed the existence of $2.3 billion in off–balance sheet transactions. The Rigas family, which had founded Adelphia and taken it public, controlled the corporation and had co-borrowed the $2.3 billion debt and couldn't provide much detail about the transactions to the SEC. The company's founder, John Rigas, and his two sons were eventually convicted of defrauding the company of more than $1 million. John was sentenced to 15 years in jail, and his son, Tim, received a 20-year sentence. Additionally, the Rigas family was ordered to turn over most of their assets, which were estimated to be about $1.5 billion, to a disgorgement fund to help compensate defrauded investors.

Adelphia stock plummeted 33 percent in May 2002, when Adelphia announced to a scandal-sensitive public that it was delaying its 10-K filing and restating its earnings.

Four Squeaky Clean SOX Objectives

In the months after the Enron collapse, no less than two dozen SOX-related bills were proposed in Congress. The SEC issued a comprehensive response during a February 2002 press release, and President Bush announced his own "ten-point plan." The following objectives emerged from the extensive testimony, press conferences, and thick packets of proposed legislation and protracted hearings that ensued:

- ✔ **Make management accountable.** Several provisions of SOX seek to ensure that management, accountants, and attorneys are held directly accountable for information that makes it onto a company's financial statements on their watches.

- ✔ **Enhance disclosure.** SOX's provisions address the fact that several key events and relatively shocking transactions relating to corporate scandal escaped scrutiny simply because they weren't required to be disclosed to the public.

- ✔ **Conduct regular reviews by the SEC.** SOX requires the SEC to look at companies more often and more closely. This objective is a reaction to the SEC's declining to review Enron's records for several years preceding its bankruptcy filing and consequential loss to investors.

- ✔ **Hold accountants accountable.** SOX seeks to purge the accounting industry of the conflicts of interest, financial self-dealing, and plain-old poor judgment that placed the investing public at risk when relying on "certified" financial statements.

These objectives continue to be the core of SOX legislation today.

Where are the Enron execs now?

The Enron-related trials made headlines routinely until 2007. Curious what happened to all of the Enron executives who swindled away investors' money? Take a look at this list to find out:

✔ **CEO Jeff Skilling:** Skilling began quietly serving a 24-year, 4-month prison sentence at the Federal Correctional Institution, in Waseca, Minnesota. Skilling was sentenced for 31 counts of fraud, conspiracy, insider trading, and lying to auditors.

✔ **CEO and Chairman Ken Lay:** On July 7, 2004, several years after the other Enron-related indictments, Ken Lay was indicted by a grand jury on 11 counts of securities fraud and charges relating primarily to his efforts to conceal the financial condition of the company from shareholders and the public as it collapsed. Lay was found guilty on May 25, 2006, of 10 counts against him. Each count carried a maximum 5- to 10-year sentence, which meant that Lay could have faced 20 to 30 years in prison. However, he died suddenly when vacationing in Snowmass, Colorado, on July 5, 2006, which was about three and a half months before he was to be sentenced. An autopsy revealed that he died of a heart attack. As a result of his death, the law required the federal district court judge who presided over the case to vacate Lay's conviction (which meant that no financial sanctions could be imposed as a result of it). Of course, this provoked further public outrage.

✔ **Accountant Richard Causey:** Causey pleaded guilty to securities fraud and agreed to help pursue convictions against Lay and Skilling. He received a sentence of seven years and agreed to forfeit $1.25 million to the government under a plea deal.

✔ **CFO Andrew Fastow:** He pleaded guilty in January 2004 to two counts of conspiracy, admitting openly to orchestrating schemes to hide the company's debt and inflate profits. He also provided the prosecution with a wealth of detailed information as to how he did it. He cooperated with prosecutors and claimed to be a changed man. As a result, Fastow got a "bargain" ten-year sentence, which began in July 2006.

✔ **Andrew Fastow's wife, Lea Fastow:** She completed a yearlong sentence last July for a misdemeanor tax charge for signing a tax return reporting her husband's kickbacks as "gifts." She was originally charged with six tax felonies emanating from her knowledge of her husband's activities at Enron and for disguising money from an Enron side deal as gifts. She planned to plead guilty to one felony, but changed her plea when the presiding judge refused to accept the five-month prison deal prosecutors recommended in the plea bargain.

The judge who sentenced Lea Fastow admitted she was a prime candidate for a less restrictive minimum-security camp, but the judge refused to allow her to serve her sentence under those usual conditions that are given to other first-time tax offenders. The judge didn't publicly state why that decision was made.

✔ **Treasurer Ben Glisan, Jr.:** He's currently completing a five-year sentence for his role in the Enron scandal.

✔ **Two former Merrill Lynch & Co. executives:** These execs were sentenced to short prison terms for their roles in helping Enron falsify 1999 earnings through a sham sale of Nigerian power barges.

How SOX Protects the Investing Public

It used to be that corporations were fixated on reporting results, and the investing public was obsessed with reading those results. Prior to SOX, the general view was that if companies provided regular financial statements, the public could simply examine them and make informed investment decisions. However, when Enron and WorldCom and other companies' financial statements had to be restated because they were off by millions, the public felt they had been duped. Congress and the SEC decided that requiring regularly filed financial statements wasn't enough to protect the public. There needed to be much stricter regulation as to how information included on the financial statements was compiled.

Because reporting problems can trigger serious and tragic consequences for investors, SOX focuses both on how companies arrive at the results they report and the reliability and credibility of the reporting process. It also holds management, directors, attorneys, and auditors accountable for the end product. This section breaks down those objectives, further explaining the different sections of SOX.

Creating a Public Company Accounting Oversight Board

One of the key components of the Enron crisis was the demise of the nation's largest public accounting firm, Arthur Andersen. In response to perceived lapses in judgment and objectivity of the accounting profession as a whole, SOX establishes a Public Company Accounting Oversight Board (PCAOB), which I discuss more fully in Chapter 7. The PCAOB is charged with the following tasks:

- Registering public accounting firms

- Making rules for "auditing, quality control, ethics, independence, and other standards relating to the preparation of audit reports for issuers"

- Conducting inspections of accounting firms

- Performing investigations and disciplinary proceedings and imposing appropriate sanctions on firms that violate the rules established for their conduct

- Enforcing compliance with SOX professional standards, securities laws, and other board rules

- Setting the board's budget and managing its staff

- Performing such other duties or functions as necessary or appropriate

Under SOX, the PCAOB is required to have five full-time, financially literate members who are appointed for five-year terms. Two of the members must be or must have been CPAs, and the remaining three must not be CPAs. The chair of the board can be a CPA, but he or she can't have practiced as one in the prior five years.

In 2004, the PCAOB issued Auditing Standard No. 2, which was intended to provide guidelines for audit firms in complying with SOX. However, it soon became apparent that the standard was encouraging auditors to subject companies to extensive, detailed, and costly audits. The auditors were profiting enormously and blaming their big bills on PCAOB requirements. Auditing Standard No. 2 was subsequently withdrawn and replaced with a more liberal Auditing Standard No. 5.

Clamping down on auditors

An *audit* isn't necessarily an adversarial process, but it's supposed to be an objective one. An audit is a process of verifying information and identifying information that isn't consistent with Generally Accepted Auditing Standards, or GAAS (see Chapter 4). One purpose of an audit is to allow accountants to *certify* financial statements that are prepared in accordance with Generally Accepted Accounting Principles (GAAP); certification assures anyone who reviews them that the statements are GAAP-compliant.

SOX addresses the issue of auditors becoming too chummy with the clients that they're auditing. Accounting firms, like any service company, have a financial incentive to cater to clients that pay their fees. A tense audit, for instance, could strain the client relationship and result in the accounting firm getting fired. This conflict of interest is exacerbated if the accounting firm provides other lucrative services to the client besides the audit.

Accordingly, SOX Section 201 limits the scope of services that can be performed by auditors (see Chapter 6 for coverage of prohibited services). SOX provides that it's unlawful for a registered public accounting firm to provide any nonaudit service to an issuer along with the audit. These unlawful nonaudit services include the following:

- Bookkeeping or other services related to the accounting records or financial statements of the audit client
- Financial information systems design and implementation
- Appraisal or valuation services, fairness opinions, or contribution-in-kind reports
- Actuarial services
- Internal audit outsourcing services

   ✔ Management or human resources functions

   ✔ Broker, dealer, investment advisor, or investment banking services

   ✔ Legal and expert services unrelated to the audit

   ✔ Any service that the board determines, by regulation, is impermissible

SOX does allow accounting firms to perform some services that aren't included in the above list. For example, accountants traditionally perform tax return preparation services.

Rotating auditors

SOX presumes that an auditor's long-time familiarity with a company compromises the quality of an audit rather than makes the process more efficient each year. In other words, SOX assumes that auditors lose their objectivity when they develop a close and comfortable relationship with the client. Accordingly, SOX Section 203 provides that the lead and concurring audit partners must rotate off the audit every five years.

Creating committees inside companies

SOX creates a new class of worker bees within public companies. Section 301 requires public companies that are listed with the national securities exchanges and associations to form *audit committees*. These audit committees are responsible for working with the independent auditors and getting them the information they need as well as for establishing procedures on related issues such as record retention and hearing complaints.

Each member of the audit committee must be a member of the board of directors of the issuer and must be independent. Accountants and attorneys are prime prospects for board membership. Audit committee members can receive compensation for serving on the committee.

The audit committee of an issuer is "directly responsible" for the appointment, compensation, and oversight of the work of any registered public accounting firm that's hired by the company to audit its financial statements. It's also the audit committee's job to establish procedures for the "receipt, retention, and treatment of complaints" received by the issuer regarding accounting, internal controls, and auditing concerns.

SOX requires that companies pay the costs of audit committees and give them the authority to hire independent counsel or other advisors to carry out committee functions.

Holding management accountable

CEOs and CFOs are likely to be much more proactive in making sure that their companies' financial statements are accurate now that they have to personally vouch for the statements and risk doing time if they aren't accurate.

SOX Section 302 provides that CEOs and CFOs must personally certify the "appropriateness of the financial statements and disclosures contained in the periodic report, and that those financial statements and disclosures fairly present, in all material respects, the operations and financial condition of the issuer." A violation of this section must be knowing and intentional to give rise to liability.

In addition, Section 302 requires that the CEO and CFO disclose all significant deficiencies and material (financially significant) weaknesses in controls over financial reporting to both the independent accountants and the audit committee. Disclosure prevents management from taking a passive attitude toward serious weaknesses.

SOX also suggests — but doesn't require — that a corporation's federal income tax return be signed by the CFO of the corporation in order to emphasize its accuracy.

SOX Section 303 now specifically provides that it is "unlawful" for any officer or director of an issuer to take any action to fraudulently influence, coerce, manipulate, or mislead any auditor engaged in the performance of an audit for the purpose of rendering the financial statements materially misleading. (How could anyone ever think this type of thing was *lawful?*)

Taking back bogus bonuses

CEOs and CFOs may be required to give back their bonuses if financial statements have to be restated after an audit because of "material noncompliance" with financial reporting requirements due to fraudulent activity.

SOX Section 304 provides that CEOs and CFOs must "reimburse the issuer for any bonus or other incentive-based or equity-based compensation received" during the 12 months following the issuance or filing of the noncompliant document. They must also reimburse the issuer for "any profits realized from the sale of securities of the issuer" during that period.

Banning blackouts

SOX Section 306 prohibits officers and directors from pulling "a Fastow." In other words, officers, directors, and other insiders aren't allowed to sell their stock during blackout periods, as Kenneth Lay did during Enron's blackout period when its stock plummeted more than $5 per share.

Any profits resulting from sales in violation of Section 306 are recoverable by the issuing company. If the company fails to sue under this provision, a suit can be initiated by "the owner of any security of the issuer," meaning any shareholder.

SOX Section 306 is the only section of the statute that shareholders may use to sue a company directly on their own behalf. Under other sections of SOX, only the SEC may initiate a lawsuit against a company.

Ratcheting up reporting

Federal securities law is based on the premise that investors in a public company have a right to know the facts and circumstances that would reasonably and fairly influence their decisions to invest in the company.

SOX attempts to ensure that investors are fairly well informed by adding the following provisions to existing law:

- ✔ **Reflection of accounting adjustments:** SOX Section 401(a) requires that companies' financial reports "reflect all material correcting adjustments . . . that have been identified by a registered accounting firm."

- ✔ **Disclosure of off–balance sheet transactions:** SOX requires that a company's annual and quarterly financial reports disclose all material off–balance sheet transactions and other relationships with "unconsolidated entities" that may have a material current or future effect on the company's financial condition. Chapter 4 contains more coverage of off–balance sheet transactions.

- ✔ **Real-time reporting of key events:** Companies need to disclose information regarding material changes in their financial conditions or operations on a rapid and current basis on Form 8-K reports (see Chapter 3).

Purging company conflicts of interest

Under SOX, auditors can't accept jobs with their clients until they have taken off a complete audit cycle. This restriction makes sense because an auditor may otherwise hesitate to alienate a prospective employer.

Under SOX Section 206, CEOs, controllers, CFOs, chief accounting officers, and persons in equivalent positions can't have been employed by the company's audit firm during the one-year period preceding the audit. Because it's a conflict of interest, it's also unlawful under SOX Section 402(a) for a company to lend money to any director or executive officer. Under Section 403, directors, officers, and 10-percent owners must report designated transactions by the end of the second business day following the transaction so that the public can follow what the "insiders" are doing.

Exercising internal control

The dreaded SOX Section 404 requires companies to include in their Form 10-K annual reports an *internal control report* that states the following:

- ✔ Management's responsibility for establishing and maintaining an adequate internal control structure and procedures for financial reporting

- ✔ Management's assessment of the effectiveness of the internal control structure and procedures of the issuer for financial reporting (The assessment must include disclosure of any identified "material weakness" in the company's internal control over financial reporting existing at the company's fiscal year-end.)

- ✔ The framework used by management to evaluate the effectiveness of their controls

- ✔ That the company's auditor has attested to the adequacy of management's assessment and the company's internal control over financial reporting

Chapter 12 covers these requirements of Section 404 in-depth.

Looking at lawyers

SOX was one scandal in which lawyers weren't directly implicated — no high-profile ones went to jail or had to do the perp walk on the 6 o'clock news, but that doesn't mean they emerged unscathed. SOX increases the level of regulation, which applies to lawyers as well. Section 602(d) establishes rules setting minimum standards for professional conduct for attorneys practicing before the SEC. However, lawyers are required to report misconduct of clients that causes them to withdraw as counsel under the so-called "noisy withdrawal" rules.

The SEC's so-called "noisy withdrawal" rule has received much criticism from the legal profession. Attorneys expressed concern about the rule's effect on confidential attorney-client relationships. Responding to this concern, the SEC proposed a revision to the noisy withdrawal provision that would require the issuer, as opposed to the attorney, to report an attorney's withdrawal to the SEC. As of this date, the SEC hasn't issued final rules as to whether to require noisy withdrawal reports by attorneys or issuers.

Waiting seven years to shred

Under SOX Section 802(a), it's a felony to knowingly destroy or create documents to "impede, obstruct, or influence" any existing or contemplated federal investigation. This is a SOX section that impacts the criminal provisions of the law and thus impacts all organizations, not just public companies. Under this section, auditors are required to maintain "all audit or review work papers" for seven years from the dates their reports are issued.

Putting bad management behind bars

SOX subjects white-collar criminals to the same tough-sentencing trends that have been imposed on other types of criminals. It also enhances some existing penalties, such as increasing maximum penalties for mail and wire fraud from five to ten years. Criminal penalties including fines up to $5 million and prison terms of up to 20 years for securities fraud are imposed for certain actions: For example:

- ✔ It's a crime under SOX to tamper with a record or otherwise impede an official proceeding (in other words, shredding documents will get you in trouble).

- ✔ Individuals who misstate financial statements filed with the SEC can expect maximum penalties for "willful" violations.

- ✔ Sections of SOX impose prison time of up to 20 years and fines for individuals who corruptly alter, destroy, mutilate, or conceal any document with the intent to impair the object's integrity or availability.

SOX extends the statute of limitations on civil fraud claims to the earlier of five years from the fraud, or two years after the fraud was discovered. (Prior to that it was three years from the fraud or one year from discovery.)

Freezing bonuses

The SEC is authorized to freeze an extraordinary payment to any director, officer, partner, controlling person, agent, or employee of a company during an investigation of possible violations of securities laws.

Blackballing officers and directors

The SEC may issue an order to prohibit, conditionally or unconditionally, permanently or temporarily, any person who has committed securities fraud (specifically, violated Section 10(b) of the Securities Exchange Act of 1934) from acting as an officer or director of a public company if the SEC has found that his or her conduct "demonstrates unfitness" to serve as an officer or director.

Providing whistle-blower protection

Whistle-blowers are employees who report information about corporate fraud or mismanagement. Under SOX, employees of issuers and accounting firms are extended *whistle-blower protection*. These protections prohibit employers from taking certain actions against employees who disclose information to, among others, parties in a judicial proceeding involving a fraud claim. Whistle-blowers are also granted a remedy of special damages and attorney's fees. (For more on whistle-blowers, check out Chapter 18.)

Rapid Rulemaking Regrets

With the passage of SOX, Congress required the SEC to make substantive rules to be enforced by the agency in 19 major areas. This requirement meant that there was only a short period of time for both public commentary and the drafting process itself. Undoubtedly, many aspects of these rules will be subject to interpretation or revision as enforcement efforts unfold.

Chapter 3

SOX and Securities Regulations

*T*he Sarbanes-Oxley Act, or SOX, which passed in 2002, is the most far-reaching attempt to protect investors since Franklin Delano Roosevelt's Securities Act of 1933 following the Great Depression. Like the New Deal securities laws of the 1930s, SOX comes on the heels of widespread disillusionment about corporate integrity. It signals a new era in the relationship among business, government, and the investing public.

SOX is a broad piece of legislation that the Securities and Exchange Commission (SEC) is in charge of administering. It administers this legislation by passing specific rules for companies, audit firms, and stock exchanges to follow. The SEC has issued many comprehensive rules that provide much of the guidance that companies need. These rules help to clearly spell out the requirements of SOX.

I cover the rules in this chapter, and I also give you an overview of securities law and the important historical context of SOX. Understanding the objectives of securities law and how SOX serves those objectives can help you better understand your company's current reporting obligations and can help you prepare for future legislative trends.

SOX isn't a stand-alone piece of legislation: It's only a part of the complex tapestry of federal securities regulations and statutes that have been carefully woven by Congress over the last seven decades.

Pre-SOX Securities Laws

To develop a sound SOX strategy for your company, you need to be aware of the securities laws that define the legal context of SOX and that are altered by its provisions. SOX amends many of the securities laws discussed in this section.

In the 1930s, the idea of laws to protect the investing public took hold among a hardworking generation that had seen the devastation of a stock market crash. Just prior to his 1932 reelection bid, President Franklin Delano Roosevelt assigned a former Federal Trade Commissioner, Huston Thompson, the task of drafting a securities law proposal to woo a depression-dazed electorate on the campaign trail.

Huston and the committee that convened to review his draft were faced with an early dilemma: Should the role of government be to protect the public from poor investments (a *merit system*) or simply to make sure that the public had enough information to evaluate investments on their own (a *disclosure system*)? In the end, the draft legislation opted for the disclosure approach, which is still used today. (For more on the disclosure system, see the sidebar "Disclosure and merit at the state level.")

The laws that ultimately emerged from Huston's draft are the Securities Act of 1933 (also known as the 1933 Act) and the Securities Exchange Act of 1934 (also known as the 1934 Act). Decades after their drafting, these two statutes remain the backbone of the federal securities regulation system. The objective of these laws goes beyond simply ensuring that companies fill out the right forms; the disclosures required are designed to provide all the information necessary for an investor to determine the true value of an investment that's offered to the public.

Disclosure and merit at the state level

It's important to understand that the Securities Act of 1933 has always been exclusively based on disclosure and not merit. As one federal judge aptly put it, any company has the right to offer and investors to buy any "hair-brained investment scheme" as long as it's accurately described. According to Richard Kranitz, a securities attorney with more than 30 years of experience, "State merit review laws have generally been repealed because voters over time recognized that regulators were no better than investors at picking winning stocks."

The federal National Securities Markets Improvements Act (NSMIA), passed in 1996, encourages the elimination of merit review, and now only a few states still have merit rules in effect. The NSMIA preempted state regulation of national offerings but preserved the role of states in prosecuting fraud cases.

SOX is an attempt to modernize existing securities laws to ensure that they continue to meet the statutes' objective in the 21st century. The premise of federal securities law, then and now, is that government plays an important role in protecting the investing public from shaky securities.

The Securities Act of 1933: Arming investors with information

The Securities Act of 1933 is sometimes referred to as the "truth in securities" law because it requires that investors receive adequate and thorough financial information about significant aspects of securities being offered for public sale. It expressly prohibits deceit, misrepresentation, and other fraud in the sale of securities. The 1933 Act contains a detailed registration process that companies must comply with before they can offer securities to the public. The burden and expense of completing the forms is the responsibility of the registering company, which is referred to as *the issuer.*

The SEC examines all registration documents for compliance with the 1933 Act. If the SEC determines that information is missing or inaccurate, the issuer may be denied registration and may lose its right to sell its securities in the United States. (Section 5(a) of the 1933 Act provides that it's "unlawful" to offer to sell a security to the public unless a registration statement is in effect.)

Companies undergoing the registration process are required to provide information about:

- ✔ The company's properties and business
- ✔ The types of securities to be offered for sale, as in stocks, bonds, shares indentures, partnership interests, and so on
- ✔ Background on the management of the company

The registration statement must also include financial statements certified by independent accountants. (The requirements for audited financial statements are discussed more fully in Chapter 4.)

In order to comply with disclosure requirements, companies generally distribute a document called a *prospectus* to potential investors. The content of the prospectus is governed by the 1933 Act, which provides that "a prospectus shall contain the information contained in the registration statement." This instruction is somewhat misleading because companies usually create these documents in reverse — drafting a prospectus prior to preparing a registration statement and then including a copy of the prospectus in the registration statement filing.

The Securities Exchange Act of 1934: Establishing the SEC

Although the 1933 Act set ambitious goals and standards for disclosure (see the preceding section), it was silent on the practical aspect of enforcement. To plug this hole, Congress passed the Securities Exchange Act of 1934, which established the Securities and Exchange Commission (SEC) to implement the 1933 Act.

Overview of the 1934 Act

The 1934 Act established the ground rules under which the purchasers of securities may resell and trade shares by:

- Requiring sellers of securities to register as broker dealers
- Creating regulated securities exchanges
- Defining the duties of companies whose securities are traded among investors

In effect, the 1934 Act requires a company to make certain information available to the public so that company shareholders may resell their stock to members of the general public.

Half of all securities sold in the United States are private placement offerings, which are not subject to registration under the 1933 Act but are subject to the civil liability and anti-fraud provisions of the 1934 Act. (For more information about private placements, see the sidebar "Keeping offerings private under Regulation D.")

Powers given to the SEC

Under the 1934 Act, the SEC has the power to register, regulate, and oversee brokerage firms, transfer agents, and clearing agencies as well as the nation's securities stock exchanges.

Periodic reporting requirements under the 1934 Act require full disclosure of facts subsequent to filing that are material or significant enough to affect investors' decision-making processes. The 1934 Act also identifies and prohibits certain types of conduct in the markets, such as insider trading and market manipulation, and provides the SEC with disciplinary powers over regulated entities and persons associated with them.

The SEC's rulemaking authority for SOX

The 1934 Act gives the SEC the authority to supplement securities laws by making its own rules for carrying them out. The SEC passes its own regulations, which have the same force, effect, and authority as laws passed by Congress.

Keeping offerings private under Regulation D

The term *private placement* refers to the offer and sale of any security by a brokerage firm to certain investors but not to the general public.

Private offerings are "exempt from registration under the 1933 Act, subject to specific exemptions contained in Sections 3(b) 4(2) of the 1933 Act as interpreted by SEC Regulation D." However, private placements may still be subject to portions of the 1934 Act and to state securities laws requiring registration as well as to certain provisions of SOX.

Regulation D Sections 504–506 establish three types of exemptions from the registration requirements of the 1933 Act:

🖊 **Rule 504 applies to transactions in which no more than $1 million of securities are sold in any consecutive 12-month period.** Rule 504 doesn't limit the number of investors. These types of offerings remain subject to federal anti-fraud provisions and civil liability provisions of the 1934 Act if they raise more than $1 million.

🖊 **Rule 505 applies to transactions in which not more than $5 million of securities are sold in any consecutive 12-month period.** Sales of the security cannot be made to more than 35 "non-accredited" investors but can be made to an unlimited number of accredited investors. An issuer under this section can't use any general solicitation advertising to sell its securities.

🖊 **Rule 506 has no dollar limitation of the offering.** An exemption under this section is available for offerings sold to not more than 35 non-accredited purchasers and an unlimited number of accredited investors. Rule 506 requires an issuer to make a subjective determination that at the time the shares are sold, each non-accredited purchaser meets a certain sophistication standard.

For purposes of Regulation D, an *accredited investor* is defined in Rule 501(a) as someone who has the following characteristics:

🖊 Is a director, executive officer, or general partner of the issuer

🖊 Has a net worth either individually or jointly with their spouse that equals or exceeds $1 million

🖊 Has income that exceeds $200,000 per year (or $300,000, jointly with spouse) for each of the two most recent years and reasonably expects an income that exceeds $200,000 in the current year

Accordingly, the SEC is in charge of making rules to implement the broad statutory provisions of the Sarbanes-Oxley Act. In fact, SOX specifically requires that the SEC make rules in 19 different areas! Congress required that rules in 12 of these areas be passed within 12 months of the date SOX was enacted in 2002. As a result, many SOX analysts worry that with so little time for public comment, the rapid rulemaking will give rise to interpretive issues in the future.

Periodic reporting under the 1934 Act

The Securities Exchange Act of 1934 directs the SEC to require periodic reporting of information by companies with publicly traded securities. These companies must submit 10-K Annual Reports, 10-Q Quarterly Reports, and

Form 8-K for significant events. These reports are made available to the public through the SEC's EDGAR database located at www.sec.gov. (I discuss the 10-K, 10-Q, and 8-K in more detail in the section "The Post-SOX Paper Trail" later in this chapter.)

Additionally, the 1934 Act imposes special reporting requirements on companies in the following contexts:

- **Proxy solicitations:** The SEC uses a procedure called *proxy* to allow geographically distant shareholders to participate in elections without attending meetings. Naturally, persons seeking control, including insiders hoping to retain control, solicit those proxies for their candidates. Companies must file materials with the SEC in advance of any such solicitations.

- **Tender offers:** The 1934 Act requires disclosure of important information by anyone seeking to acquire more than 5 percent of a company's securities by direct purchase, also known as a *tender offer.*

- **Exchanges and associations:** The 1934 Act requires that exchanges, brokers and dealers, transfer agents, and clearing agencies report to the SEC.

The 1933 Act covers offers and sales by *issuers* (companies whose securities are offered), while the 1934 Act defines what information those companies must make available to permit their shareholders to trade company shares after purchasing them.

Most of the SEC's rules under SOX have had deadlines requiring them to be implemented before July 15, 2007. However, the majority of companies don't have to comply with the full certification rules that require an auditor to certify the company's internal controls over financial reporting until well into 2008.

Insider trading provisions

Section 16 of the Securities Exchange Act of 1934 establishes that it's illegal for management, directors, and other people having "inside" knowledge about a company to use that information themselves or to pass it on to others so that they can use it improperly to gain a financial benefit for themselves. Every member of the public should have an equal advantage when it comes to investing in public companies.

SOX Section 403(a) strengthens Section 16 of the 1934 Act by requiring company insiders to disclose to the SEC information about their stock transactions within two business days of when they occur. These disclosures are made on an 8-K filing, which I explain in the "The Post-Sox Paper Trail" section later in the chapter.

Trading securities while in possession of information that's not available to the public is illegal if that information is material to the value of the investment.

Other securities laws

As part of an overall regulatory scheme to protect investors, the Sarbanes-Oxley Act impacts disclosures required under the following laws:

- ✔ **The Trust Indenture Act of 1939:** This act contains requirements on debt securities, such as bonds, debentures, and notes that are offered for public sale. Most of the SOX provisions amending the 1934 Act apply to securities governed under this provision.

- ✔ **Investment Company Act of 1940:** This 1940s act regulates mutual funds and companies that invest in other companies and whose own securities are offered to the investing public. SOX's accounting disclosure and management certification requirements specifically apply to investment companies defined in this act.

- ✔ **Investment Advisers Act of 1940:** This act requires that firms or sole practitioners who have at least $25 million in assets and advise others about securities investments register with the SEC. (Instead of selling a security as a broker, the advisor recommends the purchase of the security.) SOX's prohibitions on accountants performing nonaudit services (see Chapter 6) directly affect the services that can be offered by many of the firms registered under this act. Also, SOX provides criminal provisions that directly apply to investment advisors.

The Scope of SOX: Securities and Issuers

To understand which parts of SOX apply to your company, you need to understand what type of investments are considered securities and which types of issuers are subject to or exempt from SOX.

For example, Section 807 creates a new securities fraud provision that appears in the criminal code. This provision makes it a crime "to defraud any person in connection with a security" or to obtain "by means of false or fraudulent pretenses, representations or promises, any money or property in connection with the sale or purchase of any security." In order to determine whether you've broken the law under Section 807 and can be sent to jail, you need to know if the transaction you've conducted involves a security. If it doesn't, you may still be sued in a civil action for fraud but won't serve time in a federal penitentiary under this provision.

What is a "security"?

SOX makes reference to the Securities Act of 1933 and the Securities Exchange Act of 1934 for purposes of defining what is and is not a security. Both acts contain similar specific definitions. The 1933 Act uses the following language:

> [T]he term "security" means any note, stock, treasury stock, bond, debenture, security, future, evidence of indebtedness, certificate of interest or participation in any profit-sharing agreement . . . , pre-organization certificate or subscription, transferable share, investment contract, voting trust certificate, certificate of deposit for a security . . . or warrant or right to subscribe to or purchase, any of the foregoing.

There has long been confusion about the term *investment contract* as it's used in the definition of a security along with all the other terms. The use of this particular phrase has really extended the scope of transactions that the statute covers. Those words don't have any real meaning in a commercial context, so the courts have had to interpret them in deciding when an agreement between two or more parties constitutes an investment contract that's subject to the registration and reporting requirements of federal securities law.

A famous Supreme Court case in the 1940s, *SEC v. WJ Howey Co.,* made it clear that federal securities law covers a broad scope of commercial transactions. In this case, the court held that companies that offered sections of orange groves for sale along with contracts to harvest the oranges and distribute the profits were indeed selling investment contracts subject to federal securities law and had to register such contracts with the SEC.

In the *Howey* case, the Supreme Court stated that the test to determine whether the securities laws apply in a given transaction is "whether the scheme involves an investment of money in a common enterprise with profits to come solely from the efforts of others." Although this is a pretty broad definition, not all investments are considered securities under SOX. For example, courts have also held that transactions such as purchasing a share in a cooperative housing project or participating in a pension plan funded solely by employers (with no employee contribution) aren't securities.

Under the *Howey* case, the key questions to ask in determining whether a particular transaction may be a security subject to SOX include the following:

- Is there an investment of money?
- Is this a common enterprise?
- Is there expectation of profits?
- Do profits come solely from the investments of others?

Who is an "issuer"?

SOX provides that issuers of all stock in all publicly traded corporations of all sizes must meet its requirements — that's a lot of issuers. *Issuer* is the term used to refer to companies that sell securities to the public and that either are required to register with the SEC or meet the requirements for an exemption from registration.

Your company is required to register its securities if they're going to be traded on a securities exchange or if the company meets certain criteria with respect to the number of shareholders and the amount of assets held.

Section 207(a) of SOX identifies the types of issuers that are subject to SOX, including:

- ✔ **Companies whose securities trade on a securities exchange:** Companies that offer stock to the public though the New York Stock Exchange (NYSE) or other stock exchange must register securities under Section 12(b) of the Securities Exchange Act of 1934. (For more about stock exchanges, see the sidebar "How stock exchanges work.")

- ✔ **Companies with more than 500 investors and $10 million in assets:** SOX requires issuers with more than $10 million in assets to register securities that are held by at least 500 persons, regardless of whether the securities are traded on a securities exchange. These companies are required to register under Section 12(g) of the 1934 Act.

- ✔ **Companies with more than 300 investors:** Some companies aren't required to file under 12(g) of the 1934 Act because they have less than 500 shareholders. However, if these companies have more than 300 securities holders (and therefore don't qualify for a specific registration exemption), they must file under Section 15(d) of the 1934 Act. This category of issuers often includes companies that have privately held stock but offer debt instruments (such as bonds) to the public. Offering debt instruments pushes them over the 300-investor mark.

- ✔ **Voluntary filers:** Even though they aren't legally required to do so, some companies decide to file reports with the SEC anyway. They do this for a variety of reasons. For example, to trade stocks on NASDAQ (which isn't technically a stock exchange), a company must file SEC disclosures even if it isn't otherwise required to do so.

- ✔ **Companies with registrations pending:** A company conducting an initial public offering of equity or debt securities must file a registration statement on one of the public offering forms, one of the S-series forms, or one of the SB-series forms. Then the company must file three 10-Qs and one 10-K in the first year (even if it hasn't filed under the 1934 Act). Upon filing these statements these companies become subject to many provisions of SOX.

When interpreting the requirements of SOX, it's important to look at each particular statutory provision for definitions and criteria identifying to whom that particular statute applies. Some sections of SOX apply to management, and others apply to auditors or benefit plan administrators.

The SOX surprise

Because they aren't required to register with the SEC, some companies have been surprised to learn that parts of the Sarbanes-Oxley Act apply to them. However, the fact that a company is exempt from registering with the SEC doesn't mean it's exempt from complying with SOX.

The end of some old exemptions

Historically, the 1933 Act and the SEC have held the authority to exempt certain types of small companies and securities and offerings from SEC registration in order to help them acquire capital more easily by lowering the cost of offering securities to the public.

Exemptions are based on the type of security (for example, a bank is regulated by the Banking Commission, so bank stock is exempt) or on the type of transaction (for example, sales of less than $1 million are exempt from federal registration under Rule 504 of Regulation D, promulgated under the 1933 Act). Most states exempt offers and sales to only a limited number of investors (for example, 25 persons in a single offering in Wisconsin). In 1996, Congress passed the National Securities Markets Improvements Act, which requires states to impose a uniform exemption under Rule 506 of Regulation D, which all states must obey. (For more about Regulation D, see the sidebar "Keeping offerings private under Regulation D.")

Prior to SOX, these exemptions and waivers left a regulatory gap in the securities field and meant that many companies in which the public was investing didn't have to go through the registration process and little other government oversight occurred. Arguably, some shaky companies were exempted from tough scrutiny to the detriment of the investing public. The types of offerings exempt from regulatory oversight included:

- Private offerings to a limited number of persons or institutions
- Offerings of limited size
- Intrastate offerings
- Securities offerings of municipal, state, and federal governments

SOX doesn't have any direct effect on registration exemptions. The vast majority of small offerings are exempt from registration.

How stock exchanges work

After a company decides to go public, it has some important decisions to make about how to market its shares to the public: Should it register to sell the shares on a stock exchange? If so, which exchange?

In 1792, 24 men signed an agreement to sell securities among themselves, thus creating the New York Stock Exchange (NYSE). Today, the United States has several competing exchanges. The NYSE is home to some of America's best-known corporations, including General Electric, Exxon, Wal-Mart, America Online, IBM, and Lucent Technologies. NASDAQ is a competing stock exchange on which the stock of some equally impressive companies is traded. It includes many high-tech companies such as Microsoft, Cisco Systems, and Intel. Other exchanges available to companies include the NASDAQ SmallCap Market and the American Stock Exchange (AMEX).

Companies don't directly sell shares on an exchange; rather, they're permitted to list shares on an exchange, selling them through licensed professionals.

Each stock exchange has its own listing requirements, which may include the following:

✔ Levels of pretax income

✔ Market value and share

✔ Net assets

✔ Number of shareholders

✔ Share price

In general, requirements for listing on the NASDAQ are less restrictive than those for the NYSE, which is why many newer high-tech companies elect to list with the NASDAQ.

For example, the NYSE requires companies to have either $2.5 million before federal income taxes for the most recent year and $2 million pretax for each of the preceding two years or an aggregate of $6.5 million for the three most recent fiscal years. All three of those years must be profitable. In contrast, the NASDAQ requires only $1 million in pretax income in two of the last three fiscal years. It also offers some alternative standards to pretax income that are easier for emerging companies to meet; these standards are based on factors such as assets, revenues, operating history, and market value. As for the NASDAQ SmallCap Market and the AMEX, both have low threshold requirements for listing with them.

When a company elects to list on an exchange, it must register the class of securities under the Securities Exchange Act of 1934, agreeing to make public information available and follow the other requirements of the 1934 Act. In addition to complying with federal securities law, the company may also have to comply with state securities laws, known as *blue sky laws*, in at least one state in which it operates.

According to 30-year veteran securities attorney, Richard Kranitz, "Even the most carefully planned and highly funded start-ups involve great risk, but also potential reward. They also are the source of around 60 percent of all new jobs in the United States and most of its economic growth. They need to be able to issue securities to raise capital to survive, to grow, and to prosper."

Some universal SOX provisions

Congress has made clear that it intends for some provisions of SOX to apply to all companies that sell their securities, regardless of whether these companies are required to register with the SEC.

These catch-all provisions are

- ✔ **Section 1107,** the employee and whistle-blower protections
- ✔ **Sections 802 and 1102,** the recordkeeping requirements (see Chapter 6)
- ✔ **Sections 807 and 902,** the criminal provisions requiring jail time for securities fraud and conspiracy

WARNING!

Although many provisions of SOX technically apply only to publicly traded companies, securities law experts expect that courts and legislatures will apply the standards of the statute in a variety of litigation contexts and legal actions brought by investors.

The Post-SOX Paper Trail

Registration with the SEC is a milestone for companies going public, but it's only the beginning of the reporting relationship. After a company's registered as an issuer of securities, it's subject to annual and periodic reporting

---

Cutting small companies a small break? No way!

The Sarbanes-Oxley Act doesn't contain small-company exemptions like a lot of other federal laws do. SOX is intended to protect investors regardless of the size of the public company in which they're investing. However, Congress and the SEC have both realized how much more burdensome compliance can be on small, publicly traded companies (particularly when it comes to Section 404). So, to help small companies without leaving investors unprotected, the SEC created rules that refer to companies that have less than $75 million in publicly solicited investment and debt as "non-accelerated" filers. The SEC also gave small companies more time to comply (but only after rejecting pressures and pleas to exempt small companies all together).

Under the latest extension, non-accelerated filers (including foreign private issuers that are non-accelerated filers) must include in their financial statements a management report that attests to the company's internal control over financial reporting. They have to do this until they submit their annual reports for the fiscal years ending on or after December 15, 2007. However, these filers get to delay providing the really expensive auditor's report until they submit their annual reports for fiscal years ending on or after December 15, 2008.

But remember: Non-accelerated filers that opt to take advantage of the extensions must note the omission of the management and auditors reports in their financial statements.

requirements that extend over the life of the company. SOX dramatically changes the content, depth, and frequency of the reports — the 10-K, 10-Q, and 8-K — that must be filed with the SEC.

 SOX shortens the deadlines for filing annual and quarterly reports for a certain class of large public companies referred to as *accelerated filers*. These shortened deadlines require that reports be filed within 60 days rather than 90 days after the close of the reporting period.

Form 10-K

Form 10-K is an annual report that companies must provide to their investors and make publicly available on the SEC database (see the sidebar "Researching SEC filings online"). Many companies seize this opportunity and make their annual reports glossy marketing tools that tout the growth and accomplishments of the company over the past year. They know their 10-Ks will be reviewed by existing and prospective investors as well as securities rating companies.

SOX-mandated enhancements to 10-K annual reports include:

- ✔ An internal control report that states that management is responsible for the internal control structure and procedures for financial reporting and that it assesses the effectiveness of the internal controls for the previous fiscal year

- ✔ A requirement that all financial reports filed with the SEC reflect corrections and adjustments made to the financial statements by the company's auditors

- ✔ Disclosure of all material off–balance sheet transactions and relationships that may have a material effect on the financial status of an issue

- ✔ Disclosures of changes in securities ownership by management, directors, and principal stockholders, and information on whether these individuals have adopted a code of ethics

Form 10-Q

Form 10-Q is a quarterly supplement to the annual 10-K report; it contains updates to the annual disclosures. 10-Q reports provide a more current view of financial performance than annual reports, and analysts often compare the actual data contained within the 10-Q to prior projections that may have been released by overly optimistic corporate management.

Form 8-K

Form 8-K is a short and simple form that a company must file when certain types of events occur, such as the ceasing of a commercial activity or the departure of company officers or directors. The list of events that trigger the filing of an 8-K has grown over the years, particularly as a result of SOX. The content of Form 8-K is limited to a few salient facts abut the triggering event. For more on the 8-K, see the next section "Behind the 8-K Ball After SOX."

Behind the 8-K Ball after SOX

The SEC has always required disclosure of events that are "clearly material" to the public. And to comply with this requirement, companies have always had to use Form 8-K. The important change in this area, however, is that SOX now requires earlier and more proactive disclosure of material events to the investing public.

SOX also adds several new events to the list of material events, moves other events to the 8-K from the 10-Q and 10-K forms, and imposes a special four-day rule for other events.

The enhanced 8-K requirements are a legacy of the Enron scandal, which I cover in Chapter 1. In the Enron case, corporate executives were allowed to sell off large numbers of shares — as stock prices plummeted — without alerting the public. Many of the events that foreshadowed Enron's demise but escaped public disclosure would now trigger 8-K filing obligations under the four-day rule.

Adding new events to the list

Form 8-K disclosures play an important role in keeping the public informed of occurrences in small companies that may not capture the attention of the media.

Under new rules mandated by SOX, the following events appear on the list of 8-K triggering disclosures:

- ✔ **Entry into or termination of a material agreement:** This provision is a response to the pre-Enron practice of burying news, such as the losses of clients and contracts, in the cheery language of glossy annual reports.

✔ **Creation of a new material obligation:** This requirement applies to obligations of the issuer that are either direct or arise contingently out of an off–balance sheet arrangement. Enron's off–balance sheet transactions (discussed in Chapter 2) epitomize the extent to which pre-SOX management was able to conceal a company's ailing financial position while paying themselves large salaries.

✔ **Defaulting on a financial obligation or moving up the date when an obligation is due:** A company's inability to pay its bills and the acceleration of an obligation by a nervous creditor are considered events that the public should know about.

✔ **Ceasing a commercial activity:** Investors have a right to know what business enterprises they're investing in and when those enterprises change.

✔ **Write-offs:** Reportable write-offs include disposing of or materially adjusting the value of a company asset or taking an action that will result in a material write-off on the company's balance sheet. Rather than allowing such information to be buried in the balance sheet, SOX mandates that investors be informed about material write-offs on an 8-K.

✔ **Failure to meet stock exchange reporting requirements:** Investors have a right to know about this type of event because the inability to buy and sell their stock on an exchange can dramatically impact a company's liquidity.

✔ **Restating previously issued financial statements:** If a company makes a decision to restate, or redo, financial statements that it has already issued to the public, SOX rules say that investors have a right to know the source of the error.

✔ **Departing directors and officers:** When key players are bailing, investors may want to as well. So, companies are required to report these departures.

Shuffling events from the 10-K and 10-Q

Certain events that companies used to report quarterly on Forms 10-K and 10-Q now must be reported more often. Companies can't lump the following events with other reports but instead must put them on their 8-Ks:

✔ **Significant sales:** The sale of more than 1 percent of the outstanding securities or the new issuing of that percentage of securities must be reported on the 8-K.

✔ **Changes in shareholder rights:** Shareholders of stock, debt, and all other types of securities must receive notice of any *material modifications,* or significant changes, to their rights.

✔ **Amendments to bylaws and articles:** If bylaws or articles of incorporation are amended, shareholders are entitled to receive an 8-K.

Creating four-day reporting events

SOX has greatly expanded the number of events reportable under Form 8-K "on a rapid and current basis." SOX imposes a burden on companies to rapidly inform the public of material information regarding changes in a company's financial condition or for the protection of investors. Prior to SOX, companies were required to report very few events as they happened. Instead, they were only required to report on an annual basis, leaving investors in the dark until many months after the fact.

Now some events are subject to a requirement that they be disclosed to the investing public within four days of when they occur. Events that call for these real-time disclosures include:

- Bankruptcy or *receivership* (a process in which a bankruptcy trustee manages assets of an indebted individual or entity)
- Purchase of significant financial assets
- Changes in auditors
- Changes in financial control policies
- Suspensions of employee rights to transfer 401(k) plan assets
- Changes or waivers of ethics policies for financial officers

Prior to Sarbanes-Oxley, companies had 5 to 15 days to report these events. It's nothing short of momentous that today these deadlines have been reduced to within four days for all reportable events.

The pressure on companies to collect the required information and data and review it for accuracy is enormous. Additionally, the SEC has been criticized for making the 8-K form confusing and the instructions vague. However, many new software products have been developed to help companies comply with the 8-K reporting requirements imposed by SOX.

Providing protection in the safe SOX harbor

To keep lawsuits from clogging the courts, the SEC contains a safe harbor for companies that fail to file their 8-Ks in the required time frames. As long as the disclosure is made in the company's next periodic report, the SEC won't prosecute or allow a cause of action to be made under the fraud provisions of the Securities Exchange Act of 1934. The SEC also doesn't allow parties to sue a company simply because it failed to file an 8-K.

This safe harbor doesn't apply to material misstatements or omissions, and companies that don't file 8-Ks are still subject to SEC penalties for failing to meet their reporting obligations. Reporting failures also may cause the SEC to more carefully review and scrutinize the future activities of a company, as I explain in the next section.

Annual SEC Scrutiny after SOX

SEC Chairman Arthur Levitt championed many of the SOX reforms long before they were enacted. However, in the late 1990s, the SEC (under Levitt's watch) declined to review Enron's books for the prior three years and even gave Enron specific exemptions from securities laws. "Never again," said Congress and the SEC. New rules now make periodic review by the SEC mandatory.

Mandatory review rule

SOX requires the SEC to review a public company's annual and quarterly reports at least once every three years. Taking things a step further, the SEC has publicly stated that the largest public companies can look forward to being audited as often as once every year. It's up to the SEC to exercise its discretion in deciding how and when to conduct its review process.

SOX Section 408 provides that the SEC will use the following criteria in determining how often to review a company:

✔ Whether the issuer has had to make substantial corrections (restatements) to previously issued financial statements

✔ Whether the company has experienced a lot of volatility in its stock price

✔ How many shares are issued and the cost per share (referred to as *the size of the issue*)

✔ The disparity of the company's stock price to its earnings (called the *price to earning ratio*)

✔ The influence the issuer can exert over a particular segment of the economy

✔ Other factors the SEC considers relevant

Remedies for inaccurate registration materials

By law, the SEC requires that the information provided in the publicly disclosed registration documents be accurate. However, the SEC doesn't guarantee that companies always follow this rule, so you can't sue the agency for failing to do its job if a problem arises.

Investors who purchase securities and suffer losses must prove in court that the registration documents or periodic filings included incomplete or inaccurate information. This cause of action, generally, is limited to suing the company and not the federal government.

Why Privately Held Companies Care about SOX

Do you think that only publicly traded companies need to worry about SOX? Think again. Private companies that fail to concern themselves early on with the standards set by SOX may significantly limit their growth potential and find themselves on the losing side of court controversies. This section looks at a couple of reasons why a privately held company may want to be SOX compliant as it grows.

Bolstering the bottom line

SOX is becoming a model for governing corporations of all sizes. It provides nonpublic companies with a template of "best practices" so they don't have to develop structures from scratch as they grapple with governance issues.

Adopting SOX standards can ratchet up a company's credibility because SOX structures and procedures are easily recognizable in today's financial and business environment. This familiarity inspires trust for investors, creditors, prospective purchasers, and joint venture partners.

Privately held companies that voluntarily adopt SOX standards can expect to realize financial benefits that bolster their profits as a result of the following dynamics:

> ✓ **Financial institutions and lenders may rely on the company's internal control and governance systems in streamlining their own due diligence process.** Companies with good governance and internal control

are attractive to institutions that have to assess these processes and procedures as part of their decision-making process. Good governance and internal controls inspire the confidence of lenders, investors, and other decision makers.

Researching SEC filings online

Registration statements and information documents, which are sometimes also called *prospectuses,* become public shortly after filing with the SEC. You can access these documents for free on the EDGAR database located on the SEC Web site at www.sec.gov. The figure in this sidebar shows a portion of an 8-K statement for Toys "R" Us, Inc. on the database.

You can search the database for any of the following filings for a specific company:

- Prospectuses

- Annual reports (Form 10-K)

- Quarterly reports

- Proxies solicitations

- Tender offer disclosures

- Filings by mutual fund companies

The EDGAR database is surprisingly current: You can retrieve 8-Ks and other documents that were filed as recently as the previous week.

Tip: Your search on a particular company may pull up hundreds of documents, so it's helpful to limit your search to a particular time period.

- ✔ **Insurance companies may offer lower premiums for officers and directors.** Good governance and internal control are rapidly becoming an unofficial underwriting criteria that allows companies to shop for more competitive rates.

- ✔ **It may be easier to attract qualified board members who are wary of serving on the boards of companies that lack adequate controls.** No board member wants to feel like he's just stepped into a quicksand of questionable practices and lax controls by agreeing to serve on a board. SOX ensures that good procedures are in place, which can help the company recruit more qualified board members.

- ✔ **A company with good governance structures and internal control is more attractive to a prospective purchaser.** A purchase involves considerable due diligence, and adopting SOX standards reassures prospective buyers that the company's financial statements can be relied on.

- ✔ **The company may be more desirable as a candidate to participate in joint ventures when adequate internal control is a selection criterion.** No company wants to be affiliated with a scandal-ridden partner in a joint venture situation. These joint ventures can be particularly lucrative to small companies. Nonpublic companies can more effectively compete for joint venture deals by voluntarily adopting SOX standards. This practice may make them stand out among other competing companies.

Defending company practices in court

Even if your company has no imminent plans to go public, it may want to adopt SOX standards in order to posture and present itself in court should the unfortunate need ever arise.

In civil lawsuits and criminal litigation, courts must develop and apply standards of conduct. Courts are likely to look to SOX in evaluating the conduct of privately held companies and in developing judicial standards. If your company is sued, undoubtedly it will fare better before a judge or jury if it has embraced the principles and objectives of SOX, such as adequate financial controls and management accountability.

Moreover, several provisions of SOX, such as its criminal and whistle-blower protections, apply to companies that aren't publicly traded in the traditional sense.

Going public after SOX

Most budding entrepreneurs dream of developing a business that's so successful they can earn the prestige of *going public,* or selling shares of the business's stock. As soon as a company realizes this dream, it comes under the scope of SOX and, more specifically, Section 404's compliance requirements.

Why would a company want to go public? For those that satisfy the SEC registration requirements and willingly submit to SOX standards, the payoff can have the following advantages:

- ✔ **Consistent capital (if a liquid market for the securities can be achieved):** Many successful businesses survive their early years on successive rounds of borrowed funds. A successful public offering may yield important working capital that's needed to expand the business.

- ✔ **Control:** In the early stages of business, venture capitalists may want significant control of a company in exchange for their financial contributions. A public offering can represent an important opportunity for a company's founders to raise necessary cash without relinquishing or concentrating significant control in the hands of a small group of investors.

- ✔ **Compensation:** For an entrepreneur living on a shoestring budget while developing a business that's worth a lot of money, the prospect of going public can represent the opportunity to cash in on the success of the enterprise by selling some of his or her stock in the business.

- ✔ **Acquisitions:** A public company that wants to acquire another company can do so by issuing stock to finance the acquisition rather than financing through borrowing.

Taking a company public can cost hundreds of thousands — or even millions — of dollars in legal and underwriting fees and millions more to comply with ongoing SEC reporting requirements. And if a company isn't in compliance with SOX at the time of registration, taking the necessary steps to comply can delay the registration and significantly increase the costs associated with it. On the other hand, if a company has already been implementing practices consistent with SOX, the process can be simplified (although still expensive).

Weighing the risks and benefits of going public

Do SOX compliance costs discourage some privately owned firms from going public? It's difficult to tell. But certainly SOX has made attracting independent board members more competitive for smaller companies.

Staying private and raising money through private equity instead of tackling SOX head-on is something that companies at least consider as an option. However, going public isn't only an important vehicle for exposure to greater numbers of investors; it's also an important consideration in attracting money from those investors who want to be sure they have an exit strategy should they decide that they no longer want to invest in the company in the future.

Additionally, the costs for complying with SOX for start-up companies may be less burdensome than for existing small companies because start-up companies have fewer structures (and boards) in place that they would have to replace or demolish. Because they aren't tied down, these start-ups can implement SOX internal controls as they build from the ground up.

Because small companies are such an important engine of economic growth and technological innovation, the ripple effects of SOX will be felt throughout the economy. By raising the cost of access to the capital markets, SOX likely will slow down the economy in the long run.

Driving companies into dark corners?

SOX has been accused not only of making it more difficult for companies to go public, but also of driving some companies to *delist,* or go private. The problem with this trend is this: If it were true, it would mean that less information is available to investors because only public companies are required to meet most of the SEC filing requirements that make information available to the public.

But the evidence of this trend is inconclusive at best. For large public corporations, SOX-related costs are a relatively small burden — certainly not of the significance that would cause them to delist. One study claims that many companies delisted in 2003, but overall most experts agree that the benefit of having additional capital available outweighs the burden of SEC compliance after SOX.

Some of the benefits companies give up by delisting include the following:

- **Loss of credibility:** It's difficult to delist without attracting attention and unwanted publicity.
- **Loss of value:** Investors and prospective purchasers place a value on assets and liabilities that they can verify (and they can't count on verifying information if a company hasn't gone public).
- **Diversification of risk:** Publicly owned companies spread the risk of doing business among a greater number of owners and investors.
- **Ability to attract capital:** Few companies can privately raise the level of capital that's possible by offering shares to the public.
- **Allowing the owners to eventually cash out:** Publicly traded stock is far more liquid than an ownership interest in a privately traded company.

Nevertheless, the numbers of small, publicly traded firms that choose to delist soon may increase dramatically because the final 2008 deadlines for obtaining an accountant's certification of their internal controls over financial reporting are looming.

Adding up the effect of SOX on acquisitions and mergers

An area in which SOX seems to get a bad rap is its supposed negative impact on corporate mergers and acquisitions. However, studies showed that SOX didn't deter companies from buying other companies in the time period immediately after the bill was passed or a few years into feeling its impact. In fact, the number of "M&A" deals struck under SOX actually rose, from about 7 percent between 1983 and 1984.

This increase is a pretty dramatic one, and it was quite the opposite of the cynical expectations that were expressed when SOX was initially passed. One reason for the increase may be that SOX actually greased the wheels of certain acquisitions by making some types of financial reports more readily available to prospective purchasers. Another reason that SOX may not have slowed merger activity as expected is that larger, combined entities are likely to be more readily able to absorb the significant costs of complying with SOX than smaller companies.

Chapter 4

SOX and Factual Financial Statements

*T*he Sarbanes-Oxley Act (SOX) started with scandal, and then it evolved into a law calculated to ferret out the types of practices that contributed to the collapse of Enron, the energy giant. It's true that a wave of corporate scandals that began in 2001 revealed that publicly traded corporations like Enron and WorldCom were routinely leaving critical information off their financial statements or burying it in the footnotes. However, they were also using spurious accounting methods sanctioned by auditors who looked the other way rather than risk losing their most lucrative clients. This practice meant that American investors were in the dark, because "audited" financial statements couldn't be trusted.

This chapter first considers how far we've come since it was first revealed in 2001 that the nation's largest corporations were overstating their revenues by hundreds of millions of dollars. You look at recent guidance from the Securities and Exchange Commission (SEC) as to what level of SOX scrutiny is necessary to make sure that U.S. shareholders are informed about the company's performance or financial condition.

This chapter also explains how to critically review the information on financial statements, both from the perspective of an investor and from the perspective of a company attempting to make sound judgments about its required financial statement disclosures after SOX. It also tells you how to research the new wealth of information about companies available on the SEC Web site.

Auditing the Auditors: 2007 Guidance from the SEC

One of the more interesting post-Enron revelations showed just how unreliable corporate financial statements had become. In one instance, Arthur Andersen, one of the world's most respected audit firms, approved a practice of valuing assets called *mark-to-market accounting*. This type of accounting meant that the company could simply show its assets on the balance sheet at whatever the company decided they were worth (at the market value, for instance).

Mark-to-market accounting was one of the major factors that led to Enron's collapse; executives whose bonuses depended on the performance of the company were all too eager to inflate its balance sheet assets. After SOX was passed, hundreds of major publicly traded companies across the nation were required to restate and reissue their financial statements to reflect the real values of their assets.

These confessions were a good thing for U.S. shareholders, and they undoubtedly increased the confidence of the investing public (which meant, at least in theory, companies were better able to attract investment capital). However, sometimes too much truth is a bad thing, particularly when it comes in the form of overzealous, overbilling auditors who insist on spending days and weeks reviewing aspects of a company's financial operations that have little bearing on the overall accuracy of the company's financial statements.

For this reason, in 2007, the SEC decided that it was time for the SOX pendulum to begin swinging in the other direction. It was time for auditors to take a more pragmatic approach in signing off on a company's financial statements and in certifying the level of "internal control" that companies exercise over financial reporting.

In April 2007, SEC Commissioner Christopher Cox (who incidentally held up a copy of this book when testifying before Congress) vowed to take measures to eliminate waste and duplication in the SOX compliance process. Particularly, Cox vowed to reign in the auditors so that small companies could comply without being thrown into a financial tailspin from audit costs.

The Commissioner also urged the SEC staff to continue to work closely with the Public Company Accounting Oversight Board (PCAOB), which is a special agency created under SOX to audit the auditors. (As Chapter 7 explains, after SOX, the audit profession lost the right to regulate itself.) The SEC staff subsequently urged the PCAOB to make the internal controls provisions of SOX Section 404 more efficient and cost effective.

Under SOX, PCAOB audit standards must first be approved by the SEC, and they can't take effect without a vote of the commission. Auditing Standard No. 2, which originally was passed by the PCAOB, seemed to send auditors on an auditing rampage because the standard didn't clearly define the scope of testing that the auditors were required to do prior to certifying financial statements. Because the companies themselves foot the bill for the audit, more testing meant more profit for the audit firms. It wasn't uncommon for their first-year fees after SOX to double or triple.

As this book is being written, Auditing Standard No. 2 has been repealed. In his public statement in April 2007, Christopher Cox said "These needed improvements in the Sarbanes-Oxley process are especially urgent for smaller companies, who will begin complying with Section 404 this year . . . The result of the new auditing standard for 404, together with the SEC's new guidance to management, should make the internal control review and audit more efficient by focusing the effort on what truly matters to the integrity of the financial statements."

Cox indicated that his staff would focus on the following four main areas for the new Auditing Standard No. 5 to implement SOX Section 404:

- ✔ **Defining requirements:** The SEC staff wants to better spell out SOX requirements by narrowing definitions (and thus limiting open-ended audit testing).

- ✔ **Scaling down audits to fit "facts and circumstances":** The SEC intends to encourage auditors to tailor the Section 404 audit to account for the particular facts and circumstances of companies, particularly smaller companies.

- ✔ **Encouraging auditors to use professional judgment:** The SEC hopes to infuse a rule of common sense and sound professional judgment in the Section 404 process, particularly with regard to risk assessment.

- ✔ **Eliminating redundancy:** The SEC hopes to clarify when and to what extent auditors can use the work of others as opposed to duplicating (and billing for) work that has already been done.

SOX's Recipe for Seeking Out Cooked Books

U.S. businesses prepare two major types of financial statements — the income (profit and loss) statement and the balance sheet. The *income statement* is designed to fairly reflect the income and expenses of the company, while the *balance sheet* discloses assets and liabilities. However, as this section discusses, even after SOX, many companies may have liabilities, risks, and exposures that don't show up in the account balances on these statements.

This section shares some basic information to help you read both types of statements with some healthy post-SOX skepticism.

Reviewing what the income statement reveals

The income statement (also called the *profit and loss statement*) is a financial report that covers the business's revenues and expenses over the fiscal year. SOX is intended to ensure that this information is accurately reported and that profits aren't inflated with false promises to lure investors.

A new income statement is prepared at the end of each fiscal year. This means that companies start with a fresh income statement each accounting period, and each account on the statement has a balance of zero at the beginning of the year.

Most income statements follow a variation of this general format:

```
Sample Income Statement for ABC Company

Income from Operations
Net Revenue

Less: Cost of Goods Sold

        Minus: Expenses from Operations
        Minus: General and Administrative Expenses

= Operating Profit
        Minus: Interest Expenses
        Plus: Other Revenue or Gains
        Minus: Other Expenses or Losses

= Earnings Before Taxes
        Minus: Taxes

= Earnings Before Irregular Items
        Plus/Minus: Discontinued Operations
        Plus/Minus Extraordinary Items
        Plus/Minus: Adjustments for Changes in
        Accounting Principle

= Net Income
        Retained Earnings
        Earnings Per Share
```

Some key sections and terms disclosed on the income statement include the following:

✔ **The income section:** The income section may include information about returns, allowances, discounts, and cost of goods sold. Generally Accepted Accounting Principles (GAAP) allows these items to be shown as part of the income section of the profit and loss statement when your company feels that such placement makes the information easier to understand.

✔ **Net revenue:** This category usually includes the company's sales, presented as its total (gross) sales minus sales discounts, returns, and allowances.

✔ **Cost of goods sold:** This is the amount it costs the company to make a product.

✔ **Income from operations:** The number you get when you subtract sales, general, and administrative expenses from net income is sometimes referred to as *income from operations.* This amount is the income earned in the normal course of doing business.

✔ **Expenses from operations:** The expense section of the income statement shows the costs of goods and services that are used by the company to produce income or revenue. This section includes sales, general, and administrative expenses.

Some common financial statement terms

The following are some common terms that you'll see on financial statements and in the media when it reports on a corporate scandal:

✔ **Discontinued operations:** This is where you'll find income or expenses from shifting a business location or permanently discontinuing production.

✔ **Extraordinary items:** This section reflects accounting events that are both unusual and infrequent. Examples include natural disasters, government expropriation, or changes in laws.

✔ **Changes in accounting principle:** These are changes in income that result from changing a method of accounting. For example, a company's change in the method of computing depreciation could affect income.

✔ **Earnings per share (EPS):** EPS is the amount of income per share of stock. It can be computed in several ways, including using the average shares outstanding or some other method. For example, "diluted" EPS is a calculation that includes convertible stock options in the calculation.

✔ **Nonoperating expenses:** Large expenses unrelated to the operations of the company (such as legal fees) can be a red flag signaling future losses or lagging profits. Look for an explanation in the footnotes. (See the section "Looking for funky footnotes" for more information.)

✔ **Retained earnings:** The profit or loss at the end of each year is summarized in the retained earnings account.

✔ **The "other" income and expense categories:** Sometimes a company has income from events that aren't a normal or ongoing part of its business, such as the sale of an asset. These items may be shown as "other revenue and expenses" to give investors a clearer picture of the company's performance.

Examining balance sheet (and off–balance sheet) transactions

One of the major aspects of the Enron fraud was the existence of so-called *off–balance sheet transactions.* Sham foreign subsidiaries were created, and Enron's losses were recorded on the subsidiaries' books instead of on its own, thus inflating both income and owners' equity.

The information shown on a balance sheet is always presented in a specific order: assets, liabilities, and finally the owner's equity accounts. The information shown on the balance sheet should reflect this equation:

Assets + Liabilities = Owner's Equity

Here's a very simple balance sheet format:

```
Balance Sheet Format

ASSETS

Current Assets
Checking/Savings
Accounts Receivable
Other Current Assets
Total Current Assets
Fixed Assets

= TOTAL ASSETS

LIABILITIES AND EQUITY

Liabilities
Current Liabilities
Accounts Payable
Credit Cards
Other Current Liabilities
Total Liabilities
Equity

= TOTAL LIABILITIES AND EQUITY
```

The year-end balance in the net income account shown on the income statement is added to the retained earnings account in the equity section of the balance sheet. The equity section (which is sometimes called *stockholders' equity*) reflects the value of the shareholders' ownership interest in the company.

Looking for funky footnotes

Footnotes on financial statements can include important information that doesn't show up in a company's income and balance sheet accounts but nevertheless affects the financial condition of the company. And whenever the law permits them to do so, companies love to bury unfavorable information in the footnotes to their financial statements.

For example, the footnotes to financial statements may reveal information about the following:

- ✔ **Pending litigation and other contingent liabilities:** If a company is being sued or expects to be sued, the legal exposure that it faces doesn't show up on its income or balance sheet. There's no actual transaction or reduction in assets to record. Rather, information about the company's financial exposure to these sorts of events usually appears in the footnotes.

- ✔ **Outstanding debt:** Financial accounts show the existence of a debt but not how soon it's due. Large debts due before revenues are expected to come in obviously signal trouble for any business.

- ✔ **The accounting methods used on the financials:** Footnotes explain the major accounting policies of the business, such as how inventory costs and asset values are determined. The footnotes also reveal any other significant accounting policies that the company feels shareholders should know about.

- ✔ **Special disclosures:** Footnotes may provide information about exposures and financial deficiencies that don't fit in the financials. For example, a footnote may disclose underfunded pension plan liabilities or anticipated business interruptions.

Complying with GAAP and GAAS

Each type of business has its own peculiar types of transactions, investments, and subsidiaries. However, all financial statements filed with the SEC must adhere to Generally Accepted Accounting Principles (GAAP) and Generally Accepted Auditing Standards (GAAS), which are set by the American Institute of Certified Public Accountants (AICPA).

Some fuzzy footnote language

A problem with footnotes is that they aren't required to be presented in any standard format, which means that companies may try to obscure disclosures by using highly technical terms and jargon. Here are few examples of footnotes meant to confuse their readers:

✔ *We have received informal inquiries from the staff of the Securities and Exchange Commission (the "SEC") with respect to the accounting treatment and disclosures . . .*

   Translation: The company may be facing a costly SEC investigation.

✔ *We received a request from the U.S. Justice Department for the voluntary production of documents and information concerning . . .*

   Translation: The company may be facing a criminal investigation.

✔ *A number of purported class action complaints were filed by holders of our equity and debt securities against us, our directors, and certain senior officers during 2001 . . . made false or misleading statements.*

   Translation: A lot of our shareholders are suing the company (so many that they aren't suing us in their individual capacities but have banded together and met the complicated legal requirements for forming a "class").

✔ *We may be unable to prevent our competitors from selling unlawful goods bearing our trademark . . .*

   Translation: We can't protect ourselves from illegal knock-offs that cut into our revenues so significantly that we have to disclose the losses on our financial statements.

GAAP embodies all the written and unwritten pronouncements and policies of the following:

✔ American Institute of Certified Public Accountants (AICPA)

✔ Financial Accounting Standards Board (FASB)

✔ Securities and Exchange Commission (SEC)

✔ American Accounting Association (AAA)

✔ Other bodies such as the Financial Executives Institute (FEI)

✔ National Association of Accountants (NAA) and state boards that regulate the accounting profession

GAAS is a set of systematic guidelines used by auditors when conducting audits. It is designed to ensure the accuracy, consistency, and verifiability of auditors' actions and reports.

Adherence to these standards makes it possible for investors to look at a company's financial statements and understand and compare that company's performance to others. (For more on GAAP and GAAS, turn to Chapter 6.)

Finding Financial Information

Investors can find a company's financial information from a variety of sources, both for free and for a fee. The primary advantage of using fee-based services is that they sometimes present the data in a more convenient report format than the free services provide. However, the public can generally get much the same information about a company using the free resources available.

This section examines both types of resources and gives tips on finding specific information.

The free stuff

If the company is a public company required to register with the SEC, investors can find its financial information on EDGAR, the SEC's Electronic Data Gathering, Analysis, and Retrieval System. EDGAR's Web site, shown in Figure 4-1, is located at www.sec.gov/edgar.shtml.

All SEC-registered companies, whether foreign or domestic, are required to file registration statements, periodic reports, and other forms electronically through EDGAR. Anyone can access and download this information for free.

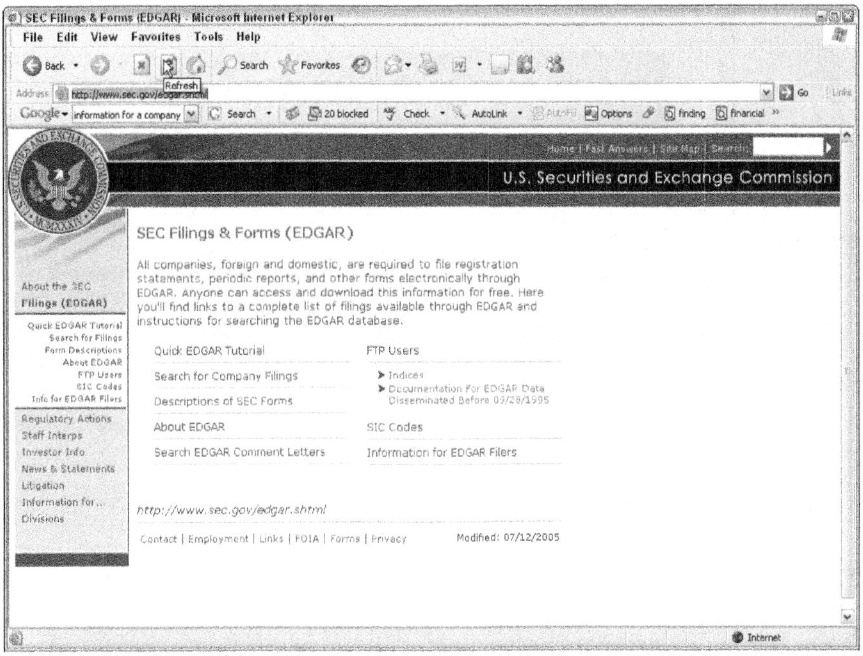

Figure 4-1:
The SEC
EDGAR
database.

Investors can also get a wealth of information from a company's Web site. Many companies, like the one for this book's publisher, John Wiley & Sons, Inc. (see Figure 4-2), put special links on their home pages for investors (or prospective investors) to access the companies' annual reports. For more on annual reports, see the section "Accessing Annual Reports" later in this chapter.

The fee-based stuff

The fee-based information services are particularly useful for creditors, competitors, or people who want to obtain marketing-related information about a company. Many of these services have tools to help investors and other folks search for a number of companies that meet certain criteria. Some of the more popular fee-based Web sites for obtaining financial information include:

✔ **Dun & Bradstreet:** D&B reports provide a summary analysis of a company's financial position based on the information you would find on the SEC Web site if you were to search it. You can order D&B reports from the firm's Web site, located at www.smallbusiness.dnb.com. As of this writing, reports cost about $150 each.

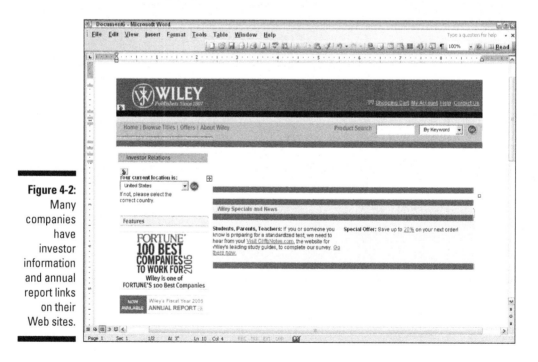

Figure 4-2:
Many companies have investor information and annual report links on their Web sites.

✔ **Hoovers Online:** This subscription-based service features special tools to help you search for companies that meet specific criteria and evaluate potential new markets. You can access this resource by visiting www.hoovers.com.

✔ **Morningstar:** This resource, located at www.morningstar.com, is a favorite among investors for its wealth of services. It provides analyst reports, portfolio management tools, and popular stock and fund screening tools that can help you identify stocks and funds that meet criteria you select.

Accessing Annual Reports

Every public company issues an annual report, which it sends (free) to its shareholders and to anyone else who requests one. Most companies also post copies of their annual reports on their Web sites, with links to the reports on their home pages.

The glossy pictures and the real figures

The annual report is primarily useful to tell you about a company's goals, vision, and future product lines, but most annual reports look more like magazines than financial documents. They're usually slick-looking promotional documents with lots of color and hype about the growth and future prospects of the company.

Annual reports often address various aspects of a company's business, including goals and products, as you can see from the example in Figure 4-3. Since the passage of SOX, most annual reports also contain information about corporate governance and ethical issues (see Figure 4-4).

Problems such as declining revenues or cash flows usually are downplayed in the glossy part of the annual report. However, they can't be hidden in the financial statements, which must be prepared according to GAAP and GAAS, as discussed in Chapter 6. The company's financial statements also appear in its annual report, though generally further back from the promotional part at the beginning.

Figure 4-3:
This annual
report
excerpt
contains
information
about the
company's
products,
customers,
and brands.

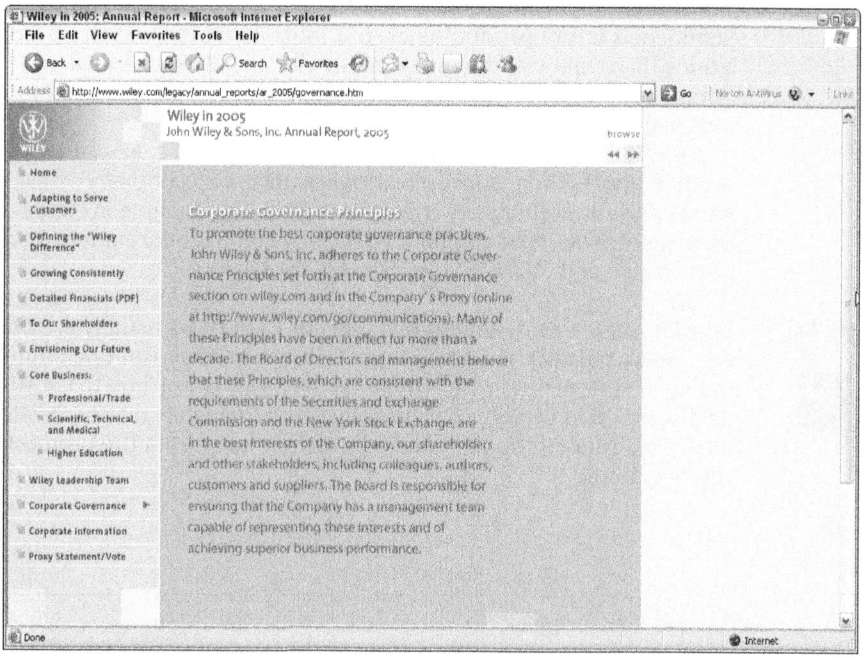

Figure 4-4:
Since the
passage of
SOX, annual
reports often
contain
governance
information
as shown
here.

Management's Discussion and Analysis

Accompanying the financial statements in an annual report is a section labeled *Management's Discussion and Analysis* (MDA). This section, which was required long before SOX was passed, summarizes the company's results for the year. It's sort of a combination of the glowing optimism of the glossy part of the annual report and the reality of the financial statements. The MDA gives you management's spin on the financials and contains information such as:

- ✔ Discussion of risks
- ✔ Year-to-year comparisons
- ✔ Breakdowns of financial results according to sectors and geographic locations

Surfing SEC Filings

The Securities Act of 1933 requires companies that accept investments from the public to make their financial information public, and the Securities Exchange Act of 1934 created the SEC to monitor this process. (For more on securities legislation, turn to Chapter 3.) The SEC requires publicly traded companies to issue reports at regular intervals, providing financial data and other relevant information to investors.

Twenty-four hours after they're filed with the SEC, these documents are accessible online through EDGAR. You can access and download a company's financial information for free through EDGAR's Web site, `www.sec.gov/edgar.shtml`. On the site, you can either run through the quick EDGAR tutorial or move straight to searching for company filings. Figure 4-5 shows the EDGAR file for this book's publisher, John Wiley & Sons, Inc., with links to the documents the company has filed with the SEC.

This section covers some of the specific and particularly useful documents you can find on the EDGAR Web site.

10-K reports

Every company has to file a 10-K report with the SEC each year. The Form 10-K is a more objective version of the annual report, without smiling photos and glossy graphics (see "Accessing Annual Reports" earlier in the chapter). The Form 10-K is likely to contain more complete financial statements than the annual report, and those statements may contain critical footnotes pertaining to issues such as pensions, contingent liabilities, and taxes.

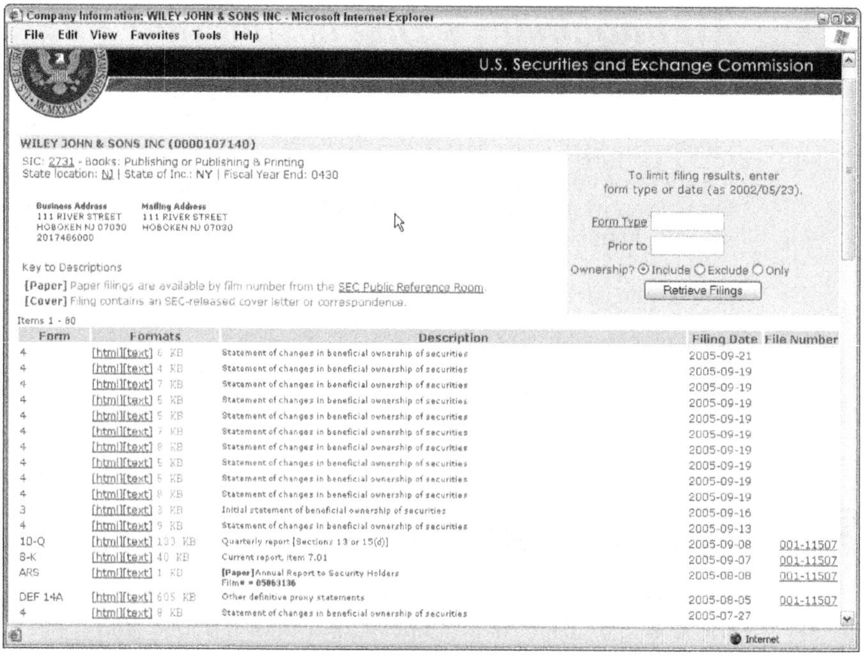

Figure 4-5:
The EDGAR
database
provides
links to all
documents
that John
Wiley &
Sons, Inc.
has filed
with the
SEC.

The Form 10-K requires the following information that isn't included in the company's annual report:

- **A detailed business description:** A breakdown of the company's performance by geographical region and business segment and a detailed description of its business (The business description is always at the beginning of the Form 10-K.)

- **Disclosure of legal proceedings:** A description of any legal proceedings in which the company is involved (This disclosure is especially important in industries such as tobacco and pharmaceuticals.)

- **How much everyone gets paid:** A list of all the company's executives and how much they're paid

- **A rundown of the competition:** Detailed discussion of the risks involved in the company's business and the major sources of competition it faces

- **Legal documents:** The company bylaws and other legal documents

Other useful forms on EDGAR

In each of the three quarters that a company doesn't have to file a Form 10-K, it has to file a quarterly report, or 10-Q, with the SEC. The 10-Q doesn't contain as much general information as the Form 10-K; instead, it simply updates the financial statements and the MDA.

In addition to the 10-Q, other useful documents you can find on the SEC Web site include:

- ✔ **Form 8-K:** This form of interim report announces any material events or corporate changes that occur between quarterly reports. SOX has substantially expanded the number of events that require the filing of an 8-K, as discussed in Chapter 3.

- ✔ **Prospectus (S-1) Form:** The S-1 Form is a prospectus for a stock offering. Reviewing the information on this form is particularly helpful when you're evaluating an initial public offering because the S-1 discloses the amount of stock being offered for sale and what the company plans to do with the proceeds.

- ✔ **Form 20-F:** This is the annual report form that foreign companies are required to file with the SEC.

- ✔ **Form 13-D:** This form discloses information about ownership of a firm's shares. Any person who acquires more than 5 percent of a class of the company's stock must file a Form 13-D within ten days of the acquisition.

Chapter 5

What's New for Non-Accelerated Filers

*N*ormally people think of publicly traded companies as huge conglomerates with billion-dollar budgets, global offices, six-figured CEOs, and armies of internal audit staff at their disposal. Guess again. Many public companies have mere millions at their disposal and are considered to be local enterprises. However, the Sarbanes-Oxley Act, or SOX, applies to companies that are listed on any exchange, regardless of size. In general, small and mid-size companies that have less than $75 million in public debt and equity are known as "non-accelerated filers" who need to comply with SOX, but at a more relaxed pace.

This chapter takes a look at how smaller companies that sell their stock to the public are being treated under SOX. I also discuss what these smaller companies can expect from pending Public Company Accounting Oversight Board (PCAOB) regulations, which will spell out what they must do to comply with SOX now that the last of the extensions appear to be coming to an end.

A SOX Update for Small Companies

In December 2006, the Securities and Exchange Commission (SEC) and the PCAOB each issued separate press releases promising to provide guidance to small companies in complying with SOX Section 404. There was a certain drama to these announcements, and a tense expectancy among small businesses across the nation. After all, most non-accelerated filers hoped for additional delays or for complete exemption from the provisions of SOX Section 404 for small companies. But that wasn't to be the case.

No relief for non-accelerated filers

A *non-accelerated filer* is a company with less than $75 million in market capitalization (which is the money a company gets from the public). A 2005 SEC study found that non-accelerated filers were spending $1.14 on auditing fees per $100 in revenues, compared with 13 cents per $100 for businesses with a market cap of more than $1 billion.

New guidelines approved by the SEC on May 23, 2007, indicated a certain loosening of the most stringent audit requirements, but in the end these guidelines left the existing rules in tact. However, four years after the large-company accelerated filers were first required to comply with SOX, much clearer guidance is now available from the SEC as to management's responsibilities. The PCAOB has also put forth directives that auditors are to take a more cost-effective and common-sense approach in complying with SOX Section 404.

Looking at what the rules require

In 2007 and 2008, small companies must begin complying with SOX Section 404 requirements for two types of reports to be issued: one by auditors and one by the management. In order for the auditors to issue a clean bill of health to the company, the company must complete the dreaded and generally costly Section 404 audit.

Current rules require management of even the teeniest publicly traded companies to issue a report on the design and operating effectiveness of the internal controls over financial reporting as of December 31, 2007. The report must be included in the company's annual Form 10-K, and it must identify all "material weaknesses" in the company's financial reporting procedures (which are know as "internal controls over financial reporting") that existed as of December 31, 2007.

Management's report must contain

> *(1) a statement of management's responsibility for establishing and maintaining an adequate internal control structure and procedures for financial reporting; and*

> *(2) management's assessment, as of the end of the company's more recent fiscal year, of the effectiveness of the company's internal control structure and procedures for financial reporting.*

These requirements don't mean that management must certify that the company is free from fraud or error. Rather, with these rules, chief financial officers (CFOs) and chief executive officers (CEOs) are basically being required to state that they have controls in place and believe that they're effective controls. In other words, the management's report doesn't address issues relating to some evil-doer within the company who's deliberately circumventing controls that are well-designed and for which there's a reasonable expectation that they'll be effective.

Getting the Auditor's Opinion

SOX Section 404 requires a company's auditor to attest to and report on management's assessment of the effectiveness of the company's internal controls and procedures for financial reporting. In other words, the SEC is looking for the auditors to back up management's assessment. Generally this means testing, testing, and more testing until the auditors are satisfied that they've done all the testing that the PCAOB requires them to do. Of course, there are some auditors that like to test (and bill clients) far more than the PCAOB has deemed necessary. That's why the PCAOB withdrew its old audit standards and implemented new, relaxed ones, which are discussed in the next section.

The good news is that with these new standards, there's no requirement for a report on internal control to be issued by auditors in 2007. Companies don't have to provide an auditors' assessment until 2008. Nevertheless, it's expected that most companies will be immersed in heated discussions with their auditors about testing long before then. However, many smaller companies that didn't have internal controls in place prior to SOX will be scrambling to document them and describe them to the outside auditors.

Ultimately, many heated discussions will likely take place over what financial data and testing the outside auditors can accept from the company's staff, and what testing they need to redo (at their hourly rate).

A kinder, gentler audit

On May 24, 2007, the PCAOB voted to approve Auditing Standard No. 5, which supersedes previous standards for audits of internal controls under SOX Section 404. These new standards tend to be kinder and gentler to the small companies who have to comply with SOX Section 404. Here are the most significant changes resulting from Auditing Standard No. 5:

 ✔ It eliminates the requirement to audit the management's assessment, and it directs auditors to concentrate on the internal controls themselves.

✔ It directs auditors to focus on areas where the actual risk to investors is highest (instead of just testing for the sake of testing), and it requires them to tailor audit procedures to small companies.

✔ It directs auditors to focus on the matters most important to internal control issues and to make a genuine effort to eliminate unnecessary procedures.

Auditing Standard No. 5 is good news for small companies, and it should go a long way in reigning in overzealous auditors and combating disproportionate SOX compliance costs for small companies.

Touting a top-down approach

A new term that has made its way into SOX vernacular is the *top-down approach*. With this approach, the PCAOB has directed auditors to make audits more suitable to the size of the company and less complex. It's the same philosophy that Auditing Standard No. 5 urges auditors to adopt.

The top-down approach basically says that auditors and companies should emphasize higher-risk areas in their Section 404 testing, and these areas should be placed at the top of the priority list. Auditors are encouraged to spend less time testing low-risk areas. Management and auditors also should tailor a specific audit agenda to fit the facts and circumstances of a particular company, starting with the largest, highest risk accounts on the financial statements and working their way down.

For example, a company with a large proportion of accounts receivable would likely spend more time and money testing the controls and procedures ensuring that the amounts shown in that particular account are accurately stated (testing for pattern false entries, phantom accounts, or understated or overstated billings to customers, for instance). Recent directions from the SEC give management a lot of flexibility in determining what constitutes adequate high and low-risk areas for their particular companies. These directions allow auditors to take different testing approaches.

Tips for adopting a new "audit-tude"

Just because the SEC has loosened the rules, small companies shouldn't lose sight of what's being required of them under SOX Section 404. Many companies have procrastinated in designing internal controls because they figured that the SEC was going to let them off the hook. Their hopes didn't come true, and now they're going on crash programs.

Arguments in favor of exempting small companies from Section 404 compliance

No group has been more vocal in opposing SOX than small, publicly traded corporations with float of less than $75 million. These smaller companies have been subject to the full range of SOX requirements, including Section 404, which requires companies to develop "internal controls" for information that makes its way onto their financial statements. Section 404 also requires those detailed processes to subsequently be reviewed and retested by an outside auditor. These companies argue that as they emerge as start-ups and would otherwise grow to fuel the U.S. economy, SOX is draining needed capital. Instead of protecting the investors of these small companies, SOX is draining needed capital, thereby hurting the companies, their employees, and their shareholders.

As of this writing, companies with less than $75 million in public debt and equity (called *public float*) have received lots of deadlines and extensions for complying with new SOX legislation. All the while the SEC is trying to work out the most burdensome bugs. Small businesses argue that they shouldn't be subjected to the same rules as huge corporations like Enron and WorldCom. They point out that their expenses of complying with SOX are proportionately much greater in relation to their revenues.

Many of these smaller companies ominously predict that they'll be required to "delist" their stock so they aren't subject to the stringent reporting requirements. Delisting their stock means that the stock wouldn't be offered publicly, and the consequence of that could hurt their ability to obtain capital. Delisting also makes less information publicly available to a company's investors in the long run.

Here's the collective argument of the small companies: Because it's so burdensome for us to comply with SOX and because we can't do the same damage to our shareholders as Enron could, why should the identical rules apply to us?

The SEC didn't find their argument to be a trivial one. While the SEC debated whether the expense of SOX was more likely to hurt businesses with thin margins and relatively low revenues than protect investors, it gave smaller companies more time to comply with SOX. It even granted four separate extensions after the first one. Because of the differences in the deadlines that apply to smaller companies, they're referred to under SEC regulations as *non-accelerated filers*.

Most companies now view SOX as a cost of obtaining public financing and of selling their shares in the public market. Experts predict that the need to go public to get capital and the relaxing of audit standards make it unlikely that any significant proportion of these companies will delist. Additionally, because many companies are new entrepreneurial ventures, they can implement SOX governance structures and financial reporting standards during their start-up phase.

If your company is one that has to adopt a new audit attitude prior to the 2007 deadline for a management's report (discussed earlier in this chapter), consider these tips:

- ✔ **Start by documenting your company's processes.** Your company will spend far more money on the audit if the auditors first have to figure out what the processes are before they can actually test them.

- ✔ **Document the review process for financial control processes.** Auditors report that the review process for financial control processes is a common problem area. For example, a company may have a requirement that says a supervisor must verify that an account balance is in place, but oftentimes the company has never formally documented the procedure. This means that the auditors can't give them kudos for having it in place.

- ✔ **Review your company's policies for segregation of duties.** In other words, multiple persons should have overlapping checks-and-balances responsibility for key financial operations.

- ✔ **Take advantage of checklists and software solutions.** Many large companies have already had to comply with SOX Section 404. As these companies went through the compliance process, they created lots of good checklists that you can use for your own company. Just because you're a smaller company doesn't mean that you have to reinvent the wheel.

Part II
SOX in the City: Meeting New Standards

The 5th Wave   By Rich Tennant

"My favorite pastimes? What do I look for in a man? Are you certain this is a questionnaire for Sarbanes-Oxley compliance?"

In this part . . .

SOX is a major piece of legislation, so it shouldn't be surprising that it's chock-full of reforms to the corporate status quo. This part takes a look at the reforms carried out under SOX and outlines what's required of companies, committees, and boards of directors. The chapters in this part also address the consequences of noncompliance and the possible collateral benefits for those companies who do embrace the ethical governance principles of SOX.

Chapter 6

A New Audit Ambience

In This Chapter

▶ Changing the audit profession

▶ Looking out for what happened to Arthur Andersen

▶ Replacing accounting self-regulation

▶ Making auditors independent from the clients they audit

▶ Understanding how CPAs are affected by SOX

▶ Examining SOX Section 404

*B*eginning in 2002, a wave of accounting scandals, involving such companies as Enron, WorldCom, Adelphia, and Global Crossing, prompted Congress and the public to ask "Where are the auditors?" The CPAs who performed audits on the scandal-ridden companies and who failed to detect financial impropriety were blamed (and sued) for profiting while fraud flourished on their watches.

This chapter explores how the audit profession as a whole came to be viewed as ethically ailing and incapable of self-regulation following waves of scandal. It explains how standards set by the Sarbanes-Oxley Act (SOX) and Securities and Exchange Commission (SEC) regulations impact the audit profession.

How SOX Rocks the Accounting Profession

Both SOX and the 2003 SEC rules passed to further the legislation regarding corporate America fundamentally change the accounting profession. These rules take aim at auditors who unquestioningly accepted large fees from corrupt corporate clients and performed only cursory audit testing before signing off on the engagement.

SOX now mandates the following:

- ✔ **Audit of internal control:** Under SOX Section 404, the company's independent auditors must conduct an audit on the company's internal control practices over financial reporting and must come up with two opinions; one on management's assessment and another on the effectiveness of the company's internal control over financial reporting.

- ✔ **New standards for auditor independence:** SOX introduces a new set of independence rules and regulations that affect accounting professionals who are performing audits. These new standards include a list of prohibited services.

- ✔ **A shift from self-regulation:** SOX signals a fundamental shift in regulating the accounting industry, from a primarily self-regulated environment to a public approach (see the section "SOX as a Substitute for Self-Regulation" later in this chapter).

- ✔ **Establishment of the Public Company Accounting Oversight Board (PCAOB):** This board has the direct authority to oversee and discipline the accounting profession.

- ✔ **Records of retention rules:** Auditors must save and store all records related to an audit for seven years.

An Example of Audit Failure: Arthur Andersen

In March 2002, Arthur Andersen, one of the world's largest and most prestigious audit firms, was indicted by the U.S. Department of Justice on charges of obstructing the course of justice in the Enron case. The Justice Department claimed that Andersen personnel shredded many documents related to its work for Enron while Enron was being investigated by the SEC.

By the end of 2002, Arthur Andersen had ceased operations and was a mere line on a resume for hundreds of out-of-work accountants, consultants, and support staff. The firm has come to symbolize the unethical environment in which audit firms operated in the 1990s and the pervasive conflicts that were deemed acceptable in the audit industry to the detriment of the investing public.

Chronology of a collapse

The following are the key events in Arthur Andersen's downfall:

1. **The shredding policy memo:** On October 19, 2001, just as Enron's collapse became public, Nancy Temple, a lawyer for Arthur Andersen, sent an e-mail to employees reminding them of the company's policy of "routine" document shredding. Two tons of documents were destroyed just prior to Andersen receiving notification that it was under investigation by the SEC.

2. **The criminal indictment:** On March 14, 2002, the Justice Department announced the criminal indictment of Arthur Andersen. The indictment contained a single count of obstruction of justice based on Arthur Andersen's destruction of Enron documents.

3. **The criminal conviction:** On June 15, 2002, the jury handed down a guilty verdict on the charge of obstruction of justice.

4. **Disbanding of the firm:** In response to the criminal conviction, Arthur Andersen announced it would cease operations as of August 12, 2002.

5. **The vindication:** In June 2005, the U.S. Supreme Court overturned the criminal conviction against Andersen.

The court fined Arthur Andersen only $500,000, the maximum criminal penalty permitted under the statute. However, the fine was miniscule compared to the exposure the firm faced from pending civil lawsuits emanating from its audits of Enron, Global Crossing, WorldCom, and other former clients plagued by accounting scandals. The criminal conviction in the Enron case virtually assured huge verdicts against the firm in all of these cases.

A vindicating verdict . . . years later

Ultimately, in 2005, the Supreme Court overturned the Arthur Andersen verdict on the basis of faulty instructions given to the jury by the federal judge in the case. The nine Supreme Court justices concluded that the jury in the case had been given vague and overly broad instructions by the presiding federal judge.

Because of the faulty instructions, the court concluded that Arthur Andersen was convicted without legal proof that its document shredding was intended to undermine the pending SEC investigation. The Supreme Court held that the jury should have been instructed that the law required the government to prove that Andersen knew it was breaking the law and acted intentionally.

Unfortunately, the successful Supreme Court appeal came three years too late to save Andersen and to prevent the "Big Five" audit firms in the United States from becoming "the Big Four." At the time of its 2002 conviction, more than 28,000 professionals were employed by the company. By the time of the verdict, Arthur Andersen had a staff of only 200.

On the brighter side, the favorable appeal may help Andersen and its malpractice insurers defend the firm in pending shareholder suits related to its work for Enron, Global Crossing, and other former clients. It also may help some individuals defend or fight criminal prosecution.

Some lawyers speculate that the Supreme Court's 2005 decision to overturn the Arthur Andersen conviction reflects concern about the provisions of SOX, which allow the government to aggressively prosecute CPAs and audit firms.

Bridging the GAAP

During congressional hearings on SOX, Congress was outraged to learn that Enron's auditors at Arthur Andersen had suggested several adjustments to the company's financial statements. Andersen had indicated it was unwilling to give Enron an "unqualified" opinion that its financial statements were prepared in accordance with *Generally Accepted Accounting Principles,* or GAAP. (As I explain in the section "The GAAP all financial statements must fall into" later in this chapter, an unqualified opinion is the type most firms need to have.)

The adjustments proposed by the auditors would have reduced Enron's reported net income for the year from $104 million to $54 million. When Enron's management refused to make the adjustments, Andersen gave in and eventually certified the financial statements anyway.

In response to this revelation, SOX amends the Securities Exchange Act of 1934 to deter auditors from giving in to clients in the future. The revised law states what perhaps should have been assumed from the very beginning:

> *ACCURACY OF FINANCIAL REPORTS — Each financial report that contains financial statements, and that is required to be prepared in accordance with (or reconciled to) generally accepted accounting principles under this title and filed with the Commission shall reflect all material correcting adjustments that have been identified by a registered public accounting firm in accordance with generally accepted accounting principles and the rules and regulations of the Commission.*

SOX as a Substitute for Self-Regulation

Prior to SOX, the accounting profession was self-regulated in that CPAs formed an organization known as the *American Institute of Certified Public Accountants* (AICPA). One of this organization's main functions was to set rules and standards for its own members, which it did by maintaining its Generally Accepted Accounting Principles (GAAP) and Generally Accepted Auditing Standards (GAAS) as well as a Code of Professional Conduct.

Not surprisingly, Congress and the SEC viewed the events tied to Enron, WorldCom, Adelphia, and Global Crossing as evidence that the self-regulation system didn't work, and so it established a new government entity to take over the task.

Congress decided that it needed to do more than make a lot of new rules for auditors to apply to themselves. So instead it created the *Public Company Accounting Oversight Board* (PCAOB) to fill the regulatory gap.

The standards set by the PCAOB not only impact large accounting firms, but they also apply to any CPA who's actively providing an audit opinion to a publicly traded company. The five-member PCAOB has the authority to set and enforce the following standards for auditors of public companies:

- Auditing
- Attestation
- Quality control
- Ethics (including independence)

Many of the PCAOB's responsibilities overlap with the AICPA, including:

- Registering public accounting firms that issue audit reports for publicly traded companies
- Establishing auditing, quality control, ethics, independence, and other standards for audit firms relating to their preparation of audit reports
- Conducting inspections of registered public accounting firms
- Conducting investigations and disciplinary proceedings and imposing appropriate sanctions on audit firms and auditors

The PCAOB's powers, duties, and procedures are discussed in more detail in Chapter 7.

Shifting the role of the AICPA

Despite the establishment of the PCAOB, the AICPA continues to play a critical role in setting GAAP and GAAS that the PCAOB enforces. The AICPA remains primarily responsible for establishing critical day-to-day accounting and standards for the profession. The difference is that it now answers to the PCAOB in deciding how to apply and enforce those standards.

As of April 16, 2003, the PCAOB essentially adopted all GAAS by the AICPA as interim standards for audits of public companies. However, the PCAOB also announced on the same day that it wouldn't rely on the AICPA in the future but would instead be preparing its own standards.

The AICPA continues to set standards for CPAs in the United States, the District of Columbia, Guam, Puerto Rico, and the Virgin Islands. By creating the PCAOB, Congress and the SEC weren't suggesting that AICPA rules and standards be abandoned. Rather, Congress took the position that the profession needed outside intervention to enforce them.

The GAAP all financial statements must fall into

In reviewing a company's financial statements, auditors render opinions that are included as part of the company's required SEC disclosures. (See Chapter 3, where I discuss the documents companies must file with the SEC.) The auditor's opinion, along with the other SEC documents, is made available to the public.

Auditors can be sued by investors, creditors, and other parties who rely on financial statements that they've audited.

The AICPA Code of Professional Conduct dictates that licensed CPAs must strictly adhere to GAAP in rendering their opinions. An *unqualified opinion* (which is the kind every company ultimately aspires to get) means that the CPA has found that the financial statements or other financial data is "presented fairly . . . in conformity with generally accepted accounting principles." If any information contains any departures from GAAP, the CPA must either render a *qualified opinion* explaining the departures from GAAP or refuse to render an opinion at all.

GAAP is particularly concerned with issues of consistency. An audit opinion not only must state whether the financial statements have been prepared in conformity with GAAP but also must address whether these principles have been applied consistently from one year to the next.

If the auditors aren't confident that a company's financial statements "present fairly" all the necessary information that the public and the SEC need in order to be informed, management may be asked to make *audit adjustments,* adjusting or adding information to financial statements before the auditors issue an unqualified opinion.

Footnotes often contain the information that auditors require companies to include because they think it's necessary for the reader to properly interpret the financial statements. A great deal of important information (such as long-term obligations or pending lawsuits) may be "buried" in the footnotes.

If the auditors can't issue an unqualified opinion, they may instead render a qualified or adverse opinion or disclaim an opinion. The basic format for each type of opinion is pretty much the same, except that in a qualified or adverse opinion, an additional paragraph is added for each problem that's found within the financial statements. A disclaimer of opinion is issued when the auditors are unable to complete the entire audit for some reason.

The GAAS audits run on

Generally Accepted Auditing Standards, or GAAS, have been around since 1941, when the president of a large drug company, McKesson & Robbins, Inc., and his three brothers embezzled company funds. A very public investigation ensued.

In response to the McKesson case, the AICPA developed GAAS for auditors to follow while conducting the audit of a company's or government entity's financial statements. These standards are maintained and updated by the AICPA to this day, and because of SOX, the PCAOB helps enforce the standards and discipline accountants who disobey them.

GAAS are divided into three categories:

- ✔ **General Standards:** Deal with technical training and proficiency, independence, and due professional care
- ✔ **Standards of Fieldwork:** Address issues pertaining to the planning, supervision, examination, and evaluation of internal controls
- ✔ **Standards of Reporting:** Are concerned with the auditor's function of determining whether the financial statements are presented in accordance with GAAP

Whose turn is it to watch the CPA?

Under GAAS, an auditor must remain independent of the client at all times and avoid any situations that may jeopardize that independence. These standards are short on specifics, so SOX and the SEC have concentrated considerable effort to clarify them.

Figure 6-1 shows how CPAs, the PCAOB, and the AICPA fit into the overall regulatory process established by SOX.

Is There an Independent Auditor in the House?

During their exhaustive hearings on the objectives of SOX, Congress and the SEC identified *auditor independence* (or the lack of thereof) as the smoking gun in many major accounting scandals.

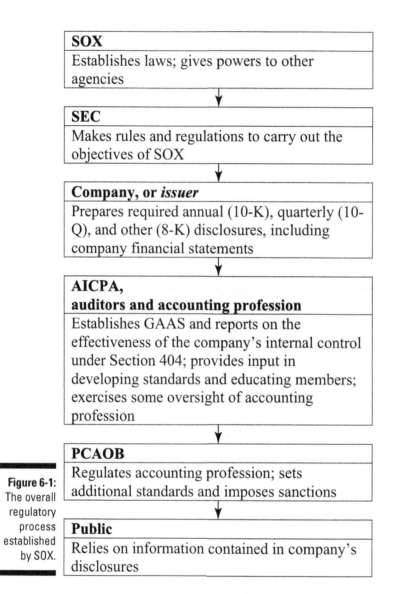

SOX
Establishes laws; gives powers to other agencies

SEC
Makes rules and regulations to carry out the objectives of SOX

Company, or *issuer*
Prepares required annual (10-K), quarterly (10-Q), and other (8-K) disclosures, including company financial statements

AICPA, auditors and accounting profession
Establishes GAAS and reports on the effectiveness of the company's internal control under Section 404; provides input in developing standards and educating members; exercises some oversight of accounting profession

PCAOB
Regulates accounting profession; sets additional standards and imposes sanctions

Public
Relies on information contained in company's disclosures

Figure 6-1:
The overall regulatory process established by SOX.

The importance of audit independence

Auditors are the arbiters of integrity when it comes to financial statements; they certify that the financial reports and disclosures fairly reflect the financial picture of a company and that they were prepared in accordance with GAAP.

It's an anomaly of the U.S. financial reporting system that auditors are hired and paid for performing an audit by the very companies they're auditing.

Despite this symbiotic relationship, an auditor is expected to remain distanced from the client/auditee both in appearance and in fact.

Some of the ways Congress and the SEC seek to ensure auditor independence involve imposing the following general restrictions on the profession:

- ✔ Banning auditors from performing certain types of nonaudit services to audit clients
- ✔ Requiring auditors to get preapproval from the company's audit committee before doing nonaudit services not banned by SEC rules
- ✔ Mandating the rotation of the lead partner on a company's audit every five years
- ✔ Requiring a five-year timeout period for members of an audit engagement team before they can work for an audit client

Every auditor's dilemma

Accounting firms don't live on audits alone. Virtually all accounting firms perform some sort of consulting or advisory services (such as tax-related work) in addition to carrying out the audit function.

When these advisory services are rendered, the question of independence emerges. Can an audit firm objectively examine financial statements prepared by management while relying on management to renew a lucrative consulting contract? This is an ongoing dilemma that SOX attempts to address.

The auditor independence provisions of SOX were strongly influenced by the fact that Arthur Andersen received $25 million in audit fees and $27 million in consulting fees from Enron in the years prior to its bankruptcy filing.

What SOX Says to CPAs

The SEC has high expectations for the accounting profession, and it views the auditor's opinion as an important instrument in protecting the public. The agency has stated that the auditor's opinion "furnishes investors with critical assurance that the financial statements have been subjected to rigorous examination by an objective, impartial and skilled professional, and that investors, therefore, can rely upon them."

In order to ensure that auditors are "objective, impartial and skilled," SOX and the corresponding SEC rules impose upon them the requirements that I cover in this section.

Give the whole team a cooling-off period

It used to be that accounting clients openly recruited members of an outside audit staff to fill positions in their own accounting departments, which explains why a lot of CFOs and controllers started as auditors.

Now, however, both SOX and corresponding SEC final rules require a one-year cooling-off period before any member of an audit engagement team can go to work for a former audit client. This cooling-off period is intended to prevent undue influence on audit quality. The concern is that a former member of the audit team may attempt to influence that team in order to benefit his or her new employer.

Prohibit services that cause conflicts

After SOX, many auditors find that they may have to choose between performing an audit and performing other equally lucrative services for a client. Most banned services are related to consulting or advisory services that could create a conflict of interest for independent auditors.

Under SOX Section 201 and SEC Regulation SX Rule 2-1(c) (4), auditors are no longer permitted to provide the following types of services to the clients they're auditing:

- **Bookkeeping:** Auditors can't keep books, maintain accounting records, or provide other related services to a client. Doing so destroys the auditor's independence, as defined by SOX and SEC rules. If bookkeeping services weren't prohibited, auditors would potentially be auditing records and financial statements they themselves prepared.

- **Information systems:** An auditor can't help a company design or implement financial information systems because ultimately the auditor must evaluate those same systems for control and compliance.

  Prior to SOX, installing and maintaining computerized accounting systems for large clients were very lucrative consulting services offered by many big accounting firms. Because this activity was first banned in 2000 (prior to SOX), many accounting firms have sold off their computer consulting divisions.

- **Appraisal and valuation services:** These systems involve determinations of fairness and reasonableness of exchanges of property and money. The value assigned to these assets directly affects the balance sheet and other financial statements.

- **Actuarial services:** Because actuarial services involve a determination of amounts recorded in the financial statements, auditor involvement can lead to a conflict of interest if questions regarding the audit arise.

✔ **Internal audit outsourcing services:** Sometimes a company needs extra manpower to perform its accounting functions and may hire a third-party service provider for this purpose. Examples of outsourced services include payroll, internal audit functions, or financial information gathering. Because these outsourced services are related to some of the information that must be audited, auditors can no longer perform them for the clients they audit.

✔ **Management functions:** Auditors can't act temporarily or permanently as directors, officers, or employees of an audit client.

✔ **Human resources:** Auditors can't act as so-called headhunters and help the client company find candidates or do background checks on candidates for positions in managerial, executive, or director positions.

✔ **Broker-dealer, investment advisor, or investment banking services:** Auditors can't act as brokers, promoters, or underwriters on behalf of a client they're auditing; nor can they assist in making investment decisions.

✔ **Legal services:** Auditors can't provide any service to audit clients that could be provided only by someone licensed to practice law.

✔ **Expert services unrelated to audit:** Auditors can't give their clients expert opinions on matters that may be the subject of the audit. For example, an auditor can't write his client a memo containing his opinion about a regulatory issue.

All these prohibited service areas are covered in more detail in Chapter 23.

What economic impact does the list of prohibited services have on the accounting profession as a whole? In the end, it means that the large accounting firms simply work for more companies, and the companies themselves work with multiple accounting firms.

Get prior permission for potential conflicts

Services not banned outright by SOX Section 201 and the SEC rules may be permitted if auditors jump through the right hoops. If a service isn't on the prohibited list, such as tax services, for example, it's permitted only if the auditor gets permission from the client's audit committee before doing the work. (Services that are banned outright are covered in the preceding section.)

The SEC rules require that the company disclose on its financial statements *any* fees it pays to its auditors. Companies must separately disclose fees that they pay their auditors to perform audit and nonaudit services.

Tax services are one area in which audit firms have been given some leeway. Generally, an audit firm may give tax-planning services and advice to a client but can't represent the client in a pending tax proceeding.

Everybody change partners!

Both SOX and SEC rules prohibit long-term client/auditor relationships. Specifically, these rules limit the time that a partner can serve on a client's audit to five consecutive years. Apparently, the SEC and Congress have determined that the value of experience is outweighed by the risk of losing one's objectivity.

Wait seven years to shred

SOX introduces a seven-year storage rule for accounting firms. With this rule, the firms must retain all records relevant to the audits and reviews of any companies that file reports with the SEC.

Records that can't be purged or shredded under SOX Rule 802 include work papers as well as electronic records that contain conclusions, opinions, analyses, and financial data related to the audit or review. Specifically, the SEC requires accounting firms to retain any documentation that's "inconsistent" with conclusions reached by the auditors in the course of the audit.

Recognize when auditors are "impaired"

It's the job of a company's audit committee to identify situations in which an auditor's independence is impaired and recommend appropriate action. Want to know what happens under the new stringent standards introduced by SOX when an auditor's independence is somehow compromised? A violation of the independence rules (see the section "Is There an Independent Auditor in the House?" earlier in this chapter) may result in a company being forced to change auditors midstream, before the audit is complete. This interruption in the process can result in considerable cost to the company for duplicative services.

If the auditor's impairment isn't remedied during the audit, the consequences may be even worse — financial statements may be required to be restated or reissued.

Section 404: The Sin Eater Provision

SOX requires CEOs and CFOs to certify that financial sins haven't been committed on their watches at the expense of shareholders. It further requires that the auditors certify management's reports. Two levels of review and accountability mean that more professionals and their malpractice insurers share any potential liability for corporate wrongdoing.

CEOs and CFOs signing off

SOX Section 404 requires CEOs to evaluate and report on the effectiveness of their company's internal control. This report is included in the company's Form 10-K annual report, which is filed with the SEC.

The SEC has passed rules to specifically implement the requirements of Section 404. The concept of internal control and the specific contents of management's report are discussed more fully in Chapter 10.

In addition to providing the required report on internal control, the company's CEO and CFO are required to sign certifications that are attached to the company's 10-K and 10-Q quarterly reports.

CPAs certifying the certifications

The PCAOB issues standards for auditors to follow in certifying management's report on internal controls. The new PCAOB Auditing Standard No. 5 replaces the old Auditing Standard No. 2. It directs auditors to focus less on minutiae by using a "top down" approach to direct the greatest testing resources to the areas that pose the most risk to companies. It also directs auditors as to how and when they may rely on testing by third parties.

Chapter 7

A Board to Audit the Auditors

*A*uditors are arbiters of fairness and accuracy in the world of securities and investing. Their job is to ensure that the information that appears on a corporation's financial statements is an accurate, objective reflection of its financial operations.

The Sarbanes-Oxley Act (SOX) ends an era of self-regulation previously enjoyed by the accounting firms that audit public companies. Specifically, SOX created a new *Public Company Accounting Oversight Board* (PCAOB) to register, supervise, and discipline these firms.

When you really get down to it, the PCAOB has the enormous task of overseeing ethics and conflict-of-interest issues in the audit world. However, the board wasn't without controversy. It had to withdraw its most comprehensive auditing standard amid horror stories of excessive audits and uncontrolled costs that were eating into corporate profits and adversely affecting shareholders.

In this chapter, I take a look at the reasons for establishing a special oversight body for the auditing profession, which has historically regulated itself. I also discuss what the PCAOB has passed (and withdrawn) in the way of standards for auditors, and I explore the messages it's sending to the audit profession and corporate America.

Taking a New Approach to Audit Oversight

The need for increased auditor oversight became a potent political mantra in the United States during congressional hearings in the post-Enron era (around 2001). The media ran heavy coverage of a flawed audit process followed by the demise of public companies. The public questioned why accountants had been permitted to govern themselves for decades through their own professional organizations and affiliations without government intervention. As the expected response to these questions and concerns, SOX established unprecedented government oversight of the accounting profession by the Securities and Exchange Commission (SEC) through its newly created arm, the Public Company Accounting Oversight Board, or PCAOB.

Unfortunately, the PCAOB got off to an unfavorable start. Harvey Pitt, the first guy who was appointed to head the board, resigned after it came to light that he was director of a board under investigation. So the PCAOB held its first meeting without a chair (during which it voted on a $400,000 salary for each member). Subsequently, William J. McDonough, current chair, was ensconced only to resign two years later.

This section looks at some history of accounting oversight, including the responsibilities held by the SEC, in order to further highlight the need for the PCAOB and closer government monitoring of accounting firms.

The old ad hoc system of accounting oversight

Prior to SOX, the SEC, individual states, and the accounting profession shared regulatory authority over accounting firms that audited public companies. Their influence broke down as follows:

- **The SEC** maintained standards for financial statements submitted with filings required by the Securities Act of 1933 and the Securities Exchange Act of 1934 (as discussed in Chapter 3). It also prohibited certified public accountants (CPAs) from practicing if they weren't in good standing.

- **The states** held the responsibility of licensing and registering CPAs.

- **The accounting profession** established the American Institute of Accountants, which later became the American Institute of Certified Public Accountants (AICPA). This private entity developed standards for certifying accountants and governing the profession, the content of financial statements, and the conduct of audits. The AICPA's standards were followed by most states admirably and without incident until the major corporate scandals of the new millennium (see Chapter 18 for details).

Alphabet soup of accounting regulation

The SEC has only become involved in the business of setting accounting or auditing standards on a sort of peripheral basis, leaving most of the job to the accountants themselves via the AICPA. To a great extent, the PCAOB is expected to defer to AICPA standards rather than rewrite them. This section offers an aerial view of the patchwork landscape of regulations in place before the PCAOB came on the scene.

FASB pronouncements

In 1973, the AICPA created an independent body with the responsibility of crafting accounting standards. The seven-member Financial Accounting Standards Board (FASB) is administered by a not-for-profit organization called the Financial Accounting Foundation (FAF), which appoints FASB members and funds that board's activities. SOX creates a mandatory funding scheme for the FAF and FASB but doesn't otherwise alter the authority or function of FASB or the weight that its pronouncements carry.

ASB standards

The AICPA established the Accounting Standards Board (ASB) in 1978 to provide technical assistance and support to the accounting profession. The ASB distributes publications that provide "auditing, attestation and quality control standards and guidance." (*Attestation* refers to the process of verifying the information reported on financial statements or in other documents.) The SEC has traditionally deferred to the ASB's auditing standards and is expected to continue to do so after SOX.

The prior POB

An interesting note in the annals of accounting self-regulation is the fate of the Public Oversight Board (POB), an ill-fated predecessor to the PCAOB. The POB was created by the SEC in 1978 to enhance audit quality and help ensure adequate internal control within audit firms. The POB was intended, among other things, to administer peer review and quality control programs within the profession. Under POB standards, accounting firms that audited the financial statements of public companies were required to go through a peer review process conducted by another audit firm every three years.

When many accounting firms balked at the cost of paying for the peer review process, the POB lacked the support necessary to enforce its policies. Frustrated with its own ineffectiveness, the POB voted itself out of existence in 2002.

Primary Purposes of the PCAOB

For the majority of public companies, accounting firms, and auditors, self-regulation was a concept that worked remarkably well. That's why much of the new Public Company Accounting Oversight Board's function is to promote public trust and a sense that the government is monitoring the accounting profession. While the PCAOB provides an added layer of enforcement, it continues to look to the profession itself to suggest and maintain technical standards for conducting audits and reporting financial information.

The PCAOB's role is primarily one of enforcement, added analysis, and discipline. The SOX sections that create the PCAOB are directed at sorting out the profession's bad apples; they aren't by any means focused on overall accounting standards or procedures.

It only makes sense that the PCAOB not scrap the accounting profession's well-defined standards that have taken decades to develop. Rather, the focus is on shoring up enforcement of these existing standards and tightening them as necessary. After all, who understands the nuances of the accounting profession better than the accountants themselves?

Goals of the PCAOB

The functions and scope of the PCAOB were hotly debated and extensively discussed during congressional hearings on SOX. In the end, Congress, the SEC, and, to some extent, the accounting profession agreed on the following objectives for the PCAOB:

- ✔ **Revamp standards for the accounting profession.** The PCAOB takes a good look at the standards that the AICPA has put into place for accountants over the last several decades and decides which standards stay, which ones go, and what new rules should be imposed.

- ✔ **Investigate questionable conduct by auditors.** Prior to the PCAOB, the accounting profession investigated its members by way of a loose system that was largely based on volunteer committees within the AICPA that were assisted by a few paid staff whose salaries were funded with members' dues. The disciplinary process was perceived by many as subject to cronyism and arbitrariness, with small firms far more likely to be sanctioned and CPAs in large firms left alone. During the post-Enron hearings, however, Congress seemed to take the view that as a volunteer organization, the AICPA lacked resources, training, and government support to police the entire profession. And that's when the PCAOB received its new duty of investigating questionable auditor conduct.

✓ **Discipline errant auditors.** In its capacity as the new disciplinary authority for errant CPAs, the PCAOB is charged with administering sensible
sanctions in an even-handed manner.

✓ **Ensure that the auditing profession keeps up with changing times.** As
information technology and the nature of business conducted by public
companies evolves and in response to the increasing globalization of the
U.S. economy, the PCAOB faces the challenge of making sure the auditing profession doesn't fall behind the times.

The seven statutory duties of the PCAOB

Administrative agencies often have overlapping functions and therefore can
be prone to turf wars with other agencies. To avoid having the PCAOB step
on the toes of other state and federal regulatory bodies, Congress carefully
spells out what it actually intended the PCAOB to do — and not to do. SOX
Section 101(c) lays out the following seven statutory duties of the PCAOB:

✓ Register public accounting firms that prepare audit reports

✓ Establish, or adopt, by rule, "auditing, quality control, ethics, independence, and other standards relating to the preparation of audit reports
for issuers"

✓ Conduct inspections of accounting firms

✓ Conduct investigations and disciplinary proceedings, and impose appropriate sanctions

✓ Enforce compliance with the Sarbanes-Oxley Act, the rules of the PCAOB,
professional standards, and the securities laws relating to the preparation and issuance of audit reports and the obligations and liabilities of
accountants with respect thereto

✓ Set the budget and manage the operations of the PCAOB and its staff

✓ Perform such other duties or functions as necessary or appropriate

Some Practical PCAOB Matters

As I mention earlier in the chapter, the Public Company Accounting Oversight
Board is the child of the Securities and Exchange Commission. In its capacity
of protecting the investing public, the SEC appoints members of the board
and oversees them. In turn, the PCAOB works with the AICPA to ensure the
quality of audits and financial statements.

Who's on the board?

The PCAOB is required to have five full-time, financially literate members who are appointed for five-year terms. (*Financially literate* generally means able to understand and assess the information in the financial statements based on professional experience doing so.) To balance the perspective of the board, two of the members must have backgrounds as CPAs (either currently holding that job or held it in the past), and the remaining three members must *not* be CPAs. The board chairperson can be a CPA, but he or she can't have practiced as one in the prior five years. SOX also stipulates that no member of the PCAOB is permitted to "share in any of the profits of, or receive payments from, a public accounting firm."

Who pays for the PCAOB?

Under SOX, an accounting firm must register with the PCAOB and pay registration and annual fees before it can audit a public company. Essentially, auditors are paying for their own PCAOB audits through these mandatory fees. This arrangement has a certain logic to it; public companies currently pay the bill for their own audits. The PCAOB is authorized to set these fees at amounts that are sufficient to recover the costs of processing and reviewing applications and annual reports.

The mandatory dues also pay the costs of setting standards and disciplining the profession. The PCAOB needs research and support staff in order to issue standards or adopt standards set by other groups or organizations, and PCAOB dues fund inspections and investigations of public accounting firms as well as disciplinary hearings and proceedings.

In addition to mandatory registration and annual fees, the PCAOB also establishes by rule a reasonable *annual accounting support fee*. This fee is charged only as necessary or appropriate to maintain the board, and the fee is assessed on issuers only.

PCAOB Rules: Old Meets New

Under SOX, the PCAOB is required to "cooperate on an on-going basis" with designated professional groups of accountants. The PCAOB also has the authority to amend, modify, repeal, and reject any standards it doesn't like, which includes deciding which FASB and AICPA rules and pronouncements to keep.

The PCAOB must report its standard-setting activity to the SEC on an annual basis.

Sticking to the ol' standby rules

The PCAOB technically gets to pick and choose which rules of the FASB, ASB, and other AICPA-created bodies it wants to keep "to the extent that it determines appropriate." However, the SEC, which oversees the PCAOB, is separately authorized to "recognize, as 'generally accepted' . . . any accounting principles" that are established by a standard-setting body that meets SOX's criteria.

To be considered *standard-setting,* a body must:

- ✔ Be a private entity (as opposed to a public charity or not-for-profit organization)

- ✔ Be governed by a board of trustees (or an equivalent body), the majority of whom are not or have not been associated with a public accounting firm for the past two years

- ✔ Be funded in a manner similar to the PCAOB

- ✔ Have adopted procedures to ensure prompt consideration of changes to accounting principles by a majority vote

- ✔ Consider, when adopting standards, the need to keep them current and the extent to which international convergence of standards is necessary or appropriate

For the short term, the PCAOB is expected to keep existing standards in each of the following areas:

- ✔ **Auditing:** Generally Accepted Auditing Standards (GAAS) developed by the AICPA and the ASB remain in force.

- ✔ **Attestation and quality control:** The PCAOB continues to use the Statements of Position developed by the ASB for engagements that require auditors to attest to the accuracy of documents.

- ✔ **Ethics and independence:** The PCAOB relies heavily on the AICPA's existing Code of Professional Conduct, which covers recommendations on things such as an auditor's obligations to third parties who may be relying on financial statements and when impermissible conflicts of interest may arise in particular situations.

Adjusting to some new rules

New boards bring new rules, and thanks to the PCAOB, not everything is business as usual for the accounting profession. As I explain in Chapter 6, CPAs have many new burdens, obligations, PCAOB pronouncements, and SEC rules to follow. The PCAOB is directly involved in implementing the changes covered in this section.

Inspections of registered public accounting firms

Public accounting firms are subject to regular inspections with respect to their audits of public companies. The frequency of the inspections depends on how many public companies a firm audits. For example:

✔ Firms that audit more than 100 public companies are inspected annually.

✔ Firms that audit fewer than 100 companies are inspected every three years.

In addition, the SEC or the PCAOB may order a special inspection of any firm at any time.

Maintenance of work paper trails

The PCAOB is responsible for making sure that registered public accounting firms "prepare, and maintain for a period of not less than 7 years, audit work papers, and other information related to any audit report, in sufficient detail to support the conclusions reached in such report."

Supervision of internal quality standards and reviews

The PCAOB is in charge of ensuring that accounting firms carry out certain SOX mandates with respect to public accounting firms' internal supervision and review. Namely, SOX requires that a second partner review and approve audits of reports and that each accounting firm adopt its own quality control standards.

Standards for reviews of Section 404 audits

SOX requires the PCAOB to oversee and implement standards for public accounting firms to use as they conduct Section 404 audits, a special type of audit that pertains to a company's internal control (see Chapter 10).

Section 404 requires auditors to:

✔ Evaluate whether the internal control structure and procedures include records that accurately and fairly reflect the transactions of the company

✔ Provide reasonable assurance that the transactions are recorded in a manner that will permit the preparation of financial statements in accordance with Generally Accepted Accounting Principles (GAAP)

✔ Include a description of any material weaknesses in the internal controls

Evolving PCAOB Policies and Issues

The practical implications of establishing the PCAOB as an unprecedented arm of the SEC are ongoing. The public and the accounting profession can expect further SEC rules to define the PCAOB's powers and limitations. More importantly, pronouncements issued by the new PCAOB profoundly impact the accounting profession in a direct way. This section highlights a few key policies that have emerged with respect to the role of the PCAOB.

Sanctioning sloppy auditors

The PCAOB is empowered to police public accounting firms with an unprecedented range of enforcement and oversight mechanisms. As directed by SOX, the PCAOB regularly inspects registered accounting firms' operations and follows up to investigate potential violations of securities laws and accounting standards.

The PCAOB has the authority to conduct full-blown investigations and hearings, including requiring testimony or documentation, to determine if an accounting firm has committed a violation. The PCAOB also can refer matters to the SEC for investigation, or, with the SEC's approval, to the Department of Justice, state attorneys general, or state boards of accountancy.

If the PCAOB decides to conduct the investigation itself, it can directly impose an array of formidable sanctions, including civil penalties, revocation or suspension of an accounting firm's registration, and prohibition of the CPA firm from auditing public companies. If an accounting firm violates rules passed by the PCAOB, it's subject to the same penalties imposed for violations of SEC rules under the Securities Exchange Act of 1934. (For more on this legislation, check out Chapter 3.)

Keeping an eye on small CPA firms

Even accounting firms that don't audit any public companies may be subject to the long arm of the PCAOB if their state laws permit. Under SOX, state regulators are directed to independently decide whether PCAOB standards should apply to small and mid-size nonregistered accounting firms within their borders.

Extending authority internationally

Sometimes foreign accounting firms perform all or part of an audit. This arrangement may be the case, for example, when foreign subsidiaries or operations are reported on a company's U.S. financial statements.

SOX provides that foreign accounting firms that "prepare or furnish" audit reports involving U.S. registrants are subject to the authority of the PCAOB. Additionally, if a U.S. accounting firm relies on some or all of the work of a foreign accounting firm, the foreign firm's audit work papers must be supplied to the PCAOB upon request.

Communicating with the SEC

The PCAOB is required to notify the SEC of pending investigations involving potential violations of the securities laws, and it also must coordinate its investigation with the SEC Division of Enforcement as necessary to protect ongoing SEC investigations.

The PCAOB also must notify the SEC when it imposes "any final sanction" on any accounting firm or associated person because the board's findings and sanctions are subject to review by the SEC. The SEC may enhance, modify, cancel, reduce, or require remission of such sanctions.

When the PCAOB Doesn't Perform

SOX is a piece of legislation that leaves nothing to chance with respect to accounting oversight and regulation. The statute even provides for the contingency that the PCAOB may become compromised or ineffectual; it states that the SEC shall have "oversight and enforcement authority over the board," which means that the SEC can require the board to retain certain records and can inspect the PCAOB itself.

Also, the SEC may, by order, "censure or impose limitations upon the activities, functions, and operations" of the PCAOB if it finds that the board has violated the securities laws or has failed to ensure that accounting firms comply with applicable rules.

Struggling for Standards

In 2004, the PCAOB unveiled Auditing Standard No. 2 to provide for an integrated audit of both internal control over financial reporting and the financial statements themselves.

Companies everywhere cried "uncle" as swarms of auditors billed them billions in response to the testing standards contained in Auditing Standard No. 2. Because of this new standard, corporate America was experiencing "audit shock." The PCAOB and SEC once again worked in tandem by withdrawing Auditing Standard No. 2 and fashioning Auditing Standard No. 5 to address the collective experience of corporate America with SOX Section 404. The following sections explain both standards.

Adapting to Auditing Standard No. 2

In 2003, the PCAOB had its work cut out for it. It was a new agency regulating a profession that had previously regulated itself. It had to draw on other sources to develop its first Auditing Standard No. 2, which was to provide direction to auditors. In drafting this standard, the PCAOB had to define new tasks and roles for auditors who were accustomed to auditing financial statements rather than internal controls, as required by SOX Section 404.

Some argue that in the PCAOB's eagerness to get it right and in the audit profession's anxiousness not to come under further negative scrutiny, testing under Section 404 went into overdrive. Corporate America and Congress began crying foul with respect to costs, and investors were concerned that profits were being drained by overzealous auditors.

Why did these problems arise? Auditing Standard No. 2 required auditors to

- Plan the audit
- Evaluate management's assessment process
- Obtain an understanding of internal control and issue a report
- Test and evaluate design and operating effectiveness
- Evaluate the sufficiency of testing
- Formulate an opinion on the effectiveness of internal control over financial reporting
- Communicate findings to the audit committee and management

Although auditors had routinely carried out most of the preceding steps when performing a financial statement audit, the audit of internal control under SOX required more extensive procedures. Specifically, Auditing Standard No. 2 required auditors to perform the following new tasks:

- ✔ Differentiate between management and auditor responsibilities
- ✔ Identify entities to include in the consolidated group
- ✔ Select testing locations
- ✔ Distinguish design effectiveness from operating effectiveness
- ✔ Consider issues related to the "as of" date
- ✔ Decide on the extent of control testing
- ✔ Use the work of others
- ✔ Distinguish between a material weakness and a significant deficiency
- ✔ Report results to management and financial statement users

In an attempt to get all of these steps right, auditors billed clients endlessly. They justified this excessive billing by citing the requirements that Auditing Standard No. 2 had brought about. That's when the PCAOB withdrew Auditing Standard No. 2. It did so largely in an effort to restrain the auditors who seemed to have gone to the other extreme from their pre-Enron days of laxity.

Implementing Auditing Standard No. 5

In its new Auditing Standard No. 5, adopted in 2007, the PCAOB sent a message to the nation's auditors that testing under SOX Section 404 was to add value to American corporations, not to needlessly drain profits.

In passing the new standard, the PCAOB was attempting to correct all the bug-a-boos, overtesting, and overbilling by auditors that it found in the two years that it monitored the implementation of its earlier effort, Auditing Standard No. 2.

The overriding principals of SOX Auditing Standard No. 5 are the following:

- ✔ **Zero in on the big-ticket items.** The PCAOB has directed auditors to focus on areas of financial reporting that present the greatest risk of a company's internal controls failing to detect or prevent a material misstatement in its financial statements.

✔ **Use a "top-down approach."** The PCAOB now requires auditors to use a top-down approach. With this approach they begin with the financial statements and company-level controls, and then perform further testing only on those controls within the company that actually impact the accuracy of the company's financial reporting.

✔ **Look at the whole environment.** The PCAOB wants auditors to recognize the importance of a company's entire "control environment." It doesn't want them to miss the forest for the tiny testing trees.

✔ **Streamline sensibly.** The PCAOB has directed auditors to eliminate procedures that that are unnecessary or controls that don't actually make financial statements more accurate. The PCAOB especially wants auditors to use experience gained in previous years' audits to make audits in subsequent years more efficient.

✔ **Scale back.** The PCAOB has directed auditors to implement testing that makes sense and is based on a company's size. In other words, the audit should be tailored to fit the company.

Chapter 8

The Almighty Audit Committee

S OX requires the board of directors of every public company to form an audit committee. Despite their name, these committees don't actually audit anything. Rather, they have direct responsibility for monitoring the independent CPA firm that conducts the audit of the company. This responsibility includes hiring and firing the firms, preapproving their services and fees, resolving disputes with management, and monitoring the quality of the audit.

An audit committee of a publicly traded company is composed of independent or outside directors. Committee members are usually drawn from members of the company's board of directors. For companies subject to Sarbanes-Oxley (SOX), audit committee members are required to be independent from management, and they must be financially literate. This chapter explores how companies implement new standards for audit committee independence, expertise, and objectivity.

Deliver or Delist: Rules of the Stock Exchanges

If you want your company to be listed on a stock exchange, such as the NYSE (New York Stock Exchange), AMEX (American Stock Exchange), or NASDAQ (National Association of Securities Dealers Automated Quotations), your company must follow the particular rules of these organizations. All of these exchanges have their own requirements for the companies that list with them. (The NASDAQ rules, for example, are more liberal and more easily met by smaller companies, as discussed in Chapter 3.)

When it comes to audit committees, the NYSE and NASDAQ require corporations listed with them to have independent audit committees. Under SOX, the Securities and Exchange Committee (SEC) requires the exchanges to impose specific standards for audit committees of publicly traded companies and increases the exchanges' supervisory role over audit committees.

Under the Securities Exchange Act of 1934, the SEC is responsible for supervising the NYSE, NASDAQ, and other exchanges. For further discussion of exchange history and securities legislation, check out Chapter 3.

SOX Section 301 amends the Securities Exchange Act of 1934 to include the following specific requirements for audit committees, which I cover in more detail later in this chapter:

- ✓ **Independence:** Audit committee members must be selected from members of the company's board of directors and can't be compensated by the company or its affiliates for any reason other than for serving as directors.

- ✓ **Complaint procedures:** Every audit committee must have procedures in place for receiving and handling complaints about the company's "accounting, internal accounting controls or auditing matters," including procedures for "the confidential, anonymous submission by the employers . . . of concerns regarding questionable accounting or auditing matters."

- ✓ **Authority to engage advisors:** A company must permit its audit committee to bring on board independent auditors that it "determines necessary to carry out its duties," and it must pay the cost of hiring such advisors.

- ✓ **Company funding:** Companies have to pay for the operations of their audit committees.

The Cynthia Cooper story

In 1997, Cynthia Cooper, the General Auditor for WorldCom, made a startling discovery. Her small audit team uncovered billions of dollars of operating fee expenses paid to local telephone companies. Instead of correctly reporting these expenses in the company's profits and losses, the company executives moved them to the balance sheet, treating them as assets, or *capitalizing* them.

Ms. Cooper and her audit team realized that WorldCom management had perpetrated an accounting fraud of massive proportions on the investing public. She confronted CEO Bernard Ebbers with her findings and then alerted the company's audit committee. Ms. Cooper was promptly terminated. (Today, whistle-blowers like Ms. Cooper are protected under SOX. See Chapter 18 for more on these protective guidelines.) Incidents such as this underscore the importance of independent audit committees within the corporate structure.

From the Audit Committee Annals

The need for more effective auditor oversight didn't go entirely unnoticed before SOX. In 1998, for instance, SEC Chairman Arthur Leavitt expressed uneasiness over the rather capricious oversight that corporate boards of directors exercised over the audit process. It wasn't until the corporate scandals of 2001 and 2002, however, that Leavitt's concerns struck a chord with Congress and the public.

Mr. Leavitt's Blue Ribbon panel

At the urging of Arthur Leavitt, chairman of the SEC, the NYSE, AMEX, and NASDAQ sponsored a Blue Ribbon Committee on Improving the Effectiveness of Corporate Audit Committees in 1998. This panel suggested a number of changes that became the basis for SEC, NYSE, and NASDAQ rule changes in the following year and later for the statutory mandates of SOX.

Enron impetus

The Senate subcommittee that investigated Enron in 2001 concluded that the company's audit oversight committee didn't oversee much. Expert witnesses at the hearings testified that the audit committee had not challenged management's refusal to make recommended adjustments to correctly reflect earnings and losses or management's omission of significant loss transactions from the company's financial statements.

The quest for consistent committee rules

In 2002, at the request of the SEC chairman, the SEC, NYSE, and NASDAQ took steps to harmonize their rules on corporate governance and, in particular, the required policies for corporate audit committees. In 2003, the SEC approved the new NASDAQ and NYSE rules, which were drafted to correspond to the standards set forth in SOX.

SOX Section 301 reflects many of the policies and practices established by the stock exchanges as well as the recommendations made by the Blue Ribbon panel that convened in 2003. The Senate version of SOX gave a nod to the Blue Ribbon panel, stating, "[C]onsistent with their recommendations, the bill enhances audit committee independence by barring audit committee members from accepting consulting fees, or being affiliated with persons of the issuer or the issuer's subsidiaries other than in the member's capacity as a member of the board of directors or any board committee."

Starting with a Charter

The NYSE and NASDAQ both require audit committees of publicly traded companies to adopt written charters. A committee's charter is a set of rules and guidelines intended to direct the committee in performing its oversight function.

The NYSE and NASDAQ rules require an audit committee's written charter to address the committee's:

- ✔ **Purpose:** SOX states that this purpose "at minimum" must be to ensure the integrity of the company's financial statements, its compliance with legal and regulatory requirements, and the independent auditor's competence and independence.
- ✔ **Role within the company:** The charter must spell out the specific duties of the audit committee with respect to ensuring the quality of the company's audited financial statements.
- ✔ **Policies:** The charter must address the audit committee's policies with respect to risk assessment and management.

A sample audit committee charter appears in Appendix C.

The Audit Committee Interface

Because audit committees at such companies as WorldCom and Global Crossing saw themselves as extensions of management, Congress and the SEC enacted legislation to clarify the role of the audit committee as distinct from management.

Audit committees are responsible for evaluating management and auditors, and they must retain objectivity regarding both. The committee monitors management's effectiveness in providing auditors with the information needed to determine whether the company's financial statements are prepared in accordance with Generally Accepted Accounting Principles (GAAP) and Generally Accepted Auditing Standards (GAAS), as discussed in Chapter 4.

Audit committees shouldn't get involved in performing audits; rather, they should facilitate them. The internal audit committee provides an essential objective interface between a company's management and its independent (outside) auditors to ensure that, at all times, the auditors' opinions and certifications are based on full and accurate information about the company's operations.

SOX Section 301 amended the Securities Exchange Act of 1934 to define the role of the audit committee as follows:

> *The audit committee of each issuer, in its capacity as a committee for the board of directors, shall be directly responsible for the appointment, compensation and oversight of the work of any registered public accounting firm employed by that (including the resolution of disagreements between management and the auditor regarding financial reporting) for the purpose of preparing or issuing an audit report, or related work, and each such registered public accounting firm shall report directly to the audit committee.*

SOX makes audit committee members "directly responsible" for disagreements that crop up regarding specific accounting issues during an audit, including "the resolution of any disagreements between management and the issuer." This provision is intended to keep committee members from giving in to management when auditors seek to impose policies and adjustments that reflect less favorably on the earnings of the company, and hence management.

Audit committees are responsible for ensuring that a company maintains a work environment that

- ✔ Enables auditors to perform necessary testing.
- ✔ Encourages employees to come forward with issues that may be relevant to the audit process (see "Handling complaints" later in this chapter for more).

Some Stricter NYSE Rules

The audit committees of companies that trade on the NYSE are subject to some requirements that are more stringent than the ones directly imposed by SOX. For example, NYSE rules require that

- ✔ A company's audit committee has a minimum of three members.
- ✔ A company conducts internal audits to assist management and the audit committee in assessing the company's accounting systems and internal control.

The NYSE listing rules state that a company may "choose to outsource" the internal audit function to "a third party service provider other than its independent auditor."

The NASDAQ listing requirements can be found at www.nasdaq.com/about/listing_information.stm.

Membership Requirements

Members of the audit committee are drawn from the corporation's board of directors. By law, the board of directors is made up of a majority of members who are financially independent from the company they audit (see Chapter 9 for a detailed explanation of the criteria that must be met for a director to be deemed financially independent). These independent directors may be eligible to serve on the company's audit committee if they meet the other requirements discussed in this section.

A few independent members

To ensure that audit committees are fair and objective advocates for effective audit procedures, SOX requires that committee members be financially independent from the company in two respects:

- ✔ **Compensation:** SOX prohibits an audit committee member from receiving any type of compensation or fee other than payment for being a director of the company. Audit committee members can't be paid for providing accounting, consulting, legal, investment, banking, or financial advisory services to a company or for working for companies that provide these services.

    Compensatory fees don't include payments to an audit committee member who's serving as a shareholder and who doesn't have enough stock in the company to control it.

- ✔ **Affiliation:** A member can't be affiliated with the company through family or employment relationships. Unfortunately, SOX Section 302 doesn't define an *affiliated person;* it merely states that if you are one, you're prohibited from serving on an audit committee. However, the legislative history of SOX and past practices of the SEC make it possible to determine who will be deemed an affiliated person and thus ineligible to serve on your company's audit committee.

    The definition of *affiliated person* that's used in most other sections of securities laws applies to SOX as well. Under this definition, a director is considered an affiliated person if he or she has a direct or indirect influence over the management of the company's business or affairs other than solely by virtue of being a director. Controlling shareholders also are considered affiliated persons and are therefore ineligible to serve. But, again, the SEC rules don't specify who's a *controlling shareholder;* the only qualification is that the person directly or indirectly owns more than 10 percent of the company's voting stock or equity. However, owning more than 10 percent of the voting stock doesn't automatically make someone an affiliate. In the case of a controlling shareholder, the SEC looks at all relevant facts and circumstances to determine whether the individual has enough control to be deemed an affiliate.

SOX gives the SEC the power to make exceptions to the independence requirements; however, few exceptions are anticipated.

Figure in a financial expert

At least one person on a company's audit committee must be a financial expert. Generally, the SEC considers a person a financial expert if he or she has, through education and experience, an understanding of Generally Accepted Accounting Principles (GAAP), financial statements, and internal accounting controls.

The SEC doesn't consider former CEOs to be financial experts.

SEC rules require that a public company disclose in periodic reports whether any of its audit committee members are financial experts. If none are, the SEC requires an explanation as to why not, and then the audit committee is expected to hire an outside consultant to provide the committee with the equivalent expertise.

Day-to-Day Committee Responsibilities

NYSE and NASDAQ rules increase the audit committee's authority beyond its former role of simply recruiting and paying the company's auditors. This section summarizes the new roles and responsibilities of internal audit committees under SOX.

Who sits on audit committees?

A report published by the Huron Consulting Group shows that each year since SOX was enacted in 2002 accountants have occupied an increasing number of seats. The report made the following findings:

✔ Accountants make up 12 percent of audit committee rosters today, up from 6 percent five years ago.

✔ Twenty-three percent of the audit committees examined were chaired by accountants, up from about 10 percent in 2002.

✔ Forty percent of audit committees had at least one accountant.

✔ The report defined "accountants" as "certified public accountants, controllers/comptrollers, accounting professors, and those who served on accounting boards or other similar oversight boards."

The NYSE and NASDAQ technically exempt foreign companies from their audit committee requirements. However, SOX doesn't include an exemption from its audit committee requirements for non–U.S. companies. So if these companies want to trade on U.S. markets, they have to convene committees that comply with the requirements imposed by SOX as well as the NYSE and NASDAQ listing requirements.

Monitoring events and policing policies

The audit committee must not only be a corporation's internal moral compass but it also must monitor external publicity and events that can impact the audit process and make sure that the company responds appropriately.

Under NYSE rules, the audit committee is responsible for reviewing and monitoring the following:

- ✔ The annual audited financial statements and quarterly reports filed by the company
- ✔ Press releases and financial information provided to the public
- ✔ Policies for risk management within the company
- ✔ Problems that occur during an audit as well as management's response to such problems
- ✔ The role and performance of the company's internal auditors
- ✔ Changes in company accounting policies
- ✔ Issues regarding internal controls and audit adjustments
- ✔ The policies and procedures of the committee itself

Interfacing with the auditors

The audit committee, in the broadest sense, is responsible for the appointment and compensation of the company's outside audit firm. Under SOX, the company's audit firm must report directly to the audit committee. This arrangement is a departure from pre-SOX days, when auditors also reported to management on a variety of issues. This change occurred when Congressional hearings revealed an inherent conflict in the interaction between management and the auditors who were, in effect, evaluating the effectiveness of management's policies.

The audit committee is expected to prevent management from influencing audit outcomes. SOX specifically states that the committee's role includes the resolution of disagreements between management and outside auditors regarding financial reporting. To properly understand and resolve these disputes, the committee must have a full understanding of both events that affect the company and the company's operations.

Under SOX, auditors are required to report the following information directly to the audit committee:

- ✔ All critical accounting policies and practices to be used

- ✔ All alternative treatments of financial information within GAAP that have been discussed with management, the ramifications of using alternative disclosures and treatments, and the treatment preferred by the auditor

- ✔ Any other material or written communications between the auditor and management, such as a management letter or schedule of unadjusted differences

Additionally, under NYSE rules, the committee must obtain a report "at least annually" from the independent auditors. That report must disclose the following:

- ✔ The audit firm's internal control procedures

- ✔ Any quality control issues raised about the audit firm by peer reviews (reviews by other audit firms) or government investigations

- ✔ All relationships between the independent auditors and the company

Preapproving nonaudit services

The audit committee has sign-off authority for audit services, which means that it must authorize every accounting service the company's audit firm provides, including confirmation letters and compliance with the financial reporting requirements of regulatory agencies.

In particular, the committee must make sure that the accounting firm performing the company's audit doesn't perform any of the following nonaudit services prohibited under SOX (Chapter 6 explains prohibited nonaudit services in more detail):

- ✔ Bookkeeping or other services related to accounting records or financial statements

- ✔ Financial information systems design and implementation

- ✔ Appraisal or valuation services, fairness opinions, or contribution-in-kind reports

- ✔ Actuarial services

- ✔ Internal audit outsourcing services, management or human resources functions

✔ Broker or dealer, investment advisor, or investment banking services

✔ Legal services or expert services unrelated to the audit

If a nonaudit service isn't on this list, it's permitted provided that the audit committee approves the service before the audit firm provides it. With respect to services that aren't specifically prohibited, SOX contains a *de minimus exception*. This exception applies when the services provided aren't significant; a service is considered de minimus if the total amount of nonaudit services in a fiscal year doesn't exceed 5 percent of the total fees to the auditor. If the de minimus exception applies, preapproval isn't required. However, in this case, the audit committee must approve the service prior to completion of the audit.

A company is required to disclose all nonaudit services that its auditors provide in the statements it files with the SEC, including those services that were deemed de minimus. The audit committee is responsible for making sure that these disclosures are made.

Handling complaints

Every audit committee must have procedures in place for receiving and handling complaints about the company's accounting, internal accounting controls, or auditing matters. These procedures must maintain employees' confidentiality and allow them to anonymously submit information that they uncover regarding questionable accounting or auditing actions taken by the company. The audit committee is also responsible for maintaining policies about the disposition of complaints about the company.

The audit committee serves as a resource for employees, management, and the auditors who put themselves on the line to provide essential audit information. With its complaint procedures, the audit committee complements SOX's whistle-blower provisions, which I discuss in Chapter 18.

Receiving CEO and CFO certifications

Under SOX Section 301, every public company's chief executive officer (CEO) and chief financial officer (CFO) are required to certify in annual and quarterly reports that they have disclosed the following to the auditor and the audit committee:

> *(1) All significant deficiencies and material weaknesses in the design or operation of internal controls that could adversely affect the company's ability to record, process, summarize, and report financial data*

(2) Any fraud, whether or not material, that involves management or other employees who have a significant role in the company's internal controls

The audit committee must make sure that any relevant information gleaned from the certifications is brought to the attention of the audit firm. If appropriate, the audit committee may also be required to bring such information directly to the attention of the SEC.

Monitoring conflicts and cooling-off periods

The audit committee is expected to know which public accounting audit firms are eligible to perform its company's audits and which are not. In determining who's eligible, the committee must be mindful of SOX's provisions that auditors are barred from performing any audit service if the company's CEO, CFO, chief accounting officer, controller, or any person serving in an equivalent position was employed by the auditor and participated in any capacity in an audit of the company during the one-year period preceding the commencement date of the current audit.

Ferreting out improper influence

SOX Section 303 regulates the relationship between the audit committee, the auditors, and management with a catch-all provision to discourage company management from improperly influencing audits and auditors. This SOX section directs the SEC to adopt rules prohibiting officers and directors of public companies or any person acting under the direction of an officer or director from fraudulently influencing, coercing, manipulating, or misleading any outside auditor engaged in an audit for the purpose of making the audited financial statements misleading.

Rotating the audit partners

SOX requires public accounting firms to rotate the following individuals every five years:

- ✔ The audit partner primarily responsible for a company's audit
- ✔ The audit partner responsible for reviewing the audit

The audit committee is responsible for making sure that this rotation actually happens.

Audit committee rules for private companies

Companies whose stock isn't available for trade on a public exchange are also affected by SOX Section 301. This section provides that these "over-the-counter" traded companies must disclose in their proxy statements

✔ Whether they have an audit committee.

✔ Whether the members of the committee are independent under the rules of the public stock exchanges

Engaging advisors

The audit committee may be involved in hiring more than just the auditors. Under SOX, the committee must have authority to engage independent counsel and other advisors as it deems necessary to carry out its duties. The law also requires companies to provide their audit committees with appropriate funding for hiring these advisors.

Providing recognition in annual reports

SOX requires a complex communication matrix: Auditors report to the audit committee, the committee reports to management, management reports back to the committee, the committee reports to the securities exchanges, and everyone reports to the SEC and the shareholders.

Because of this complicated communication trail, SOX requires that the names of all audit committee members be identified in the company's annual reports. If the company doesn't have a separately designated audit committee, it must state that the entire board of directors is acting as the audit committee.

Chapter 9

Building Boards That Can't Be Bought

"Board governance" is a buzz phrase circulating throughout corporate America in the wake of scandals involving such companies as Enron and WorldCom. Historically, the term has been used to refer to the policies and procedures that a company's board of directors uses to govern a corporation. However, after the Sarbanes-Oxley Act (SOX), the meaning of the term has expanded to include the selection process for directors and their duty to put the company's interests above their own.

The most shocking aspect of the corporate scandals that seemed to engulf corporate America after Enron was the behavior of the companies' boards. The media revealed that the boards governing the nation's largest corporations routinely strategized to overstate revenues, ignored auditors' proposed adjustments to financial statements, and sold stock during periods of plummeting prices when company employees were prohibited from doing so. Some directors even made loans of corporate funds to themselves to finance their own shaky side ventures. Prior to the passing of SOX in 2002, these activities were all business-as-usual in corporate America, leaving shareholders and employees holding worthless stock and underfunded retirement plans.

This chapter explores how new standards of board governance imposed by SOX make boards more accountable. I provide you with some general information about boards of directors and their functions, and I touch on some examples of board governance gone bad.

Some Background about Boards

Every corporation is run by its board of directors, who in turn answer to the shareholders that elect them. SOX ends an era of autonomy for board directors who, with the consent and consensus of the other board members, were able to embark corporations on ruinous courses.

SOX contains the following provisions to make boards more accountable:

✔ Requiring "majority-independent" boards

✔ Changing how directors are nominated

✔ Regulating how compensation for directors and senior management is set

What does a director do?

Directors manage corporate assets on behalf of the company's shareholders. A corporation's bylaws generally establish the board of directors and specify how many people will sit on it; typically, the number is no less than seven and no more than ten. However, there may be more or fewer directors depending on the specific provisions of the bylaws.

The role of the board isn't to manage the day-to-day operations of the corporation but rather to review the company's long-term strategies and make critical decisions. Typical tasks faced by a board of directors include

✔ Identifying the long-term goals of the company

✔ Hiring a chief executive officer (CEO) to run the company

✔ Receiving reports from the CEO as to the company's actions

✔ Making decisions about mergers, acquisitions, and dispositions of corporate assets

✔ Deciding what lines of business the company will continue

✔ Deciding whether to enter into new lines of business

✔ Directing reorganizations of the company structure, including issuing new classes of stock

✔ Handling lawsuits and litigation

✔ Making major decisions about borrowing on behalf of the company

Looking at some bad, bad boards

Prior to SOX, boards governed companies; seldom did shareholders have the opportunity to delve into their dealings. After the Enron debacle and other corporate scandals, many misdirected directors found themselves in the media spotlight. To really understand the kind of conduct SOX's new board governance is intended to prevent, consider SOX's provisions in light of the following scandals:

✔ **Enron:** In 2001, during what's referred to as a *blackout period,* Enron employees were prohibited from selling their stock for a period of time while the company that administered their retirement plans was being changed. (The average employee had about 62 percent of his or her stock invested in Enron stock.) Ken Lay, Enron's chairman of the board during this period, enjoyed an exemption for board members. This exemption allowed him to sell substantial amounts of his stock as the price plummeted during the blackout from $13.81 to $9.98.

Additionally, Enron's board approved the creation of several *special purpose entities,* which the company's chief financial officer, Andrew Fastow, owned. These entities were used to hide corporate losses and get them off Enron's balance sheet so shareholders and employees remained unaware. These off–balance sheet transactions were an important factor in Enron's eventual downfall. (For more on off –balance sheet transactions, see the nearby sidebar "Off–balance sheet transactions after Enron.")

In what is perhaps one of the biggest understatements of the Enron era, the Senate subcommittee investigating the Enron collapse concluded that the Enron board of directors "failed to safeguard Enron shareholders and contributed to the collapse." Congressional hearings detailed numerous red flags waved in front of the directors and recounted how they repeatedly ignored these warning signs. The subcommittee concluded that the Enron board was hopelessly compromised because of financial ties between the company and certain board members.

✔ **Tyco:** In 2002, it came to light that the CEO of Tyco International, Dennis Kozlowski, had paid one director a $10-million fee and contributed $10 million to the director's pet charity. Also, the Tyco board had approved millions of dollars in questionable loans and bonuses to Kozlowski, who was later convicted of conspiracy, securities fraud, falsifying records, and stealing millions of dollars from the manufacturing and service company.

✔ **Xerox:** In 2002, Xerox settled a Securities and Exchange Commission (SEC) civil fraud complaint relating to its accounting irregularities. As part of the settlement, Xerox agreed to appoint a committee of outside directors to review its accounting practices and policies.

- ✔ **WorldCom:** In 2002, WorldCom, the second largest long distance carrier in the United States, filed bankruptcy after shocking shareholders with the revelation that the company had overstated cash flows by more than $3.8 billion for the previous five quarters. It was discovered that the board had approved more than $366 million in loans and loan guarantees to CEO Bernard Ebbers to assist him in concealing losses as stock values declined.

- ✔ **Global Crossing:** In 2002, Global Crossing, one of the nation's largest telecommunications companies, declared bankruptcy amid allegations that the board had sanctioned long-term strategic planning that involved swapping unused fiber-optic capacity with other companies and using phantom revenues to boost the company's shaky bottom line.

- ✔ **Adelphia:** In 2002, Adelphia Corporation, the world's sixth largest cable television operator, disclosed that it had loaned $2.3 billion to entities controlled by the Rigas family, which founded and controlled Adelphia. When the SEC began looking into these transactions, management came up short on details. The transactions never showed up on the company's balance sheet, so investors in Adelphia's publicly traded stock had no way of knowing about them.

In Search of Independent Directors

There's a historical correlation between corporate fraud and boards of directors dominated by insiders. For example, the Senate subcommittee that investigated Enron concluded that "independence of the Enron board of directors was compromised by financial ties between the company and certain board members." The subcommittee recommended that, first and foremost, Congress require the SEC and stock exchanges to "strengthen the requirements for director independence at publicly traded companies."

Under SOX, stricter board governance requirements are primarily implemented by the listing requirements of stock exchanges such as the New York Stock Exchange and the National Association of Securities Dealers Automated Quotations, better known as NYSE and NASDAQ, respectively. For example, the rules of the NYSE now require that "[l]isted companies must have a majority of independent directors." Companies must also identify which directors are independent and disclose the basis for making that determination. To be considered independent, directors must meet all the criteria discussed in this section.

Off–balance sheet transactions after Enron

The term *off-balance sheet* has received a bad rap because of Enron. However, not all off–balance sheet transactions are shady. A company can use off–balance sheet transactions for a variety of legitimate purposes; therefore, it's important to distinguish what was off-color about Enron's off–balance sheet transaction from what a legitimate off–balance sheet transaction may be.

Essentially, Enron's board of directors approved deals for banks to loan funds to the special purpose entities (SPEs) owned by chief financial officer Andrew Fastow. A *special purpose entity* is a company (a partnership or another corporation) formed to achieve a particular purpose or accounting objective for the company.

Enron's board did question Fastow's apparent conflict of interest. The loans to the SPEs weren't shown on Enron's balance sheet because, as the board knew, they were "non-recourse" to Enron, meaning that Enron couldn't be sued if the SPEs defaulted on the debt. The loans to the SPEs were collateralized by shares of appreciating Enron stock. The deal unraveled when Enron's shares began declining in value. To placate the banks, Enron agreed to guarantee the debt. However, because the obligation was never reported to shareholders, it made Enron's publicly filed financial statements fraudulent.

The following are examples of off–balance sheet transactions that boards can legitimately approve:

- ✔ **Operating leases:** Operating leases are popular in industries that use expensive equipment. The leases are disclosed in the footnotes of the company's published balance sheet because the company doesn't own the assets.

- ✔ **Building leases:** A company may enter into an arrangement with a bank in which the bank buys a building and leases it to the company instead of the company borrowing the money to purchase the building. These leases appear in the footnotes of the company's published balance sheet.

- ✔ **Special assets:** Many companies legitimately create SPEs to segregate special assets they use for collateral or other special purposes from assets the companies intend to keep and use in their businesses.

A board can approve many other types of legitimate off–balance sheet transactions in which there's no conflict of interest and no intent to deceive shareholders. Still, investors must read the footnotes on a balance sheet to identify such transactions.

No relationships with related companies

According to SOX, an independent director can't serve "either directly or indirectly as a partner, shareholder, or officer of an organization that has a relationship with the company." This provision is intended to apply to the company's affiliates as well as the company itself. For example, the CEO of a company wouldn't be considered an independent director if he or she served on the board of a subsidiary company.

Three-year look-back period

Both the NYSE and NASDAQ want to know what directors have done in the three years prior to joining the board. Under the rules of both exchanges, a director isn't independent if he or a member of his immediate family has been an employee or executive officer of the listed company in the three years prior to joining the board of directors.

Prohibited payments

Prior to SOX, many directors received large payments and bonuses that they were unable to justify to the SEC and company shareholders. Criminal proceedings ensued in many cases, and irreversible damage was done to the companies that directors had treated as their personal trust funds.

In response to the public outrage that these large payments inspired, the NYSE and NASDAQ have placed limits on the amount of compensation directors can receive and still be considered independent. For instance:

- ✔ **Under NYSE rules,** a director isn't independent if he or she has received more than $100,000 in direct compensation from the listed company in the last three years. An exception is made if the compensation is received for serving as a director and on the company's audit committee, which I discuss in Chapter 8. The independent status of a director generally isn't impaired if he or she received a pension or other deferred compensation because of past service.

- ✔ **Under NASDAQ rules,** a director isn't independent if he or any family member (as defined in the "Family ties" section later in this chapter) "accepted any payments from the company or any parent or subsidiary of the company in excess of $60,000 during any period of twelve consecutive months within the three years preceding the determination of independence." The NASDAQ rules contain exceptions for board or committee service, compensation paid to family members in a nonexecutive capacity, and benefits paid from retirement plans.

Family ties

Securities exchanges not only look at what directors themselves are doing (or have done) to determine their independence, but they also look at the directors' immediate family members.

NYSE rules provide that a director isn't independent if an immediate family member is employed by the firm (or has been for the last three years) or is compensated in any manner that would be directly prohibited for a director. (I discuss these requirements in the previous section.)

SOX defines an immediate family member as any

- ✔ Spouse
- ✔ Minor child or stepchild
- ✔ Adult child or stepchild sharing a home with the director

When it comes to identifying a director's family members, NASDAQ listing requirements have a broader and therefore stricter definition than the NYSE. For example, according to the NASDAQ, a family member is

- ✔ A spouse, parent, child, or sibling, whether by blood, marriage, or adoption
- ✔ Anyone residing in such person's home

Mandatory meetings

NYSE rules contain a new requirement that distinguishes between board members who are involved in the management of the company and those who are not. The NYSE rules state that "[t]o empower non-management directors to serve as a more effective check on management, the non-management directors of each listed company must meet at regularly scheduled executive sessions without management."

These meetings are intended to promote more open discussion about the effectiveness of a company's management. The company is required to announce the non-management meetings to shareholders and other interested persons and to provide a way for them to communicate their concerns at the meetings.

Forming Committees for Nominating Directors

The NYSE and NASDAQ take decidedly different approaches when it comes to nominating directors. Although their nominating procedures differ, both exchanges specify publicly disclosed objective criteria for selection.

NYSE nominating procedures

To fill positions on a company's board of directors, the NYSE requires the establishment of a nominating/corporate governance committee that's run pursuant to a written charter displayed on the company's Web site. The NYSE rules recommend that the charter address

- ✔ Qualifications of committee members
- ✔ How committee members are appointed to the committee and removed from it
- ✔ How the committee operates
- ✔ The criteria used to select directors
- ✔ Policies for paying fees to executive search firms to select director candidates

The nominating/corporate governance committee is permitted to delegate responsibilities to other committees as long as the other committees consist of independent directors and have written charters.

NASDAQ nominating rules

NASDAQ rules provide for director nominations either by a majority of independent directors or by a committee made of independent directors. However, "[e]ach issuer must certify that it has adopted a formal written charter or board resolution, as applicable, addressing the nominations process and such related matters as may be required under securities laws."

The NASDAQ rules include a special exception that allows a nonindependent director to serve on a nominating committee as long as the board discloses in its proxy why allowing the director in question to serve is in the best interests of the company. A nonindependent director serving on a nominating committee thanks to this exception can't serve more than two years.

Under NASDAQ rules, if a company uses a committee structure to nominate director candidates, evaluation of a candidate can't be delegated to a subcommittee.

Regulating Director Compensation

Under NYSE rules, listed companies must have a compensation committee composed entirely of independent directors to determine the compensation for the entire board of directors and management. The compensation committee is required to post a written charter on the company's Web site that addresses how the committee goes about making recommendations to the CEO and the board. The committee also is required to produce a "compensation committee report on executive officer compensation as required by the SEC to be included in the listed company's annual proxy statement or annual report on Form 10-K filed with the SEC."

NASDAQ allows compensation to be set either by a committee or a majority of independent directors who make recommendations to the board. As with the nominating committee, a special exception is made that allows a nonindependent director to serve on the compensation committee (for up to two years) if the board discloses in its proxy why allowing the director in question to serve is in the best interests of the company.

Making governance guidelines public

Every corporation listed on the NYSE must post its *corporate governance guidelines* on the company Web site. Governance guidelines need to be tailored to reflect a particular company's operations, but at a minimum, NYSE rules require that the guidelines address the following:

- Director qualification standards, including procedures for training and continuing education
- Responsibilities of directors, including obligations to attend meetings
- Policies for director access to management and independent advisors
- Procedures for determining director compensation
- Management succession policies
- A procedure for the board to conduct an annual self-evaluation (see the following section)

NASDAQ rules don't include any specific requirements for written board governance guidelines. However, most NASDAQ-traded companies are likely to adopt written guidelines both to document that they have such policies and to facilitate their practical implementation.

Evaluating the board's performance

According to the NYSE, an important component of board self-governance is self-evaluation. However, the NYSE guidelines don't specify how boards must go about evaluating themselves. Many boards tackle the self-evaluation requirement by giving board members a questionnaire that asks them to rate how well the board has performed its designated tasks. However, this approach can have unintended consequences: If the board doesn't address problems that are disclosed by negative feedback on a questionnaire, a perception may arise that the board isn't diligent about fulfilling its responsibility. Thus, the board may feel compelled to follow up on each less-than-perfect rating it receives on the questionnaires.

If a company uses questionnaires for self-evaluation, the questionnaires must be preserved because the company may be required to produce them in the event of future litigation.

For most companies, a more practical approach to self-evaluation is to hold regular meetings for purposes of board discussion and self-evaluation. During such meetings, the board can determine what further action, if any, is necessary as a result of the self-evaluation process. The issues raised in the meetings and the details about how the issues were handled should be carefully documented.

Some Exempt Boards . . . For the Moment

New board governance initiatives under SOX were primarily introduced as amendments to the Securities Exchange Act of 1934, which I discuss in Chapter 3. The board governance standards are implemented by the requirements of the stock exchanges in which stock is publicly traded. Companies that aren't publicly traded, as discussed in this section, aren't currently subject to SOX.

Nonpublic companies

Although nonpublic corporations aren't currently subject to SOX, they are accountable to their shareholders. Directors have a fiduciary duty to shareholders, which means that they must govern with loyalty to the corporation, not with loyalty to their own self-interest.

SOX ushers in new principles of independence and accountability that are likely to impact the outcome of future lawsuits brought by shareholders who claim that directors haven't acted independently or otherwise in accordance with their fiduciary duties. Accordingly, nonpublic companies are well advised to voluntarily adopt governance standards (such as installing independent board members and establishing audit committees) that reflect those mandated by SOX for public companies.

Nonprofit corporations

Nonprofit corporations aren't currently subject to the governance mandates of SOX, but many are eager to comply voluntarily because they can't afford to allow a hint of scandal to taint their organizations. Their boards of directors owe a fiduciary duty to the "stakeholders" in their missions. Stakeholders may include organizations that award federal grants, individual and corporate donors, and the intended recipients of services provided by the nonprofit organization.

According to the annual Grant Thornton Board Governance Survey for Not-for-Profit Organizations, more than 80 percent of nonprofits surveyed said that they're "very" or "somewhat" familiar with SOX.

Other exempt companies

Both the NYSE and NASDAQ exempt certain types of companies whose stocks trade on the exchanges from complying with SOX's stringent board independence and other governance requirements.

Under NYSE rules, the following types of companies are exempt:

- ✔ Companies in which an individual, a group, or another company holds more than 50 percent of the voting power
- ✔ Limited partnerships
- ✔ Companies involved in bankruptcy proceedings

NASDAQ exempts the following types of companies:

- ✔ Limited partnerships
- ✔ Issuers who have certain levels of assets to back the stock issuance
- ✔ Certain registered management investment companies

Chapter 10

SOX: Under New Management

. . . .

. . . .

*T*he Sarbanes-Oxley Act, or SOX, requires managers to do more than just manage; they must now personally sign off on an annual array of financial reports and certifications.

Requiring management to stand behind the public disclosures that the investing public relies on isn't a new concept. Prior to SOX, management was required to sign off on a representation letter included in the company's annual report. However, the reporting and certification requirements under SOX are more specific as to the representations required. SOX also imposes criminal penalties for CEOs and CFOs that acquiesce to inaccurate reports.

In this chapter, you find a road map of CEO and CFO reporting and certification requirements. It also includes some suggestions as to how managers can comply with SOX requirements in an economically beneficial way.

Chiefly Responsible: CEOs and CFOs

SOX seems to single out CEOs and CFOs when it comes to corporate ethics and public accountability. Why? The answer lies in their overall job descriptions. The following sections explain.

CEO: The chief in charge

The *chief executive officer*, or CEO, is the man or woman primarily responsible (and with the most authority) for carrying out the company's strategic plans and policies as established by the board of directors. The CEO reports to the board of directors and oversees the operations of the company. Because pretty much every employee in the company (except the board members) answers to the CEO, SOX obligates the CEO to take responsibility for maintaining sound financial practices and good control within the company.

Some typical job responsibilities of a CEO include

- ✔ **Keeping the board of directors informed:** The CEO advises and informs board members of the company's day-to-day operations and progress with respect to implementation of the board's policies.

- ✔ **Making sure the company produces profitable products and services:** Generally, the CEO oversees design, marketing, promotion, and quality of the company's products and services.

- ✔ **Budgeting:** The CEO makes budgetary recommendations to the board and manages the company's resources within the budget that the board establishes.

- ✔ **Managing tax and regulatory obligations:** CEOs usually are responsible for overseeing tax reporting policies and compliance with industry and government regulations.

- ✔ **Managing facilities and human resources:** The CEO is responsible for making recommendations to the board about company personnel and company facilities policies; he or she also implements the policies established by the board in a way that conforms to current laws and regulations.

- ✔ **Monitoring community and public relations:** The CEO is generally responsible for making sure that the company maintains a positive public image and a high level of shareholder confidence.

CFO: The financial fact finder

Traditionally, the *chief financial officer*, or CFO, of a company is held accountable for all the financial aspects of the company's operations. He or she is responsible for making sure that shareholders, creditors, analysts, employees, and management have accurate information about the company's performance. The CFO also must make sure that systems are in place to measure how well the company is achieving its financial goals.

Some of the CFO's critical duties include

- Overseeing the forecasting and budgeting process
- Maintaining relationships with investment and commercial banks or other sources of capital on which the company may be dependent
- Supervising control structures within the firm

Because the CFO exercises a great deal of authority over company finances and personnel who carry out financial policy, it makes sense that SOX requires him or her to sign off on reports and personally certify the company's financial structures.

Three SOX sections for the chiefs

Thanks to SOX, life will never be the same for CEOs and CFOs. SOX contains three separate sections that direct top executives to the two tasks they must perform on a regular basis: certifying and reporting. These three important sections are Sections 302, 906, and 404.

Sections 302 and 906 require the CEO and CFO to *certify* the accuracy of the company's financial statements. Section 404 (covered in detail in Chapters 12 and 13) further requires management officials to *report* on internal control within their companies and include these reports in the annual and quarterly reports filed with the SEC.

SOX requires management to file Section 404 reports once a year, in the company's annual report. However, the certifications mandated by Sections 302 and 906 must be filed both annually and quarterly. SEC rules require companies to perform quarterly evaluations of changes that have materially affected or are reasonably likely to materially affect their internal control over financial reporting.

Companies may also be required to file extra reports between quarters, namely an SEC Form 8-K, if important events affecting their internal control structures occur. For example, an additional 8-K may be required if the company discontinues or outsources a sensitive control activity that was previously performed in-house. (I discuss the 8-K form in more detail in Chapter 3.)

Section 302: Civil certifications

Section 302 requires the CEO and CFO of every publicly traded company to certify the "appropriateness of the financial statements and disclosures contained in the periodic report, and that those financial statements and disclosures fairly present, in all material respects, the operations and financial condition of the issuer." The required contents and mechanics of certifications are discussed in more detail in the section "A Section 302 Certification Checklist" later in this chapter.

Section 906: Criminal penalties

CEOs who willfully certify false financial statements are now subject to criminal penalties. SOX Section 906 adds a provision to the federal criminal code requiring CEOs and CFOs to file additional annual and quarterly reports. This certification is separate and somewhat redundant to the one required in Section 302 (see the preceding section), but it's mandatory. (Applicable penalties are discussed in the section "Viewing Control as a Criminal Matter: Section 906" later in this chapter.)

Overlap with Section 404: Reports

In addition to the certifications described in Sections 302 and 906, SOX Section 404 requires two types of management reports that attest to the accuracy of the company's financial statements. Here are the required reports:

- ✓ **A statement of management's responsibility:** The Section 404 report must state management's responsibility for establishing and maintaining an adequate internal control structure and procedures for financial reporting.

- ✓ **An assessment of internal control:** Management must include its own assessment of the company's internal control structure and procedures for financial reporting.

The attestations must follow the standards issued by the Public Company Accounting Oversight Board, or PCAOB (covered in Chapter 7). For more on Section 404, see the section "More Reporting Responsibilities for Management and Auditors: Section 404" later in this chapter.

A Section 302 Certification Checklist

SOX Section 302 definitely doesn't leave CEOs and CFOs guessing about what their certifications must contain, nor does it give them much wiggle room. In fact, the statute is structured to provide a checklist of what each certification must contain. Each paragraph of Section 302 identifies a particular matter with respect to the company's annual or quarterly report to which management must certify. This section discusses each of these Section 302 paragraphs; I include the text of a sample management certification in Appendix B.

Paragraph 1: Review of periodic report

First and foremost, management must certify that it has actually read the report in which the certification is being included. Paragraph 1 of SOX Section 302 requires the signing officer to certify that he or she has reviewed the report being certified.

Paragraph 2: Material accuracy

Paragraph 2 requires the signing officer to state that based on his or her knowledge, the report doesn't contain any material misstatements or materially misleading statements. The wording in this paragraph is similar to the antifraud section of the Securities Exchange Act of 1934 (Section 10b-5). (You can find out more about the Securities Exchange Act of 1934 in Chapter 3.)

Paragraph 3: Fair presentation of financial information

Paragraph 3 requires management to state that based on the knowledge of the signing officer, the financial statements and other financial information contained in the annual report "fairly presents" in all material respects the company's financial condition, results of operations, and cash flow for the periods being reported.

The SEC clarifies that *financial information* includes any information from which the financial performance of the company can reasonably be construed, including footnotes, financial data included in the report, and discussion and analysis of the financial information.

With this paragraph, the SEC also has made clear that it intends to hold management to a more stringent standard than the company's accountants. The requirement that the report "fairly present" financial information isn't limited to Generally Accepted Accounting Principles (GAAP), as discussed in Chapter 6. Rather, management is held to a higher standard of material accuracy.

Paragraph 4: Disclosure controls and procedures

Paragraph 4 of Section 302 is divided into four subparagraphs: A, B, C, and D. Each of these subparagraphs imposes a particular duty on management with respect to evaluating the company's internal control:

- ✔ **Paragraph 4(A)** imposes responsibility on the signing officers "for establishing and maintaining internal controls."

- ✔ **Paragraph 4(B)** addresses the design of the controls, directing management to make sure controls are adequate to ensure that *material,* or significant, information about the company comes to the attention of the officers.

- ✔ **Paragraph 4(C)** imposes a time frame for testing, stating that the relevant signing officers must certify that they "have evaluated the effectiveness of the issuer's internal controls as of a date within 90 days prior to the report."

- ✔ **Paragraph 4(D)** requires management to take ownership of the conclusions it has reached, requiring it to represent that it has reached its own conclusions about the effectiveness of the company's internal controls based on an evaluation. In other words, this requirement implies that management is directly responsible for the evaluation process and can't delegate this function.

The SEC recommends that management create a *disclosure committee* to help it comply with Paragraphs 4(A) and 4(C). I explain these committees in the later section "Establish a disclosure committee."

In addition to the proper disclosure of information, the SEC expects management to develop processes for reviewing and evaluating controls and procedures. Management is also responsible for setting policies for supervising people within the company who implement the internal control procedures.

Paragraph 5: Disclosure to auditors

Paragraph 5 relates to the disclosures that management must make to its auditors and audit committee about the company's internal control environment. Management must certify that the signing officers have disclosed the following:

(A) all significant deficiencies in the design or operation of internal controls which could adversely affect the issuer's ability to record, process, summarize, and report financial data and have identified for the issuer's auditors any material weaknesses in internal controls; and

(B) any fraud, whether or not material, that involves management or other employees who have a significant role in the issuer's internal controls

Paragraph 5(A) doesn't define *significant deficiencies,* but SEC rules indicate this phrase has the same meaning as under Generally Accepted Auditing Standards (GAAS). GAAS standards state that a significant deficiency is a material weakness that places the company at risk.

Paragraph 5 also doesn't define the phrase *involves management* as it's used in connection with fraud under subparagraph (B). However, Congress intended that it include a failure to supervise and detect fraud as well as an active participation in these activities by management.

Paragraph 6: Changes in internal controls

Paragraph 6 requires management to provide information about any changes in the company's internal controls. The signing officers must certify that they've indicated in the report, in which the certification is included, "whether or not there were significant changes in internal controls or in other factors that could significantly affect internal controls subsequent to the date of their evaluation, including any corrective actions with regard to significant deficiencies and material weaknesses."

Management must make sure that it errs on the side of disclosing *factors* that happen in the company that can affect internal controls. Paragraph 6 also instructs management to inform the public about *corrective actions* that could serve as a signal of ongoing problems to a wary investor. For example, if management discovers discrepancies in reconciling accounts, it may be required to disclose what actions it took to reconcile them.

Clearing Up Common Section 302 Questions

In passing Section 302, Congress was pretty specific about the content and wording of the Section 302 certification (see the sidebar "Cutting and pasting the Section 302 certification" for details). However, some aspects related to whom, when, and how the filing requirements are actually applied can be confusing. This section gives you the skinny on answers to these common questions.

What companies are required to file certifications under Section 302?

Section 302 certification requirements apply to all companies defined as *issuers* under SOX. This label generally fits companies that file quarterly and annual reports with the SEC under either Section 13(a) or 15(d) of the Securities Exchange Act of 1934 (see Chapter 3). Specifically, issuers include foreign companies, banks, savings associations, and small business issuers covered by the 1934 Act.

Which reports get certified?

SOX requires CEOs and CFOs to certify liberally. In fact, most reports filed with the SEC require management certification. The Section 302 and 906 certification rules apply to

- Annual reports on Form 10-K
- Quarterly reports on Form 10-Q
- Amendments to Form 10-K

Cutting and pasting the Section 302 certification

The SEC provides a gift to managers everywhere in the form of a *standard certification form*. CEOs and CFOs can use the form word-for-word with only a few small changes:

- **Switching from plural to singular officers:** The phrase "other certifying officers" in Paragraph 4 may be changed if a company has two or fewer certifying officers.

- **Adjusting for newly complying companies:** Until the first audit of a company's books is performed, management can omit Paragraph

4(B) pertaining to the officers' responsibility for establishing and maintaining internal control systems.

When using the standard certification form, the CEO and CFO must sign separate but identical certifications. Notarization isn't required. After they're signed, the certifications must be filed as exhibits to the report in which they're being included. I provide a copy of the SEC's general certification form in Appendix B.

Certifications don't have to be included with Form 8-K, which is used to disclose significant corporate events between quarters. (I discuss the 8-K events and reporting requirements in Chapter 3.)

Viewing Control as a Criminal Matter: Section 906

According to SOX Section 906, lack of internal control can be a criminal matter. CEOs can end up in jail if they certify false financial information in an SEC report.

Section 906 requires management to certify "that the periodic report containing the financial statements fully complies with the requirements of section 13(a) or 15(d) of the Securities Exchange Act of 1934 . . . and that information contained in the periodic report fairly presents, in all material respects, the financial condition and results of operations" of the company.

Section 906(c) provides serious criminal penalties for failing to meet these requirements, stating that whoever

> . . . *certifies any statement as set forth in subsections (a) and (b) of this section knowing that the periodic report accompanying the statement does not comport with all the requirements set forth in this section shall be fined not more than $1,000,000, or imprisoned not more than 10 years, or both; or*

> *willfully certifies any statement as set forth in subsections (a) and (b) of this section knowing that the periodic report accompanying the statement does not comport with all the requirements set forth in this section shall be fined not more than $5,000,000, or imprisoned not more than 20 years, or both.*

Most of this section's certification requirements are redundant with those required under Section 302, so some experts think that including the requirement of a separate certification under Section 906 is an SEC oversight.

SOX Section 802 imposes additional criminal penalties for altering documents, including fines and prison time.

Famous CEOs and CFOs behind bars

Prior to the Enron scandal, sentences for white-collar crimes were minimal. Embezzling executives were viewed as nonviolent and therefore tended to get off more easily than a guy who robbed a convenience store.

During the big insider trading scandals of the late 1980s, executives received their sentences and were back on the golf course within a matter of months. For example, famous fraudster Ivan Boesky, who amassed a fortune by trading on tips from corporate insiders, got a 10-year sentence but served only 22 months. Boesky cooperated with the SEC and informed on junk bond trader Michael Milken, who also served a mere 22 months of his 10-year sentence.

In contrast, nowadays judges have begun handing out prison terms of 10 to 30 years, and they intend to enforce these sentences in full. Recent sentences for high-profile CEOs and CFOs include the following:

- **Adelphia Communications:** Founder John Rigas got 15 years and his son, Timothy, landed a 20-year prison term after both were ousted from the board of directors. They were convicted on 18 counts each of fraud and conspiracy after Adelphia, the sixth largest cable company in the United States, filed for bankruptcy. During the five-month trial, prosecutors accused the Rigases of conspiring to hide $2.3 billion in corporate debt and stealing $100 million from the company so they could invest in golf courses and other personal assets.

- **Dynergy:** Jamie Olis, a former Dynergy executive, is currently serving a sentence of more than 24 years. Olis was found guilty of securities fraud for a gas trading and finance scheme dubbed Project Alpha. The deal inflated Dynergy's cash flow and created

bogus tax deductions that overstated the company's revenues to investors by as much as $300 million. When the financials had to be restated, the company's stock plummeted.

- **Tyco:** Following their convictions, Tyco CEO Dennis Kozlowski and CFO Mark Swartz received sentences of 8⅓ to 25 years in prison for misappropriating $600 million from the manufacturing conglomerate.

- **Enron:** CFO Andrew Fastow received a 10-year sentence after the Enron collapse. Fastow personally profited from partnerships that were used to move debt off the company's books. This tactic caused a $1 billion loss, required Enron to restate $600 million in inflated profits, and cost about 4,000 workers their jobs. The partnerships quickly emerged as a leading cause of what was then the largest bankruptcy-protection filing in U.S. history. (As of this writing, it's the second largest, overtaken by WorldCom.)

- **WorldCom:** Now known as MCI, WorldCom remains the largest bankruptcy in history, surpassing even Enron. Convicted on nine counts of accounting fraud, CEO Bernard Ebbers received 25 years behind bars for his role in the company's collapse.

Ironically, executives involved in these scandals, including Ken Lay, the CEO of Enron, couldn't be charged with SOX-related crimes because their misdeeds all took place before SOX was passed. It's an odd twist indeed that they couldn't be tried under the law they inspired. The reasons these execs got such tough sentences has to do with a 1987 change in federal sentencing guidelines linking prison terms to the financial losses caused by the crimes. (The 1987 law also did away with parole.)

More Reporting Responsibilities for Management and Auditors: Section 404

In addition to certifying several aspects of a company's annual report, management is now required to prepare a key component of the report: Section 404 directs that management and auditors work in tandem to report and assess the company's internal control. This section of SOX assigns specific responsibilities to each party.

What management has to do under Section 404

Under SOX Section 404, in a company's annual report, management is responsible for including an internal control report that

- ✔ States the responsibility of management for establishing and maintaining an adequate internal control structure and procedures for financial reporting
- ✔ Contains an assessment, as of the end of the company's most recent fiscal year, of the effectiveness of the internal control structure and company procedures for financial reporting

Management has a lot of leeway in choosing what methods to use in fulfilling its Section 404 responsibilities. This flexibility is appropriate considering the fact that the management of a company is in the best position to identify control issues and know where financial skeletons lie. Ultimately, management must be confident in signing off on the effectiveness of its company's internal control.

What the auditors need from management

According to Section 404, the independent auditor is responsible for attesting to and reporting on the assessment made by the management of the issuing company. Before signing off on management's internal control report, the independent auditor must make sure management has

- ✔ Accepted responsibility for the effectiveness of the company's internal control
- ✔ Evaluated the effectiveness of the company's internal control, using suitable criteria

✔ Supported its (the auditor's) evaluation with sufficient documentation

✔ Presented a written assessment of the effectiveness of the company's internal control

Taking Internal Control Seriously

CEOs and CFOs have traditionally had a wide range of responsibilities, first and foremost of which has been making their companies profitable. And prior to SOX, assessing internal control may have taken a back seat to activities like developing a global marketing plan or seeking out competitive technologies. Consequently, many CEOs (and even some CFOs) need to get up to speed on the concept of internal control and why it's important to their companies. This section takes a look at what the accounting profession, the SEC, and management have to say on the subject of internal control.

Considering the auditor's perspective

According to Generally Accepted Auditing Standard Number 60, a goal of internal control is to "reduce to a relatively low level the risk that errors or irregularities in amounts that would be material in relation to the financial statements . . . may occur and not be detected within a timely period by employees in the normal course of performing their assigned functions."

Under SOX, management is required to report on any significant "material weakness" in the company's internal control. Auditing Standard Number 60 states that significant weaknesses (as opposed to material ones) need not be disclosed in management reports, but the aggregate effect of a number of significant deficiencies may amount to a material weakness that does need to be reported.

For more information about Generally Accepted Accounting Standards as they pertain to SOX, turn to Chapter 4.

What the SEC says

SEC rules define "internal control over financial reporting" as a process designed to provide reasonable assurance regarding the reliability of financial reporting and the preparation of financial statements. The SEC says internal controls must include policies and procedures that address

✔ **Good recordkeeping:** The maintenance of records that accurately, fairly, and in reasonable detail reflect transactions and dispositions involving company assets

✔ **Recording and authorization of transactions:** Reasonable assurance that transactions are recorded as needed to permit preparation of financial statements in accordance with Generally Accepted Accounting Principles (GAAP) and that the transactions themselves are authorized by management

✔ **Fraud detection:** Reasonable assurance regarding prevention or timely detection of unauthorized acquisition, use, or disposition of company assets

Management standards criteria for controls

Although management has a lot of leeway in deciding how to create and enforce internal controls, the criteria it uses must be sensible and well recognized. SEC rules stress that management's evaluation and assessment of internal control must be based on procedures developed by a recognized nongovernmental organization. (The SEC has specifically endorsed the Committee of Sponsoring Organizations of the Treadway Commission's *Internal Control, An Integrated Framework* — better known as the *COSO framework*. I discuss the COSO framework standards in more detail in Chapter 14.)

At a minimum, management's criteria must

✔ Be unbiased

✔ Permit consistent measurement of internal control over financial reporting

✔ Include all factors relevant to evaluating the effectiveness of the company's internal controls

✔ Be relevant to an evaluation of internal control over financial reporting

Seeking Out Subcertifications

The SEC emphasizes that management must be actively involved in implementing the internal control structures it approves and that it may not delegate its responsibility for evaluating internal control to the independent auditors.

Nevertheless, in many companies, the CEO and CFO request that people within the organization certify to them that internal control structures and procedures are in working order. Some of the employees and middle managers within an organization that may have to provide such *subcertifications* include the following:

- ✔ Controllers
- ✔ Corporate vice presidents and officers
- ✔ Risk management personnel
- ✔ Managers of information technology departments

CEOs and CFOs are understandably focused on attaining the highest degree of confidence in financial-reporting documentation. It remains to be seen whether the SEC hasn't specifically sanctioned this trickle down accountability approach, and regardless, the SEC is unlikely to shift any liability from management. However, the advantages to the subcertification strategy are clear:

- ✔ It puts employees on notice as to what management's expectations are.
- ✔ It documents management's expectations.
- ✔ It may increase the likelihood of compliance with existing internal control structures.

Some Good Advice for CEOs and CFOs

Most companies already have procedures in place and hold management accountable for gathering and evaluating information to be included in their financial statements, annual reports, and SEC filings. From this standpoint, SOX doesn't really require management or companies to do anything specific. Rather, it directs CEOs and CFOs to take a greater role in these tasks and assume more public responsibility for acting on procedures that safeguard corporate assets.

No two companies have identical business operations, so SOX can't give you a "one-size-fits-all" solution for management. For example, establishing a disclosure committee may not be appropriate for all companies. The reality is that each CEO and CFO must decide what methods of information gathering and reporting constitute the best internal control for his or her organization. This section covers three common-sense suggestions that can make the jobs of CEOs and CFOs easier.

Establish a disclosure committee

The SEC suggests that companies consider establishing *disclosure committees* to assist in developing disclosure controls and procedures. The disclosure committee can consist of the company's general counsel, the principal accounting officer, the chief investor relations officer, risk managers, or other people with control-related responsibilities in the company, such as information technology or human resources personnel.

Take an inventory

The first task a disclosure committee may want to undertake (if the company establishes one) is taking inventory of the company's existing practices as well as any known weaknesses. The committee should pay particular attention to any matters raised by the company's independent auditors. This inventory can help management document what policy breaches and material weaknesses happened on their watches as opposed to that of a prior management team.

Woo the whistle-blowers

An important aspect of internal control that receives a lot of publicity is how a company currently handles whistle-blower complaints. (I discuss whistle-blower protections in more detail in Chapter 18.) *Whistle-blowers* are people inside the company who provide information about breaches in internal control, material misstatements, and internal fraud to management or government officials. Management should be familiar with audit committee procedures for handling such complaints. It can use the information gleaned from whistleblowers to fulfill its own reporting and certification responsibilities.

Chapter 11

More Management Mandates

*T*he Sarbanes-Oxley Act, or SOX, could aptly be renamed the Shareholder Advocacy Act because its primary intent is to make sure that public corporations are managed for the benefit of shareholders, even though corporate health is dependent on management.

The post-Enron wave of corporate scandals revealed audited financial statements that were fantasy sheets with phantom income on which huge management bonuses were based. Shareholders were left holding the deflated stock when massive accounting adjustments had to be made to reflect the company's true earnings.

This chapter identifies some new tools ushered in by SOX for reigning in management.

Codifying the Corporate Conscience

SOX insists that corporations codify their consciences by requiring

✔ A written code of ethics

✔ Public disclosure of the code and changes to it

✔ Prompt reporting of any potential violations of the code

The Senate Banking Committee, which drafted many management oversight provisions that were ultimately included in SOX, observed that the problems surrounding Enron and other public companies primarily "raised concerns about the ethical standard" of senior management. The report concluded that "investors have a legitimate interest in knowing whether a public company holds its financial officers to certain ethical standards in their financial dealings."

This section takes a look at the practical aspects of requiring companies to write up their ethical standards and communicate them to shareholders.

Explaining the code

SOX Section 406 requires companies to disclose in the periodic 10-K and 10-Q reports that they file with the SEC (discussed in Chapter 3) whether the company has a written code of ethics for senior financial officers. If the company hasn't established a written code, an explanation is required.

If a company changes its code of ethics, it must promptly report the changes to the public on the SEC Form 8-K, which the SEC requires for the reporting of special events.

Establishing worthwhile objectives

The SEC Regulation S-K Item 406 explains that a *code of ethics* is a set of standards that's "reasonably designed to deter wrongdoing." The regulation provides that a written code of ethics should specify the following:

(1) Honest and ethical conduct, including the ethical handling of actual or apparent conflicts of interest between personal and professional relationships;

(2) Full, fair, accurate and timely, and understandable disclosure in reports and documents that a registrant files with, or submits to, the [SEC] and in other public communications made by the registrant;

(3) Compliance with the applicable government rules and regulations;

(4) The prompt internal reporting of violations of the code to an appropriate person or persons identified in the code; and

(5) Accountability and adherence to the code.

Realizing one code doesn't fit all companies

SEC rules provide that companies may have separate codes of ethics governing different types of officers. A company also can create a broad code of ethics with special provisions to address additional topics that apply to specific persons within the company.

Disclosing amendments and waivers

SEC regulations require disclosure of any amendment or waiver of the provisions of a company's code of ethics. Amendments can be very telling when it comes to corporate culture, particularly if they're made in response to specific events. For example, if a company suddenly implements standards for disclosing off–balance sheet transactions, you may wonder whether it has had a problem with this issue in the past.

According to the regulations, the term *waiver* means the approval by the company of "any material departure from a provision of the code of ethics." SEC regulations also state that this term includes *implicit waivers,* which occur when a company fails to take action within a reasonable period of time after management or the board of directors learns of a breach of the written provisions of the code.

Expecting ethics on the exchanges

Stock exchanges, such as the NYSE and NASDAQ, require the companies trading on them to have written codes of ethics. Although the SEC, NYSE, and NASDAQ requirements are similar in many respects, the following are a few significant differences:

- ✔ SOX requires that the code of ethics apply only to senior financial officers. NYSE and NASDAQ rules require that a code be implemented to all directors, officers, and employees.

- ✔ The SEC and NASDAQ rules require any waivers of code provisions to be disclosed on SEC Form 8-K (discussed in Chapter 3). The NYSE allows waivers to be disclosed by other means, such as in letters to shareholders, press releases, or on the company's Web site.

- ✔ SEC rules require disclosure of amendments to the code of ethics on a Form 8-K, but neither the NYSE nor NASDAQ require the disclosure of amendments.

A checklist of code contents

Despite their differences (see the preceding section), it's possible to draft a single code of ethics that meets SEC, NYSE, and NASDAQ requirements.

At a minimum under all three sets of requirements, your company's code should do the following:

- State the objectives of the code, mirroring SEC Rule 406 (check out the section "Establishing worthwhile objectives" earlier in this chapter)

- Identify the persons to which the code is applicable (for example, "all directors, officers, and employees" or "exclusively senior financial officers")

- List contact people within the company who should be approached when questions about the code of ethics arise

- Impose an obligation for candid and honest conduct

- Address how conflicts of interest should be identified and handled

- Establish policies for full disclosure and representation

- Identify the obligations of people who become aware of any violations of the code of ethics, and lay out a protocol for notifying persons within the company

- Establish that people subject to the code of ethics have, at all times, an obligation to advance the company's business interests before their own

- Impose confidentiality when it's appropriate for achieving the objectives of the code of ethics

- State that a duty of fair dealing exists at all times

- Impose on all people who are subject to the code a duty to protect and safeguard the company's assets for the benefit of the shareholders

A sample code of ethics is included in Appendix D.

New Rules for Stock Selling and Telling

Prior to SOX, a huge loophole existed for the sale of company stock back to the company that issued it as opposed to selling it on the open market. Federal securities laws required executive officers and directors to report their ownership interests in the company on SEC Forms 3, 4, and 5. These forms are commonly referred to as *Section 16 reports* because they're required under Sections 16(a) and b-2 of the Securities Exchange Act of 1934. Prior to SOX, the law stated that stock sales were generally reportable 10 days after the end of the month in which the transaction occurred. However, sales of stock back to the company weren't reportable until 45 days after the end of the company's fiscal year.

During its post-Enron hearings, Congress was outraged to learn of the following pre-SOX executive antics:

- Early in 2001, Enron CEO Ken Lay sold substantial amounts of stock to the company and wasn't required to report the transaction until much later. At that time, SEC Rule 16b-3 required that a sale to the issuer only needed to be reported annually on Form 5 (rather than monthly on Form 4, which was the requirement for sales of stock other than back to the issuing company).

- Tyco International Ltd.'s CEO and CFO sold more than $100 million of Tyco stock to Tyco in late 2001, just before the company received extensive media coverage for corporate mismanagement. The CEO and CFO weren't required to report these sales under the SEC rules that were in effect at the time because those rules provided that such sales were required to be reported only on an annual basis.

- Global Crossing founder and Chairman Gary Winnick reportedly received $734 million for his stock before it plummeted into worthlessness in January 2002.

These events prompted the U.S. Senate to lament that the law should have required stock sales by executives to be brought to the public's attention "not a month or a year later when the damage has already been done."

Because of the numerous crimes and scandals of the past, SOX Section 16 changes the preexisting requirement for stock-sale reporting by company executives in several ways, which I cover in this section.

Faster disclosure

SEC rules require that stock sales by company executives be reported on SEC Form 4 within two days of the "date of execution." The revised rules also require two-day reporting of certain transactions between employee benefit plans by officers and directors. They also require that transactions involving stock options (such as grants, awards, cancellations, and repricings) be reported in the same time frame.

More disclosure

SEC Forms 3, 4, and 5 have been amended to add columns that show the exact dates that stock was purchased and sold. Under SOX, these forms must be posted on the corporation's Web site so everyone knows what management and directors are up to when it comes to selling their stock.

Owners of more than 10 percent of the common stock of any U.S. company are required to file SEC Forms 3, 4, and 5, regardless of whether they're officers or directors.

Prohibiting Personal Loans

SOX Section 402 prohibits SEC-registered public companies from making or arranging loans to their directors and executive officers. Prior to SOX, this practice was surprisingly commonplace; Enron, WorldCom, Adelphia, Quest, and Global Crossing all had authorized substantial personal loans to their executive officers.

SOX distinguishes between *personal loans* and other *extensions of credit.* Essentially, a loan isn't considered a personal loan or an arrangement for a loan if the primary purpose is to advance the business of the company, even though the loan may have the ancillary effect of enhancing the executive's personal credit. For example, some companies have employee benefit programs, such as 401(k)s, under which loans are available on the same basis to all participants. Although the company may have arranged the loan provisions of the benefits plan, the plan isn't a prohibited loan arrangement under SOX.

SOX Section 402 contains a grandfather clause that exempts credit or loan arrangements entered into between the company and its executives prior to July 30, 2002 (the date SOX was enacted), as long as the extension of credit hasn't had any material modifications or renewals since its inception.

Banning Blackout Trading

No aspect of the Enron collapse captured more media attention than the infamous management and director stock trades that took place during a blackout period. From October 29 to November 12, 2001, Enron employees were temporarily prohibited from selling the Enron stock in their 401(k) accounts while the company administering the plan was changed. During this period, the price of Enron stock dropped from $13.81 (right before the blackout) to $9.98 (right after the blackout). Enron company executives, most notably CEO Ken Lay, reportedly sold more than $1 billion in Enron stock during the blackout period, while employees lost nearly $1 billion from their retirement plans.

Avoiding media images of stricken retirees

During Enron's collapse, the media seized upon images of devastated retirees, and the effect was understandably heartbreaking and enraging. To help reassure members of the public holding stock in their employers as parts of retirement plans that their investments are secure and protected, several changes were made:

- ✔ SOX Section 306(a) contains a general statutory prohibition on stock transactions by directors and executive officers during blackout periods that are related to employee benefit plans.

- ✔ The Employee Retirement Income Security Act of 1974 (ERISA) is amended to require the administrators of retirement plans to give all plan participants at least 30-days' notice before a blackout period is imposed. The company faces a fine of $100 per day for each employee who doesn't receive such notice.

- ✔ ERISA further requires that the public be notified of any impending blackout period; the company must file a Form 8-K within four days of the date that the notice of the blackout is provided.

Making some necessary exceptions

The requirements covered in the preceding section are subject to a few notable exceptions. For the most part, these exceptions are intended to strike a compromise between employees' needs for information about blackout periods and the added administrative burden of giving notice of routine and anticipated blackout periods. Here are the exceptions:

- ✔ Neither ERISA nor SOX require notice of regularly scheduled blackout periods that are disclosed in retirement plan documents distributed to participants and beneficiaries.

- ✔ No notice is required for blackouts that must be imposed in connection with mergers, acquisitions, and divestures.

Making Managers Pay Personally

In 2005, prior to being sentenced to 25 years in prison, WorldCom CEO Bernard Ebbers agreed to pay $5.5 million in cash and turn over his mansion and $40 million in other assets to settle claims filed by WorldCom shareholders who lost billions of dollars when WorldCom collapsed in the largest bankruptcy in history. Prior to the deal, Ebbers had repaid only a small portion of the $408 million in personal loans that WorldCom made to him before the board forced him to resign.

Because of scandals like this one and others, SOX now makes it much more difficult for managers to appropriate corporate assets. New laws also permit their personal assets to be frozen or recovered under a wide range of circumstances.

The freeze factor

SOX Section 1103 authorizes the SEC to freeze the paychecks of "directors, officers, partners, controlling persons, agents, or employees" that it targets "during the course of a lawful investigation involving possible violations of federal securities laws." The way this deep freeze works is that the SEC requests a federal court to issue a temporary order placing the payments earmarked for these individuals in an interest-bearing escrow account.

The court order is effective for 45 days, during which time the SEC decides whether to file charges against the individuals in question. If the SEC doesn't bring charges and can't convince the court that it has good cause to freeze the assets for another 45 days, the funds are paid out to the individuals who were slated to receive them. In any event, the SEC can't freeze the assets for more than 90 days without bringing charges. If it does bring charges, the freeze remains in effect "until the conclusion of any legal proceedings related thereto."

The danger of disgorgement

Many CEOs and corporate executives are given bonuses and compensation based on the performance of their companies. But what at first blush may seem like a straightforward, merit-based compensation arrangement can become enormously complicated and terribly unfair when the corporate earnings on which the bonuses are based have to be adjusted downward. For this reason, SOX provides that bonuses based on previous (erroneous) earnings also have to be repaid when the restatement is attributable to management's noncompliance.

In other words, under SOX, CEOs must give back their bonuses if the company's financial statements have to be restated due to "material noncompliance" with financial reporting requirements. Specifically, CEOs and CFOs have to give back

✔ Any incentive-based compensation paid during the 12-month period following the initial publication of the financial statements

✔ Any equity in the company received as compensation during the 12-month period following the initial publication of the financial statements

✔ Profits from the sale of the company's securities

Stopping Audit Inference

In 2001, Enron was forced to report that it was required to correct (or *restate*) its 1997 earnings by $96 million, its 1998 earnings by $113 million, its 1999 earnings by $250 million, and its 2000 earnings by $132 million. During investigations, Congress and the public were outraged to discover that its accounting firm, Arthur Andersen, had been pressing for the adjustments for years but had given up when management stood firm in refusing to make them.

As a result of this and other events, SOX Section 303 provides that it shall be "unlawful" for any officer or director of an issuer or any other person acting under his or her direction to take any action to fraudulently influence, coerce, manipulate, or mislead any independent public or certified public accountant performing the audit of the issuer's financial statements.

Identifying audit interlopers

SEC rules make it clear that very little leeway is given to managers and directors who attempt to influence the outcome of their company's audits. The following activities aren't tolerated:

✔ Attempting to convince the auditors to issue financial statements that aren't in accordance with Generally Accepted Accounting Principles (GAAP; see Chapter 4)

✔ Attempting to skip or overlook parts of an audit

✔ Failing to communicate required matters to the company's audit committee

✔ Threatening to cancel audit engagements or to fire auditors (this includes undertaking the more obvious forms of blackmail threats and intimidation)

✔ Knowingly providing false, misleading, or incomplete information to auditors

Suing audit interlopers

In the aftermath of SOX, if a company were to shred documents, encourage employees to mislead auditors, or skew audit test results, it would find itself defending a lawsuit brought about by the SEC under a new provision of SOX that specifically authorizes such litigation.

SOX Section 303 and the accompanying SEC Rule 13b2-2 enable the SEC to file civil lawsuits against individuals and public companies that interfere with audits. In fact, under Section 303, the SEC can make more specific rules to prevent audit interference. Rule 303(b) also provides that in "any civil proceeding," the SEC "shall have the exclusive authority to enforce this section and any rule or regulation issued under this section." This SEC authority means that private individuals usually don't have the right to sue companies for audit interference; they have to wait for the SEC to do so. Similarly, Rule 303(c) states that the anti-interference provisions are enacted "in addition to" other provisions and don't supersede any other provisions of the law or rules or regulations that may prohibit the same conduct.

Part III
Scaling Down
Section 404

The 5th Wave   By Rich Tennant

"Thanks to Sarbanes–Oxley, we've got more internal controls than a warehouse full of Imodium."

In this part . . .

Thanks to its unprecedented documentation requirements, no part of SOX has received more adverse publicity than Section 404. Section 404 requires companies to document the internal controls that affect the financial information they distribute to the investing public. This part explains how your company can streamline Section 404 projects and avoid red herrings and tangents, based on experience with SOX over the years. It also takes a look at potential benefits, cost-savings, and competitive advantages that your company may achieve as a result of the Section 404 process.

Chapter 12

Clearing Up Confusion about Control

*B*efore the Securities Act of 1933 was passed, President Roosevelt publicly agreed with Supreme Court Justice Louis Brandies that "sunshine is said to be the best of disinfectants; electric light the most efficient policeman." Like the 1933 Act, the Sarbanes-Oxley Act (SOX) attempts to shine a bright light on financial reporting improprieties within corporations by zeroing in on "disclosure controls and procedures" and "internal control over financial reporting." However, in doing so, Congress and the Securities Exchange Commission, or SEC, have also created the inevitable uncertainty that accompanies any new legislation.

This chapter attempts to clarify the concepts of "disclosure controls" and "internal controls" introduced by SOX Sections 302 and 404. It also looks at the costs, dates, criteria, and other threshold issues associated with complying with these sections. I also explain why the term "internal control" has different definitions depending on whether it's used in connection with Section 302 or Section 404.

The Nuts and Bolts of Section 404

Congress included some broad new standards in SOX Section 404, and deliberately didn't tell companies how to implement them. The section is intentionally short on specifics. Congress instead directs the SEC and the Public Company Accounting Oversight Board, or PCAOB, to create more specific rules for companies to follow under SOX. (For more on the PCAOB, turn to Chapter 7.)

What Section 404 says

SOX Section 404 may be only 180 words, but since it was first introduced, U.S. companies have been busy interpreting every turn of phrase in order to figure out exactly what they must do to comply with the statute. Examining the wording of Section 404 can help you understand the obligations imposed under the SEC and PCAOB rules, which interpret Section 404 and more specifically define companies' obligations.

The following comes directly from Section 404. I've underlined buzzwords and key phrases for you to pay particular attention to:

SEC. 404. MANAGEMENT ASSESSMENT OF INTERNAL CONTROLS.

(a) RULES REQUIRED.—The Commission shall prescribe rules requiring each annual report required by section 13(a) or 15(d) of the Securities Exchange Act of 1934 (15 U.S.C. 78m or 78o(d)) to <u>contain an</u> <u>internal control report</u>, which shall—

(1) state the <u>responsibility of management</u> for establishing and maintaining <u>an adequate internal control structure and procedures for financial reporting</u>; and

(2) contain an <u>assessment</u>, as of the <u>end of the most recent fiscal year</u> of the issuer, of the effectiveness of the internal control structure and procedures of the issuer for financial reporting.

(b) INTERNAL CONTROL EVALUATION AND REPORTING.—With respect to the internal control assessment required by subsection (a), <u>each registered public accounting firm that prepares or issues the audit report for the issuer shall attest to, and report on, the assessment made by the management of the issuer.</u> An attestation made under this subsection shall be made in accordance with standards for attestation engagements issued or adopted by the Board. Any such attestation shall not be the subject of a separate engagement.

What Section 404 really does

The concept of internal control really isn't anything new; many companies had excellent controls and procedures in place prior to SOX. But SOX Section 404 accomplishes three objectives:

- ✔ Clarifies what's required for a company to maintain adequate internal control

- ✔ Requires management and auditors to formally certify that adequate internal controls are in place

- ✔ Specifies roles of the SEC and PCAOB in carrying out the objectives of SOX

SEC rules under Section 404

In carrying out its mandate to prescribe specific rules for implementing SOX Section 404, the SEC has focused on two critical areas:

- ✔ **Management responsibility:** Annual reports required to be filed with the SEC must state management's responsibility for establishing and maintaining an adequate internal control structure and procedures for financial reporting.

- ✔ **Effectiveness of internal control:** An annual report must contain an assessment of the effectiveness of the company's internal control structure and procedures for financial reporting as of the end of the company's most recent fiscal year.

PCAOB participation in the Section 404 process

As I mention earlier in this chapter, SOX Section 404 requires the PCAOB to create standards specifically for auditors in complying with Section 404. Under this section, auditors are responsible for attesting to and reporting on the assessment made by management. They must do so in accordance with standards for attestation engagements adopted by the PCAOB. (The role and duties of the PCAOB in regulating the audit profession are discussed in Chapter 7.)

In 2006, the PCAOB issued Auditing Standard No. 5 to replace its prior Auditing Standard No. 2. Both of these standards were designed to regulate internal control over financial reporting. However, Auditing Standard No. 5 is a "lightened up" version of the prior standard.

This newest standard directs auditors to focus on the big picture and to become more efficient (and hopefully more cost-effective to their clients). It also directs auditors to take a more focused approach and look for real financial risks to a company. This new "risk-based" testing approach is intended to be a scalable approach that can be tailored to fit companies of all sizes. This flexibility is particularly important as the compliance deadline for smaller companies looms. In addition, the PCAOB is expected to propose changes to the independence rules regarding the preapproval of nonaudit services and other conforming changes to existing interim standards.

When Do Companies Have to Comply with Section 404?

Most companies have until fiscal years "ending on or after" July 15, 2007, to comply with SOX's internal control reporting and disclosure requirements. Large companies have 60 days after the close of the fiscal year to file their Form 10-K (containing audited financial statements) with the SEC. Smaller companies with revenues of less than $75 million in equity (generally its voting and non-voting stock) have 90 days after the close of the fiscal year to file their financial statements.

Because many companies are on a calendar-year or fiscal-year basis, their date for Section 404 compliance will be December 31, 2007. However, many companies use June 30 or another date for the end of their fiscal year, and they have a longer or shorter period to comply. For example, a company with a June 30 end to the fiscal year would have to comply with Section 404 for its June 30, 2008, fiscal year end.

Accelerated and non-accelerated filers

If a company is considered a *non-accelerated filer*, it has a much longer time frame to comply with SOX than a company that's deemed an accelerated filer under SEC rules.

If a company is an accelerated filer, it meets the following four conditions at the end of its fiscal year:

✔ The market value of the voting and non-voting common equity (stock) of the company is $75 million or more.

✔ The company has been subject to the reporting requirements of Section 13(a) or 15(d) of the Securities Exchange Act of 1934 (discussed in Chapter 3) for a period of at least 12 calendar months.

✔ The company has filed at least one annual report under Section 13(a) or 15(d).

✔ The issuer isn't eligible to use certain special SEC forms for small businesses.

If a company meets the previous criteria, it's deemed an accelerated filer, which means that it was required to include management's assessment regarding internal control over financial reporting in its annual reports for fiscal years ending on or after December 15, 2007. A non-accelerated filer must begin to comply with the auditor attestation requirement in their annual reports filed for fiscal years ending on or after December 15, 2008.

As of the writing of this book, the SEC is also considering liberalizing the Section 404 requirements that apply to quarterly and other SEC reports filed during the year. It's also considering relaxing the requirements to allow more companies to qualify as *non-accelerated,* which would possibly exempt those companies with equity of as much as $125 million from having to obtain an independent Section 404 audit. For further discussion regarding which companies are currently required to do what, see the sidebar "Accelerated and non-accelerated filers."

A *fiscal year* is a year measured for financial reporting purposes, and can end on a date other than December 31, which is the year-end date for a calendar year. Many companies are on a calendar year ending December 31, so their first date for Section 404 compliance was December 31, 2007, because that's their first fiscal year "on or after July 15, 2007." Another popular date used by companies to end their fiscal year is June 30. These companies would have to comply with SOX Section 404 beginning with their June 30, 2008, annual reports.

Section 302 "Internal Control" versus Section 404 "Internal Control"

One of the biggest sources of confusion under SOX is the term "internal control." It certainly doesn't help that the SEC decided to use the term in two different sections of SOX and provide a different meaning for the term under each section.

By using different definitions, the SEC intended to make clear that SOX is aimed at two distinct types of internal controls. Under Section 302, the term internal control means *disclosure controls and procedures.* Under Section 404, the term means *internal control over financial reporting.* The following sections attempt to clarify the differences between the two.

Defining "disclosure controls and procedures" under Section 302

SOX Section 302 requires the CEOs and CFOs of a public company to certify that they have designed "internal controls" sufficient to ensure that they're familiar with material information within the company. The certification applies to the period for which each SEC periodic report was prepared. The SEC said that, for purposes of Section 302, references to internal controls mean "disclosure controls and procedures." The SEC further explained that disclosure controls and procedures encompass all the controls and procedures a company uses to ensure that information in the 10-K annual reports and 10-Q reports it files with the SEC is accurate.

The scope of the term "disclosure controls and procedures" is broader than the term "internal control over financial reporting." Disclosure controls and procedures include controls over all information that impacts company resources, not just controls on accounting and financial information.

In addition to complying with the certification requirements discussed in Section 302 to avoid civil liability, management must submit an additional certification containing similar information under Section 906. (I discuss both types of certifications further in Chapter 10.)

Section 302 requirements at the end of every period

SEC rules require management to

- ✔ Evaluate a company's disclosure controls and procedures as of the end of each period covered by the particular report.

- ✔ Make conclusions about the effectiveness of the controls and procedures that the company has in place.

To comply, most companies begin preliminary testing of internal controls and procedures early in the year that's being reported and do final testing at the end of the year to make sure management and auditors have submitted a report that's valid as of the end of the year, as required by Section 404.

Minimum Section 302 standards for every company

Disclosure controls and procedures vary according to the industries in which companies operate and to the companies' unique corporate structures. However, in every company, certain basic structures must be present in order for management to prepare its report and for the auditors to indicate that management's report is accurate.

At a minimum, a public company must have the following in place with respect to its disclosure controls and procedures:

- ✔ **Written procedures:** A company's internal controls and procedures should be written out in enough detail to provide guidance but not in so much detail that they're burdensome and difficult to follow. Disclosure controls and procedures requiring excessive detail can make the processes rigid and inflexible and create unnecessary compliance issues.

✔ **Systematic management supervision:** Management should be formally involved in supervising internal controls and procedures at a practical level. Companies should put into place a calendar for monitoring controls and procedures and for identifying milestone dates. Additionally, the SEC recommends that they form special disclosure committees, as discussed in Chapter 10.

✔ **A process for reviewing effectiveness:** Internal controls and procedures for U.S. companies should be evaluated on a quarterly basis in order to ensure that they continue to be effective.

Interpreting "internal control over financial reporting" under Section 404

Under SOX Section 404, all public companies are required to include in their annual reports a management report on the company's "internal control over financial reporting." The SEC rules describe an internal control over financial reporting as a process designed "to provide reasonable assurance regarding the reliability of financial reporting and the preparation of financial statements for external purposes."

This phrase "internal control" as it's used in Section 404 refers to the types of controls a company must have in place in order to prepare its financial statements according to Generally Accepted Accounting Principles (GAAP), which I explain in Chapter 6. Because this term relates only to GAAP, it's narrower in scope than the broader term "disclosure controls and procedures," which is used in Section 302 (this term is discussed in the preceding section).

Key elements of an internal control over financial reporting

The SEC rules require that an internal control over financial reporting satisfy three key functions:

✔ **Recordkeeping:** The process must involve maintaining records that accurately and fairly reflect (in reasonable detail) transactions and dispositions involving the company's assets.

✔ **Compliance:** The process must provide reasonable assurance that transactions are actually recorded so as to ensure that receipts and expenditures are made only when authorized by management and are recorded so that financial statements can be prepared in accordance with GAAP.

✔ **Prevention and detection:** The process must provide reasonable assurance that unauthorized use or disposition of company assets will be detected.

U.S. securities laws have required companies to maintain internal controls since 1977. SOX merely requires management and auditors to formally report on what should already be in place.

Management's evaluation responsibilities under Section 404

SOX Section 404 provides that management's report must establish its responsibilities for maintaining adequate internal accounting controls. The SEC rules warn companies that "inquiry alone will not provide an adequate basis for management's assessment." Management's procedures for testing internal controls must include both:

- Evaluation of the control's design
- Testing of the control's effectiveness

In the company's annual report filed with the SEC, management must include its own report on the company's internal control over financial reporting. In addition, the public accounting firm that audits the company's financial statements that appear in the annual report must issue an attestation report on management's assessment of internal control; this report is then filed as part of the company's annual report. With respect to quarterly reports, management is required to evaluate any change in the company's internal control occurring during a fiscal quarter that materially affects or is reasonably likely to materially affect the company's internal control.

What evaluation criteria should management use under Section 404?

Management is required to base its assessment of the effectiveness of the company's internal control over financial reporting on a suitable set of standards established by recognized experts. The SEC specifically refers to the Committee of Sponsoring Organizations (COSO) of the Treadway Commission as an acceptable framework for management's internal control assessment. The COSO criteria is covered in more detail in Chapter 14, and is the only set of standards specifically recognized by the SEC as of the writing of this book.

The directives in PCAOB's Auditing Standard No. 5 are based on the framework established by COSO. This is because so many public companies are expected to use that framework for their assessments. Other SEC-sanctioned approaches and frameworks may be published in the future. Even though different frameworks may not contain exactly the same elements as COSO, they probably incorporate most of the same testing concepts and criteria.

The American Institute of Certified Public Accountants, or AICPA, offers several resources to assist in understanding and complying with the COSO framework, including checklists for internal control testing. You can find these resources at www.cpa2biz.com.

Controlling the Cost of Compliance

Research shows that public companies have had to dig deeply into their pockets to comply with SOX. In fact, a survey by Financial Executives International (FEI), the leading professional organization of CFOs and other senior financial executives, concluded that in the first year of SOX's enactment, Section 404 cost U.S. companies $3.14 million per company. Much of this initial expense is attributed to costs for consulting, software, and the 58-percent increase in the fees charged by external auditors. (For full coverage of the costs associated with Section 404, check out Chapter 14.)

Although Congress was in a hurry to pass SOX in 2002 as a political response to the Enron crisis, it wasn't totally insensitive to the costs of compliance. For instance, simply take a look at Section 404(b). It provides that the auditor's attestation of management's assessment of internal control shall *not* be the subject of a separate engagement. In other words, Congress carefully conveys its expectation that companies not be forced to pay for duplicative audit services.

Cost-cutting measures by the PCAOB

The PCAOB, which oversees all audit firms, has attempted to make compliance as economical as possible. In an effort to reign in audit costs, the PCAOB has issued Auditing Standard No. 5. Under this standard, the audit firm must:

✔ Address the requirements for internal control over financial reporting

✔ Review management's assessment of the effectiveness of the internal control

Auditing Standard No. 5 also directs audit firms to perform two tasks required under Section 404 during a single audit engagement, rather than conducting two separate audits (and billing the company to do both). This is because the objectives and the work involved in performing both audits make them interrelated. For example, the auditor's discovery of misstatements in the financial statements may indicate the existence of weaknesses in the company's internal control over financial reporting.

In addition to issuing Auditing Standard No. 5, the PCAOB has also specially studied the impact that Section 404 costs have on companies, particularly small and medium-sized companies. The PCAOB anticipates that most companies, regardless of size, experience the highest cost of compliance with Section 404 during the first year that they're required to comply with the law.

An SEC commissioner's reflections on Section 404 costs

In a September 2005 speech before the Association of State Treasurers, summarized in *Compliance Week Magazine,* SEC Commissioner Paul Atkins blasted the SEC for its poor estimates on the costs of complying with SOX. Atkins charged that "Perhaps nothing in resent memory has illustrated the need to perform more probing cost/benefit analysis before requirements take effect than the regulatory regime that has grown under Section 404 of the Sarbanes-Oxley Act." He concluded, "As we enter the second year of the 404 process . . . it is becoming increasingly evident that everyone greatly underestimated the costs."

To support this criticism, Atkins discussed several compelling statistics. He explained "When

the SEC first released its implementation rules for Section 404, we estimated aggregate costs of about $1.24 billion or $94,000 per public company." He lamented "Unfortunately our estimates were not just low, they were incredibly low. Surveys have indicated that actual costs incurred for 404 compliance were 20 times higher than what we estimated."

Atkins also warned that compliance costs would not decrease significantly in year two. He predicted that "Cost reductions from year one will instead be in the neighborhood of 5 to 20 percent, and I predict that the reduction will be at the low end of this range."

The PCAOB has determined that the cost of complying with SOX Section 404 is related to factors such as:

- ✔ **The adequacy of the company's internal controls in previous years:** Existing control systems, ethical standards, and core values of a senior management group all help determine the costs of compliance with Section 404 and related SEC rules.

- ✔ **Whether the company does business overseas:** Large, complex, multinational companies, for example, are likely to need more extensive and sophisticated internal control systems.

- ✔ **The complexity of the company's corporate structure:** Companies with multiple subsidiaries and related entities may have increased costs of compliance simply because they have more information and locations to track. In contrast, smaller companies and companies with less complex operations may find that compliance is less burdensome than originally anticipated.

The PCAOB also has recognized that audit costs may be impacted by how much the auditor is permitted to rely on the work of internal auditors (which are paid at company salaries rather than expensive hourly rates as the auditors are). Accordingly, PCAOB Auditing Standard No. 5 provides outside auditors lots of discretion and flexibility in using the client company's personnel. The standard does, however, require the audit firm to obtain (through its own auditing procedures) a meaningful portion of the evidence that supports its opinion.

Section 404 sticker shock

A major criticism of SOX has been the huge, unexpected first-year costs of complying with Section 404. These costs are the primary reason the SEC cited when it continually pushed back compliance deadlines for smaller companies (see the section "When Do Companies Have to Comply with Section 404?" earlier in the chapter).

Decreasing costs in year two

When companies were asked about their anticipated costs in complying with SOX in year two, "85 percent of respondents said they expect nonauditor expenditures to decrease (by an average of 39 percent), and 68 percent said they believe the costs of their primary auditor will also decrease (by an average of 25 percent)," according to a recent study completed by Financial Executives International (FEI).

A great way to keep up with what other companies are doing with respect to SOX is to become a member of Financial Executives International. FEI is the "leading advocate for the views of corporate financial management." The organization has more than 15,400 members who hold policymaking positions as CFOs, treasurers, and controllers. The organization's Web site is located at www.financialexecutives.org.

According to FEI, companies believe they can reduce their SOX compliance costs after the first year by:

- ✔ Focusing on risk areas in the audit
- ✔ Reducing the degree of documentation required in general
- ✔ Being more flexible in remediating control problems uncovered by the SOX Section 404 audit

Looking for the sunny side of Section 404

Most businesses (and many politicians) are unhappy with SOX simply because the costs of compliance have been so much greater than originally expected. These costs have been viewed as a drain on productivity. And that drain puts American businesses at a disadvantage with foreign competitors.

Section 404 is the provision of SOX that businesses complain about most. However, SOX proponents argue that there will be less grumbling about Section 404 as businesses move beyond the first year of compliance, which is when the costs are the highest. After the first year, businesses may also notice benefits from Section 404 audits and increased internal control, such as elimination of fraud and redundancies in internal processes. Companies that have always operated in an ethical, above-board manner consistent with Section 404 may actually enjoy a competitive advantage. These squeaky-clean companies will have an easier time complying with Section 404 and will ultimately have to dedicate less money for compliance than companies that need to substantially scramble and revamp their internal processes in order to get a clean Section 404 opinion from their auditors.

A benefit on the horizon for businesses and investors alike is the increased reliability of financial information and reporting. This reliability is what SOX was passed to accomplish, and it appears that the law is working. According to Financial Executives International (FEI), "55 percent of companies surveyed believe Section 404 gives investors and other external audiences more confidence in a company's financial reports, and 83 percent of large companies (more than $25 billion) agree. Significantly, however, 94 percent of all respondents said the costs of compliance exceed the benefits."

Chapter 13

Surviving a Section 404 Audit

Section 404 of the Sarbanes-Oxley Act (SOX) makes it the responsibility of management to assess the company's internal control for financial reporting at the end of each year. Unfortunately, SOX Section 404 and the SEC rules passed to interpret it don't spell out exactly what *internal control* means in all scenarios. Reportedly, this omission has led to extreme scenarios in which auditors insist on verifying that all restroom keys are accounted for or insist on testing obscure computer code configurations that are unlikely to impact the company's financial statements.

This chapter examines the expanded the role of the audit firm and helps chief financial officers (CFOs), compliance officers, and audit committees identify where they can draw the line in a Section 404 audit.

Dividing Responsibilities in a Section 404 Audit

An audit of internal control is, as you might expect, a very controlled process. The Section 404 audit is a major project to which a company devotes substantial manpower and financial resources to complete. The audit process involves structured communication between management, independent auditors, the company's audit committee, and, on occasion, its board of directors. In a Section 404 audit, everyone has a specific role to play.

Management's role

Shifting focus from the pursuit of profits to the internal controls within a company is a difficult transition for many managers. Most are still adjusting to their new SOX-related responsibilities.

The major responsibilities of management with respect to the Section 404 audit are:

- ✓ Learning about the system of internal control that's in place
- ✓ Evaluating the effectiveness of both the design and implementation of internal control structures
- ✓ Preparing a written assessment at the end of the year on the effectiveness of internal control to include in management's report

The independent auditor's role

A Section 404 audit is part of the annual audit of a company's financial statements — it's not a separate process. As part of the overall audit, Section 404 requires the independent audit firm to express an opinion on management's assessment of the effectiveness of internal control. The audit firm must attest that management's assessment of internal control over financial reporting is stated fairly, in all material respects. The auditor must be satisfied that management has performed the necessary testing and has formed an accurate basis for its reporting and attestation.

An auditor can't simply take management's word that adequate testing has been done. Auditors are required to form their own opinions about the accuracy of management's reports and attestation and be able to support those opinions with evidence and data from the testing.

Because SOX forecloses audit firms from performing consulting and other nonaudit services (as discussed in Chapter 6), many are hoping to make up the lost revenues on the Section 404 audits.

The outside audit firm can get the evidence it needs in several ways, including:

- ✓ **Testing transactions:** Performing its own tests on company transactions to see if the internal controls that are supposed to be in place actually kick in
- ✓ **Verifying management's assessment process:** Retracing the steps taken by management

✔ **Evaluating and testing work done by others:** Retesting a sampling of transactions on internal control that were tested by the company's own staff (such as internal auditors) to see if their conclusions about the company's internal control can or should be used by the auditors

What will auditors look at when they're doing a Section 404 audit of your company? They're given guidance in this area by the Public Company Accounting Oversight Board (PCAOB) (discussed in Chapter 7). The PCAOB issues special standards for public auditors to guide them in complying with Securities and Exchange Commission (SEC) rules.

What Is (and Is Not) Related to the Audit

A Section 404 audit focuses on a company's internal control over financial reporting. Internal controls operate as checks on processes that impact the company's financial statements. However, not everything is within the ambit of the audit. For example, marketing decisions, unrelated administrative procedures, and most personnel policies probably aren't things your auditors should spend time and money digging in to.

Examples of internal controls the auditors may be looking for include:

✔ **Policies and procedures for maintaining accounting records:** All companies should have controls in place to ensure accurate recording of information and to protect against tampering.

✔ **Procedures for authorizing receipts and disbursements and safeguarding assets:** SEC rules require that all transactions carried out within the company should be appropriately authorized. They also state that employees and third parties should not be permitted to initiate transactions without appropriate authority to do so.

✔ **Tracking systems for use of the company's resources:** Transactions involving the company's resources should have controls to ensure that resources (such as labor and inventory) aren't diverted or misused as the transaction progresses.

✔ **Verification of balances and transactions:** Account balances and transaction amounts should be verified.

✔ **Appropriate segregation of responsibilities:** Responsibilities should be divided among different persons in a way that makes it more difficult to perpetrate fraud or error. For example, the employees authorizing payments to vendors shouldn't be the same ones cutting checks.

Taking the broad view, the auditors performing the Section 404 audit are in charge of making sure that the board of directors, management, investors, and others can rely on reported financial information when making decisions.

SOX was passed, in part, because of Congress's concern about cases in which fraudulent reporting on financial statements was initiated by management and resulted from management's ability to exploit weaknesses in internal control. Thus, under SOX, internal controls are now assessed twice: once by management and once by the auditors.

Complying with Auditing Standard No. 5

During congressional hearings regarding the Enron scandal, senior management complained to Congress that at the time, it wasn't aware of the illegal activities taking place at Enron, and the independent auditors didn't bring any problems to management's attention. To remedy this all-too-common scenario, Congress created the Public Company Accounting Oversight Board (PCAOB) as a new arm of the SEC. This board replaced the system of accounting self-regulation that had previously been in place. Section 404 directs the SEC to create rules for implementation, and the SEC in turn directs the PCAOB to create standards for auditors.

PCAOB Auditing Standard No. 2 was approved by the SEC on June 17, 2004, and was quickly withdrawn and replaced with Auditing Standard No. 5 in 2007. Auditing Standard No. 5 directs auditors to lighten up and focus their audits on the greatest risks to a company. Doing so would hopefully help the auditors become more efficient (and hopefully more cost-effective to their clients).

This new "risk-based" testing approach is intended to be a sensible approach that can be tailored to fit companies of all sizes, particularly as the compliance deadline for smaller companies looms. This approach is also effective for audits of internal control over financial reporting required by SOX Section 404(b). This section summarizes the key provisions of Auditing Standard No. 5.

Integrating the audits

Auditing Standard No. 5 provides that auditors integrate their audit of internal control over financial reporting with the audit of the company's financial statements. Even though the objectives of the audits aren't identical, the auditor must plan and perform the work to achieve the objectives of both audits.

Auditors are directed to keep costs down by designing their testing of controls in a way that will help them accomplish the objectives of both audits simultaneously. SEC rules further require management to base their evaluation of the effectiveness of the company's internal control over financial reporting on a suitable, recognized control framework (also known as *control criteria*) established by a body or group that followed due process procedures. Examples of these acceptable standards are those contained in the report of the Committee of Sponsoring Organizations of the Treadway Commission (known as the COSO report).

Planning the audits

The auditor should properly plan the audit of internal control over financial reporting and supervise any assistants. The PCAOB provides very specific guidance to auditors by directing them to evaluate whether the following matters are important to the company's financial statements and internal control over financial reporting and, if so, how they will affect the auditor's procedures:

- Knowledge of the company's internal control over financial reporting obtained during other engagements performed by the auditor
- Matters affecting the industry in which the company operates, such as financial reporting practices, economic conditions, laws and regulations, and technological changes
- Matters relating to the company's business, including its organization, operating characteristics, and capital structure
- The extent of recent changes, if any, in the company, its operations, or its internal control over financial reporting
- The auditor's preliminary judgments about materiality, risk, and other factors relating to the determination of material weaknesses
- Legal or regulatory matters of which the company is aware
- The type and extent of available evidence related to the effectiveness of the company's internal control over financial reporting
- Preliminary judgments about the effectiveness of internal control over financial reporting
- Public information about the company relevant to the evaluation of the likelihood of material financial statement misstatements and the effectiveness of the company's internal control over financial reporting
- Knowledge about risks related to the company evaluated as part of the auditor's client acceptance and retention evaluation
- The relative complexity of the company's operations

Scaling the audits

Auditing Standard No. 5 contains a special note to auditors directing them to scale their audit activities to the size and complexity of a particular company.

For instance, some larger, complex companies may have less complex units or processes. According to Auditing Standard No. 5 "factors that might indicate less complex operations include: fewer business lines; less complex business processes and financial reporting systems; more centralized accounting functions; extensive involvement by senior management in the day-to-day activities of the business; and fewer levels of management, each with a wide span of control."

Assessing the risk

Auditors are directed by Auditing Standard No. 5 to focus their energies on the most significant risks to the company. They're directed to do this by identifying the most "significant accounts and disclosures and relevant assertions" regarding those accounts. Auditors are also directed to take into account the risk of fraud in their assessments.

Auditing Standard No. 5 specifically directs that auditors should evaluate the following types of controls:

- ✔ Controls over significant, unusual transactions, particularly those that result in late or unusual journal entries
- ✔ Controls over journal entries and adjustments made in the period-end financial reporting process
- ✔ Controls over related party transactions
- ✔ Controls related to significant management estimates
- ✔ Controls that mitigate incentives for, and pressures on, management

Cutting costs by relying on the work of others

A particularly important way in which Auditing Standard No. 5 will reduce audit costs is by directing auditors to rely more on the work of others, including testing that has already been done by the company's internal audit staff. After all, what's the use in testing the same things over and over?

According to Auditing Standard No. 5, the auditor should assess the competence and objectivity of the persons whose work the auditor plans to use. This assessment allows the auditor to determine the extent to which he or she may use that work. The higher the degree of competence and objectivity, the greater use the auditor may make of the work.

Using a top-down approach

Auditing Standard No. 5 directs auditors to use a top-down approach to SOX Section 404 audits over internal control when selecting which controls to test.

Using a top-down approach means starting at the financial statement level and grasping an understanding of the overall risks to internal control over financial reporting. This approach directs the auditor's focus to accounts, disclosures, and assertions that present a reasonable possibility of material misstatement on the company's financial statements. The auditor can then verify his or her understanding of the risks in the company's processes and subsequently select for testing those controls that sufficiently address the assessed risk of misstatement to each relevant assertion.

Flunking a Section 404 Audit

Preliminary research shows that anywhere from 5 to 15 percent of public companies will flunk their Section 404 audits in their initial year of compliance. And despite already spending large amounts to comply with Section 404, these companies may need to invest even more substantial resources to correct the flaws found in the audits they fail.

How to fail a Section 404 audit

A company essentially flunks its Section 404 audit when it receives either a qualified or an adverse opinion from its auditors with respect to internal control. Both of these opinions reflect material weaknesses in internal control that, in the opinion of the auditor, render it ineffective.

A *qualified opinion* may contain the dreaded phrase, "except for the effect of the material weakness, internal control was effective." An *adverse opinion* more bluntly states "internal control over financial reporting was not effective." Both types of opinions basically mean the company has flunked its Section 404 audit with respect to the effectiveness of internal control.

If the auditor and the company's management disagree about whether a material weakness exists (that is, the auditor concludes that a material weakness exists, but management doesn't), the auditor may render an adverse opinion on management's assessment. This is another way to fail a Section 404 audit.

What to do if your company flunks

If your company receives a qualified or adverse audit opinion with respect to its internal control, there isn't much you can do to change the opinion. Effectiveness of internal control is measured at year's end, and the Section 404 audit process is intended to obtain a snapshot as of that date. However, when moving forward, the company needs to analyze material weaknesses and deficiencies and take proactive measures to correct the situation before subsequent audits occur.

Recommended proactive measures include the following:

- The audit committee should carefully review with the independent auditors the nature of the material weakness identified.

- The audit committee should hire appropriate independent consultants (neither affiliated nor related to the company or the audit firm) to decide remedial actions.

- The company should follow through with the implementation of additional controls recommended by the audit committee and its consultants and document that this action has been taken.

- Management should work to simplify and update internal control structures where possible (such as getting rid of paper ledgers).

- Management should use feedback from the prior Section 404 audit and other available information to eliminate redundant processes.

- The company should implement appropriate software solutions to enhance internal control.

- Management should elicit feedback from performing and documenting testing.

- Management should fire or reassign personnel who are responsible for lapses in implementing internal controls.

- The company should begin testing well in advance of subsequent Section 404 audits.

- Management should compare test results to that of the prior year to see if the newly implemented controls have achieved a higher level of accuracy and reliability.

These measures will help prevent fraud or financial loss that could result from ineffective internal control.

A company that receives an adverse or qualified opinion in a Section 404 audit should carefully explore its legal exposure to shareholders who may sue the company alleging that they have been damaged by management's failure to implement effective internal control structures.

Chapter 14

Taking the Terror Out of Testing

● ●

In This Chapter

▶ Controlling Section 404 project costs

▶ Streamlining documentation

▶ Figuring out who's running the risks and manning the controls

▶ Getting to know COSO and COBIT

● ●

An audit of a company's internal control under Section 404 of the Sarbanes-Oxley Act (SOX) can turn into a mushroom cloud of resources and manpower that leaves little constructive value when the smoke clears. To avoid this scenario, most companies approach the Section 404 compliance process as a series of projects, with each project having the clear objective of testing a specific type of internal control within the company. Every project in a Section 404 audit must be well managed, and the information that results from it must fit into the scheme of the Section 404 audit so that management can confidently attest to internal control within the company.

Successful Section 404 compliance under SOX means being able to see the big picture and how a lot of smaller pictures fit into it. This chapter gives you some practical guidelines for managing Section 404 projects, and it also introduces you to the useful COSO framework and auditing standard (SAS 70) developed to help companies in this area.

 SOX, in the grand scheme of things, requires companies to study their own internal processes. Under Section 404, employees responsible for generating documentation may also be empowered to come up with ideas for improving processes.

The Price of the Project

The major source of criticism of SOX Section 404 is the sheer cost of implementing it. Corporations across the country experience the sticker shock of compliance (as discussed in Chapter 12); actual Section 404 costs exceed projected ones at a staggering rate, and companies everywhere scramble to understand why. This section takes a look at some of the most common costs, financial and otherwise, associated with a Section 404 audit.

The six most common Section 404 project costs

Companies are more alike than they are different when it comes to the costs of complying with SOX Section 404. A typical Section 404 compliance project produces labor costs that fall into the following categories:

- **Documenting the company's processes:** A substantial skilled staff is required to document and chart all the processes that directly impact a company's financial statements and the controls and risks associated with each process.

- **Testing the company's process controls:** Section 404 requires considerable manpower to test controls, such as company policies, cross-checks, records, and internal accounting and audit procedures, that are associated with all company processes.

- **Documenting information technology controls:** Companies have to test the controls on their information technology systems. Examples of these types of controls include controls on data gathering, computer networks, and the company's computer hardware systems.

- **Reviewing and editing all documentation:** Additional manpower is necessary to review all the documentation collected on the company's processes and controls. (For more on these costs, check out the "Meeting massive manpower requirements" section later in this chapter.)

- **Testing documentation:** After all process-related documentation is compiled and edited, a company needs the staff to test it. Software tools, as discussed in Chapter 16, are particularly useful for helping staff in this area and thus reducing manpower requirements.

- **Audit fees:** Above all, companies must contend with large Section 404 audit fees from outside CPA firms.

Meeting massive manpower requirements

The most significant cost a company faces in complying with SOX Section 404 comes from the sheer manpower required to document the control processes and the results of the tests on those processes. SOX requires several levels of documentation, some of which may be prepared by the company and some of which must be outsourced. Generally, however, a company can save a lot of money by using its own employees to compile documentation rather than outsourcing the same job to another company. For example, if your company is able to pay employees their usual wages for compiling information about cash disbursements rather than paying a CPA or consulting firm to do it, the savings can be substantial.

To be in a position to realize this type of savings, your company must have capable employees in place to do the tasks and create the documentation required. The personnel on a payroll who are responsible for SOX compliance generally include the following:

- ✔ **Project managers:** Project managers know a little something about the employees in their departments who are assigned to a Section 404 project, so they can coordinate the employees' work to bring the project to completion. The project manager is responsible for

    - Verifying quality control of the work everyone does on the project

    - Monitoring all aspects of the project's progress

    - Reporting progress to management

    - Meeting certain milestone dates in the project's progress

- ✔ **Internal accounting staff:** Most SOX-compliant companies dedicate significant staff within their accounting departments to test accounts and accounting controls and conduct audits to determine compliance with company policies that affect internal financial controls. The outside independent audit firm may "test the tests" performed by the internal accounting staff by sampling their results.

- ✔ **Information technology staff:** A critical subject of internal control testing is information technology and how company systems and policies impact the data used to prepare financial statements. Significant staff within the information technology department must be assigned to the task of testing and compiling documentation on these controls.

If your company is of the smaller variety, with common stock valued at less than $75 million, you may be in the process of complying with Section 404. Many larger companies, however, have already complied with Section 404, and you can benefit from their experiences. Industry publications and Securities and Exchange Commission (SEC) disclosures filed by these companies (available on the SEC Web site at www.sec.gov) can yield important information that's relevant to planning your company's Section 404 projects. (For more information about how to review documents filed by companies with the SEC, take a look at Chapter 4.)

The social challenges of Section 404

Every project in a company needs the support of the people involved in executing it to realize a successful outcome. Your company can save considerable time and money on Section 404 projects by enlisting the support and cooperation of the company's board of directors, the chief executive officers (CEOs), department heads, project managers, and other key personnel.

It's more time efficient to enlist this cooperation at the outset than to contend with internal power struggles along the way. It's unlikely that staff will cooperate if their managers are equivocal about the project's benefit or skeptical about the way things are being carried out.

Most human resource experts recommend that department heads and project managers initiating a new Section 404 project call special kick-off meetings to introduce the top-level project management. This meeting offers an opportunity to explain the value of the project as well as its objectives.

Hail to the Documenters

The success or failure of most projects associated with a SOX Section 404 project depends on the quality of the documentation generated. The most skilled people on a project are usually in charge of creating, editing, and approving the documentation before the project is handed off for the next phase of the audit. This section identifies some skills and practices for generating good project documentation.

The right documentation skills

Laws, regulations, and the standards they set are what drive the documentation on a Section 404 project. The documentation must respond to all the relevant standards, answering the questions posed pursuant to those standards. Therefore, documenters must know what information can safely be discarded and what must be scrupulously retained. They also have to present the information so that compliance with the relevant standards is clearly apparent.

Documenters must understand the following standards:

✔ Standards issued by the Public Company Accounting Oversight Board (PCAOB) (see Chapter 7)

✔ Generally Accepted Accounting Principles (GAAP) and Generally Accepted Auditing Standards (GAAS) (see Chapter 6)

✔ SEC rules

✔ COSO and COBIT standards (discussed in the sections "Evaluating Control with the COSO Framework" and "A bit about COBIT" later in this chapter, respectively)

Section 404 documenters must also be skilled communicators on both technical and nontechnical levels. Specifically, they must be able to

✔ Interview other employees about their day-to-day duties to the extent that those duties impact processes covered under Section 404.

✔ Prepare flowcharts and reports of business processes.

✔ Help identify risks to internal controls and recommend how those risks can be avoided or minimized.

Well-trained documenters save a company a lot of time. Prior to preparing any documentation, the project manager should meet with the documenters to ensure that they understand the project scope and know how much detail to document.

Getting the documentation down

Before documenters can do their jobs, they need to know *how* they're going to document. In other words, every documenter needs to follow a set of pre-determined steps to document each process. The project manager is responsible for spelling out these steps in writing before work begins. Additionally, the project manager needs to assign a budget for each task and tell the documenters how long documentation is expected to take. Documenters should track the actual number of hours it takes to get the project done for each process and measure their hours against the project manager's estimate (for more on documentation and time, see the upcoming section "Time tracking").

Time tracking

Section 404 project managers have a daunting job in making sure that their projects are completed correctly and within the time frames necessary to integrate the project results into the scheme of the entire Section 404 audit process. Accuracy and timeliness are critical, but an important secondary goal for project managers is ensuring that their projects are accomplished efficiently and that inefficiencies in conducting a first-year project aren't repeated in subsequent years.

Tracking the time spent on the project by everyone involved in its execution is a valuable way of identifying inefficiencies in the testing process. These inefficiencies may be attributed to some of the following causes:

- ✔ **Vague scope definition:** If the scope and objectives of the project are poorly defined at the outset, effective time tracking systems can indicate whether staff may be forced to spend inordinate amounts of time clarifying their roles. Staff can also waste time documenting data that's extraneous to the project goals or omitting data that should have been included in the results of a particular testing project. For more on project scope, jump to the section "Scoping out savings" later in this chapter.

- ✔ **Untrained staff:** A good project manager knows the skill levels of the people involved in the project and therefore can estimate how long tasks should take. Staff members who spend excessive time on a task may be encountering unanticipated issues that require follow-up, or they may be training on the job. Time tracking helps identify skills lacking on a project in a prior year as well as staff that aren't performing up to project standards.

- ✔ **Poor budgeting and estimates:** A project may be taking too long because of unexpected glitches and adverse findings, or it may simply be that no one knew how long it was supposed to take. Time tracking can help with Section 404 project budgets in future years.

Time tracking is so vital to the economics of a Section 404 project that one or more team members may be assigned to the sole task of tracking the time spent by the rest of the project team members.

Scoping out savings

The key to working in a cost-effective manner and saving money when complying with Section 404 is to define the scope of each project at the outset. Clearly defining the scope of the project benefits the company in two ways: It prevents unnecessary and redundant work, and it ensures that only required data is gathered (so the project can be completed on schedule).

Scope definition includes identifying the following:

- ✔ **The project's objectives:** What controls is the project testing?

- ✔ **What data should be gathered:** What information is being documented to meet the objectives? What's the standard for determining whether a particular event is significant enough (material) to be reported in the project results?

✔ **Where the data should be gathered from:** Which company locations, departments, and transactions are the subject of the testing?

✔ **Acceptable procedures for gathering the data:** What tasks will be performed according to the parameters of the project?

Defining the scope of a project should be a formal, *written* endeavor. Section 404 project managers should take a page from the book of information technology managers, who almost always require a formal written scope statement for any new project. Writing out a formal project scope statement avoids backtracking and second-guessing later on; it also prevents management from attempting to expand the scope of a given project without formally authorizing it.

Taking an inventory of your company processes

A good inventory of processes presents an opportunity for saving time and money on a Section 404 project. In this context, a *process* is a collection of procedures and activities for recording company transactions. Some examples of business processes include:

✔ Preparing a requisition to buy inventory

✔ Documenting a customer sale

✔ Making a bank deposit

✔ Processing a credit card transaction

Getting 'em all

CEOs dread nothing more under Section 404 than the possibility of missing a key process in a Section 404 audit. Why? Because they must personally certify, under fear of both civil and criminal penalties, the effectiveness of their company's internal controls and processes. (For more on management and board certifications, turn to Chapter 10.)

Identifying the key processes in your company may require the following:

✔ **Looking to see what other companies in your industry have already documented:** Outside consultants who have worked with other companies in your industry may have already compiled process lists that you can work from.

✔ **Meeting with your own middle managers:** Talking to managers, department heads, project managers, and others who are familiar with key company processes can help you develop comprehensive process lists.

> ✔ **Capitalizing on "canned" lists:** Many software documentation tools on the market contain their own helpful process lists. For example, the American Institute for Certified Public Accountants (AICPA) sells a COSO Control Environment checklist on its Web site at www.cpa2biz.com. This is a good tool to start with when gathering information about your company's controls. (COSO standards are discussed in more detail in the later section "Evaluating Control with the COSO Framework.")

When documenting processes, it's important for the documenters to understand how financial processes may overlap with company processes that are considered unrelated to the financial statements. Documenters need to gather documentation on processes that are potentially relevant to financial reporting and must be wary of increasing the costs of the project by testing irrelevant controls.

For example, aspects of how a company runs its manufacturing plant (operational processes) or legal compliance measures can potentially impact financial statements. Project managers must make a determination as to what reasonably needs to be stated.

Starting with charting

Most companies use flowcharts to help them identify business processes. For instance, a company may create a detailed chart of its manufacturing or sales cycle and fill in the processes related to each stage. More flowcharts may be used in the Section 404 process to document accounting cycles. Ultimately, a final round of flowcharts may be created for the processes themselves, documenting both the steps in the process and how the processes relate to each other.

Looking at the ledger

The company's *general ledger* is likely to be an important source of information for documenting company processes because general ledgers are chronological records of the company's accounting transactions. The general ledger shows the effect of each transaction on the accounts reflected on the financial statements.

Ranking the processes

After processes are inventoried, a company has to figure out which processes are most significant. After all, it's impossible to test them all. Most companies use some sort of objective system for scoring processes to determine which are the most significant. They identify the factors that determine significance and apply those standards to each individual process in order to produce a rating. The processes that rank the highest receive priority for Section 404 testing.

Some factors that contribute to the significance value of a process include the following:

- ✔ The dollar amount associated with the process relative to the assets of the company as whole
- ✔ The risk to the company if the process isn't properly controlled
- ✔ The likelihood that the process can be subverted
- ✔ The type and availability of documentation associated with the process and the ease of reviewing that documentation
- ✔ How well employees performing the process are supervised

Creating Section 404 dream teams

Good project teams save their companies money. The first step in creating a good team is deciding what role each team member should play. Then you have to pick people with the right skills for each role.

Consider the following players when building a winning Section 404 project team:

- ✔ **Process manager:** The person in the company with management-level responsibility for ensuring that the process is correctly carried out.
- ✔ **People who perform the process:** The people who perform the financial process on a daily basis should be consulted when it comes time to test it because they're familiar with the process's intricacies.
- ✔ **Information administrators:** These people are the most familiar with how information about the process is gathered within the organization.

Communicating as colleagues

Team meetings go smoothly if everyone comes prepared, and preparation is most important during a company's initial Section 404 project team meetings.

For these meetings, the project manager should have a clear agenda, and he or she should bring information to share with the team regarding:

- ✔ The assertions being tested
- ✔ Possible risks
- ✔ Controls designed to mitigate the risks
- ✔ Procedures for documentation
- ✔ Estimates as to how long the project tasks should take

Walking through the process

One of the best ways to make sure that the Section 404 project meets its objectives is to attempt a dry run. Have your team try documenting one process, and then review that documentation. Discuss the format and completeness of what the team produces as well as changes that the team needs to make before documenting the remaining processes.

Organizing the documentation: Why form is equal to substance

A good set of forms can be a great cost-saver on a Section 404 project. The documentation gathered in all of the company's Section 404 projects should use a consistent, easy-to-read and ready-to-review format. The document forms should contain information not only about the tests performed but also about who performed the tests. Standardizing forms within the Section 404 audit helps team members work efficiently and coordinate their efforts. It also makes the forms easier to review and lessens the risks of overlooking important information.

Good Section 404 documentation usually contains the following:

✔ **Information about the process being tested:** A process is commonly explained and illustrated using a flowchart like the one shown in Figure 14-1, which examines an inventory control process.

Visio is an easy-to-use computer program for creating flowcharts for documenting processes. You can download a trial version of this program at www.visio.com.

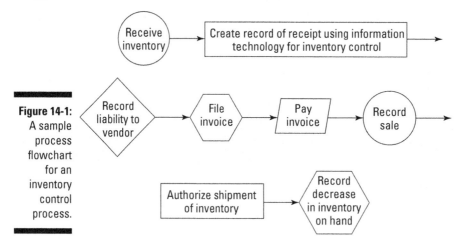

Figure 14-1:
A sample process flowchart for an inventory control process.

> ✔ **A summary of the risks and controls associated with the process:** The procedures for identifying risks are explained in the section "Caveats about Controls" later in this chapter. For the most part, risks and controls usually are identified and tracked using a software program such as SarbOxPro, which I discuss in Chapter 17.

> ✔ **Identification of the controls used to prevent the risk:** To get a clean bill of health on its Section 404 audit, a company should have at least one effectively working control for each risk. The project team should identify the controls in place on the standard project form.

Caveats about Controls

A *control* is what prevents a risk from happening. There should be at least one control for each risk. If the risk of a flawed control could allow a material error to creep into a company's financial statements, that control needs to be tested. A *material error* is one that's deemed financially significant based on a standard established by the audit committee and independent auditors. Design your Section 404 tests so that a single test covers as many controls as possible.

PCAOB standards state that the independent auditor must

> ✔ Test each relevant assertion that the company makes on the financial statements it files with the SEC

> ✔ Verify the existence and completeness of the documentation supporting each relevant assertion

As a practical matter, a financial statement assertion can form the basis of a Section 404 project within the company. For each assertion, the company should determine all the scenarios and situations that could cause it to be inaccurate. Such risks include the possibility that account balances may be understated or overstated or that assets may be undervalued or overvalued. Project managers and auditors must look at all the scenarios that could cause any of these risks to be the case. For example, an employee may be falsifying payable records to a vendor, thus overstating accounts payable; unauthorized disbursements may be lowering other account balances, or assets may be overvalued.

Although testing for all risks is impossible, companies are expected to have a control in place for every identified risk and to test key controls, which are explained in this section. This prioritization is known as the "top-down" approach (see Chapter 13 for more details).

Key controls

A control that prevents a material risk is known as a *key control.* The key controls in every company are different, because they're based on the type of goods and services that a company provides and its own peculiar accounting processes. Some questions to ask when identifying key controls at your company are:

✔ Does the control prevent fraud or inaccuracy?

✔ Does the control safeguard assets?

✔ How significant (material) could the impact be if the control failed?

Many controls will be included in the first two categories, so the question of whether a control is a key one will generally hinge on the issue of materiality. *Materiality* is usually (but not always) measured as some sort of dollar amount. Every company must decide on an appropriate level of materiality.

Some common key controls

Although company controls vary and must constantly evolve as new risk factors are identified, some controls are common to most companies. This section examines a few of these standard controls.

Segregation of duties

Segregation of duties exists when responsibility for a financial process is divided among several people so that no one individual can misappropriate company assets. For example, segregation of duties for accounts payable may be accomplished by making sure that the same person isn't responsible for more than one of the following tasks:

✔ Authorizing an accounts payable transaction

✔ Entering data for an accounts payable transaction

✔ Having custody of the assets used to pay the transaction

✔ Disbursing assets to pay the vendor

✔ Performing a control to verify the accounts payable transaction

Authorization procedures

An *authorization* control is in place when more than one person in a company has to authorize a decision or action that can impact the company's assets or financial statements. For example, several managers may be responsible for approving a disbursement.

Reconciliations

Reconciliation is a control process of verifying one account balance by comparing it to another account balance that should be affected by the same transaction. If the first account can't be balanced or reconciled using this technique, an error may be present or fraud may be occurring within the company.

Ogling the Outside Vendors: SAS 70 Reports

Almost every company that's subject to SOX outsources something, but the one thing a company can't outsource is responsibility for matters that impact its financial statements. According to Auditing Standard SAS 70, if a company outsources functions, it must establish that adequate internal control is maintained at the outside vendor.

If outside vendors perform significant financial processes or handle key controls for your company, SOX requires you to vouch for the controls in place at those third-party vendors.

Often, third-party vendors have audit reports prepared by their own auditors and are happy to hand them out to valued customers. If your company chooses to rely on such third-party reports, known as *SAS 70 reports,* keep the following requirements in mind:

- ✔ **Timing:** The SAS 70 report must be completed close enough to your company's year-end that the third-party controls described in the report can be expected to remain in place at the end of your company's fiscal year.

- ✔ **Covered controls:** The SAS 70 report must cover all the controls your company relies on given the services that the third-party vendor supplies.

- ✔ **Effectiveness of controls:** Third-party controls must be effective for detecting errors material to *your* company. Sometimes, a third-party company designates a materiality limit that's much higher than your company would consider appropriate, which means the control in place is less stringent.

The SAS 70 report provided by your third-party vendor doesn't fulfill these requirements; your company needs to perform its own audit of that process. As a practical matter, a competitive vendor will strive to provide its clients with an SAS 70 report on which they can rely. *Tip:* Design your Section 404 tests so that a single test covers as many controls as possible. To review a sample SAS 70 report, flip to Appendix E.

Evaluating Control with the COSO Framework

In 1985, the Committee of Sponsoring Organizations of the Treadway Commission (COSO) was formed to study factors that can lead to fraudulent financial reporting by businesses. In 1992, this commission issued a publication titled *Internal Control — Integrated Framework.* This document is the most widely relied upon framework and set of standards for businesses to evaluate their internal control systems in the United States. (The SEC specifically cites the COSO framework as a set of standards that managements may use permissibly in evaluating internal control.) Your company is likely to use the COSO framework in conjunction with other standards that it has developed.

How COSO breaks down companies' controls

The COSO framework views a company's overall internal control environment as consisting of five components:

- **Control environment:** How decisions and policies are made within a business and how authority and responsibly are assigned

- **Risk assessment:** How the processes performed within each department may impact the company's financial statements

- **Control procedures:** Those that limit risk

- **Information and communication:** How polices and control structures are communicated to people within the organization

- **Monitoring:** Whether controls are actually operating as expected

The COSO framework takes a very people-oriented approach to the evaluation of internal controls, viewing internal control as "a process, effected by an entity's board of directors, management, and other personnel, designed to provide reasonable assurance" with respect to the following issues that may impact a company's financial statements:

- Effectiveness and efficiency of operations

- Reliability of financial reporting

- Compliance with applicable laws and regulations

The COSO Web site (www.coso.org) explains that internal control is "a process. It is a means to an end, not an end in itself. . . . Internal control is effected by people. It's not merely policy manuals and forms, but people at every level of an organization."

COSO guidance for your company

The SEC mandates that your company develop its internal control standards with reference to those developed by COSO or a similar organization.

The COSO framework provides guidance in the following areas:

- **Project planning:** COSO provides guidelines and suggested procedures for helping your company determine how to structure project teams and documentation as well as coordinate with internal auditors.

- **Identifying control objectives:** COSO contains credible standards that your company can rely on in identifying which controls are key controls and in determining levels of materiality for testing.

- **Documenting controls:** COSO contains documentation guidelines and formats as well as discussion about coordinating your company's internal documentation with that of the independent auditors.

- **Testing and evaluating controls:** COSO provides procedural guidelines for conducting tests and standards for evaluating the reliability of particular internal controls.

When you're involved in any SOX Section 404 project, visit the COSO Web site at www.coso.org for great articles and resources on evolving Section 404 audit standards, procedures, and trends.

A Bit about COBIT

COBIT, or Control Objectives for Information and Related Technology, refers to a set of generally applicable and accepted standards for information technology. COBIT standards provide a reference framework specifically for IT control systems as opposed to financial control systems as a whole. The standards relevant to SOX include best practices for each IT process and models to assist in improving internal controls.

The COBIT standards are issued by a not-for-profit organization called the IT Governance Institute (ITGI). In 2003, the ITGI also published *IT Control Objectives for Sarbanes-Oxley,* which specifically addresses the financial reporting aspects of COBIT. Most COBIT information is available for free downloading at www.isaca.org/cobit.htm.

Part IV
SOX for Techies

"I like the numbers on this company. They show a very impressive acquittal to conviction ratio."

In this part . . .

*I*f you're a software geek at heart, this part's for you. The chapters in this part can guide you through the task of choosing the right software solution for any size company. To illustrate the types of issues SOX-specific software can solve, this part looks at a couple of simple, economical products on the market.

Chapter 15

Getting Technical with SOX

*U*nless someone is using them to manipulate financial data, the Sarbanes-Oxley Act (SOX) isn't directed at the intricacies and security features of your company's e-mail system or inventory control systems. However, SOX is directed at ensuring the accuracy of the information that appears on financial statements.

SOX also places new emphasis on where financial numbers actually come from. For example, computerized financial systems store and manipulate financial data and play a role in the accuracy and reliability of that data. Because of this new emphasis, a lot of confusion (and some overreaction) has occurred with respect to what SOX requires from information technology (IT) employees.

There are a lot of reasons to have clear documentation trails and fraud prevention in place, but these issues aren't the target of SOX — other laws and standards are in place for those issues. However, SOX does include some rules that specifically require IT departments to get involved in assuring the accuracy of financial statements and reporting events that may have a financial impact on a company.

Unfortunately, the role of the IT professional with regard to SOX still isn't completely clear. Because of the confusion, many companies are falling back on some prefabricated IT standards that were around long before SOX (one of which is specifically blessed by the Securities and Exchange Commission (SEC). These standards include COSO (the Committee of Sponsoring Organizations of the Treadway Commission) and COBIT (the Control Objectives for Information and related Technology).

Some Specific SOX Sections That Talk to Techies

SOX was never intended to directly address such things as security concerns or privacy policies. Other laws, such as HIPPA, do that. However, a few generally agreed upon SOX provisions are causing companies to look to their IT professionals to take the lead in compliance. These provisions include the following:

- ✔ SOX document retention requirements
- ✔ Mandatory reporting of events, such as computer security breaches
- ✔ Section 404 compliance regarding company computer systems

I explain each of these provisions in the following sections.

Ramping up document retention policies

Today "paperless offices" are everywhere. When an office goes "paperless," key documents and communications in a company may no longer be available in hard copy. They instead have to be accessed by e-mail, electronic files, electronic data, and reports from computer programs. SOX addresses the retention and destruction of financial documents extensively. It is now a crime to shred evidence or even relevant information.

Under SOX, anyone who knowingly alters, destroys, or falsifies information or documents in an attempt to impede any governmental investigation may be fined and imprisoned for up to 20 years. This law includes computer records and reports as well as e-mails, electronic memos, databases, and so on.

You can blame Arthur Andersen for this newest retention policy. During the Enron fiasco, Enron's auditors from Arthur Andersen began destroying e-mails and memos, claiming that they were simply following the company's document retention policy. The auditors' mistake was the inconsistency in which they "enforced" this policy. They also should have immediately suspended the policy when the investigation began. Of course, the Justice Department didn't buy their explanation.

Auditors and accounting firms share an extra burden thanks to Arthur Andersen's actions. After all, because lots of auditing work is now being performed on a combination of laptops and computer systems (in addition to traditional paper and pencil), the auditors themselves are required to maintain more computer records, and all these records must be retained for five years. Identifying, organizing, and maintaining all these records becomes quite a task for accounting firms, and they often turn to the IT profession for help.

Disclosing critical events in real time

SOX Section 409 requires companies to tell their shareholders in a timely manner when an event happens that could impact their financial status. Most times these events are unrelated to IT, but sometimes technical or IT issues can impact profits. When this happens, these events must be disclosed.

Knowing what to disclose (from an IT perspective)

Under SOX Section 409, an event such as a security breach, which can potentially impact the financial status of a company, must be reported in a timely fashion.

Here are some types of IT events that may trigger a disclosure under this section of SOX:

- **Data loss:** This category includes accidental loss of computer systems or vital computer data that can't be recovered and will have a financial impact on the company when it attempts to rebuild or restore the systems or data. Examples of this type of loss include server hard drive failure with no backups or a fire or flood that damages systems that have no offsite backups.

The changing nature of business communication

E-mail, instant messaging, and other forms of electronic communication have changed the nature of business communication. In the past, the only traceable communication was that which was written or recorded, such as letters and memos. Many times these forms of communication would account for only a small percentage of the overall communication between people. Considering the massive amounts of e-mail generated nowadays, as well as the fact that many companies don't have a well-implemented electronic records destruction policy, large amounts of communications may be stored indefinitely, sometimes unknowingly in log files, backup tapes, or on employee computers.

Log files are computer system files that are included in most IT systems. They track electronic events such as incoming and outgoing e-mail, Web sites that were visited, users who signed on, and files that were accessed. These files contain important information and shouldn't be overlooked when deciding on a data retention policy.

All this extra information can be both an asset and a liability for companies involved in an investigation or audit. In the electronic age, every e-mail, instant message, or electronic record has the potential to be tracked down and used in an investigation. Any intentional destruction of these communications while involved in an investigation could get you in trouble. However, in the end, many companies are finding that having more archived, easily accessible information is a plus. Of course, as soon as the hint of an investigation begins, all destruction of e-mails, computer data, and physical records should halt immediately.

- ✔ **New systems:** The purchase of a new system, or changes to an existing system, may financially impact a company, and so those events are required to be disclosed.

- ✔ **Major security breaches:** Any security breach that allows an unauthorized individual access to view or change financial statement information may trigger disclosure obligations. This breach could also take the form of internal fraud. For example, a company may have to disclose if an employee who's unauthorized to access a system gains access and commits fraud by changing records.

- ✔ **Potential liabilities from security breaches:** Security glitches and systems failures (which, for example, may have allowed unauthorized individuals to see customer credit or Social Security data) may have legal or financial impact to the company in the form of repayments, lost revenue, or lawsuits. Therefore, any event in this category must be disclosed.

- ✔ **The firing of key financial reporting personnel:** The loss of a chief information officer (CIO) or other IT official may prove costly to replace or may otherwise impact the financial status of the company, and so disclosures are often necessary.

Examining the case of TJX

As an example of when disclosure is necessary, take a look at the case of TJX companies. On January 17, 2007, TJX Companies, the owner of TJ Maxx, Homegoods, and Marshall's, filed a statement with the SEC to report that it had lost customer financial and credit card data.

According to the press release included with TJX's statement, an unidentified hacker had compromised its computer systems at multiple locations, and had stolen the credit card data that had been stored there. The intrusion may have started as early as 2003. It was confirmed that for at least seven months prior to December 2006, when the intrusion was discovered, a hacker had free reign over TJX's data.

As of the January 17 filing, the company didn't have enough information about the repercussions of the security breach to asses the damage to shareholders. A month later, however, TJX Companies issued a second statement relating to the issue. The statement claimed that the company reported a loss of $5 million in costs to remediate the affects of the intrusion, which didn't include losses from future lawsuits or liabilities relating to the breach.

All told, more than 40 million customers may have had credit card, Social Security, driver's license, and other financial data stolen. Due to the amount of time it took to discover the intrusion and the intruder's methods of hiding, TJX still isn't fully aware of the actual number of people who may have been affected. Currently, TJX Companies is being sued in a class action lawsuit in the U.S. District Court in Boston over the breach. Because TJX has already spent $5 million in remediation efforts, there's no question of the breach's financial impact on the company's bottom line.

However, it's interesting to note that TJX Companies was SOX compliant during the time the breach was discovered, and it was determined that TJX didn't actually break any SOX laws in reference to the breach.

IT and the dreaded SOX Section 404

Just when you thought you were finally finished with SOX Section 404, the monster again rears its ugly head. IT isn't immune to the overreaching effects of Section 404, particularly when it comes to pressures from companies that are marketing costly SOX security programs or from overreaching auditors who are looking for new testing territory.

As of the writing of this book, the debate as to whether Section 404 directly imposes significant legal requirements on the IT profession is still a hot topic. The law itself gives no detailed direction as to the specific internal controls that need to be in place. However, the SEC and Public Company Accounting Oversight Board (PCAOB) have been working for years to get standards in place that speak to this issue.

In May 2005, the SEC issued a report stating that companies need to document and test general IT controls as well as controls within computer-programs and systems. In other words, a company must ensure that information generated by its software and other IT systems can be reasonably relied on.

In reply to various requests to clarify SOX Section 404, the SEC also released a ruling clarifying that the phrase "internal controls over financial reporting" includes those policies and procedures that provide reasonable assurance regarding the reliability of financial records. IT controls and policies should ensure that:

- ✔ Records and data are maintained with reasonable detail and accuracy

- ✔ Transactions are recorded in accordance with Generally Accepted Accounting Principles (GAAP) and are authorized by management

- ✔ There's a reasonable assurance that financial data and systems are safe from unauthorized use that could have an effect on financial statements

Getting a SOX-ified System in Place When . . .

SOX poses some unique challenges for companies. After all, the specifics of what a company needs to do to maintain compliance depends on what sort of IT systems are currently in place, the size of the individual company, and the amount of money available for IT. Of course, one size doesn't fit all. This section explains the specifics from three different points of view.

. . . Your company is starting from scratch

Lots of options are available for companies that don't yet have a centralized IT system or that are looking to overhaul their current IT methods. For instance, many small companies are able to find "off-the-shelf" accounting software that meets their business needs and incorporates SOX concepts. SarbOxPro is a popular off-the-shelf program. (For more information on this program and several others, see Chapter 17.)

The drawback to off-the-shelf software suites is that many times, the particulars of a company may not match the tools available in the software, which means the software is either discarded, left unused, or supplemented with other systems, which complicates matters.

. . . Your company is already halfway there

If your company already has a well-defined IT system in place, you can consider this to be both a challenge and blessing. The challenge will center on the documentation of such systems. In other words, if your computer system has been in place for a number of years and has evolved and been customized over that time, you'll likely run into problems if you haven't updated the documentation for the software.

Many times, legacy software is undocumented, and the original developer or implementer is long gone, leaving no one who knows the particular reason why a piece of software works the way it does. In addition, some legacy software programs may be written in old languages, creating headaches for IT staff members who are no longer familiar with them.

The importance of an established program of documentation is clearly seen in such situations, and SOX compliance as it relates to IT will not only help during an audit, but will also benefit IT professionals who must support such systems.

. . . Your company has a larger budget

Larger companies with more expansive IT budgets may opt to develop custom software in-house, or they may opt for a combination of pre-written and custom software. This flexibility allows the computer and information systems to adapt to the business model of the company instead of the company having to adapt to a software package.

The drawbacks for custom software include the potential for programming errors that may impact financial data. These bugs are usually worked out in mainstream prepackaged software suites. Also, if there aren't clearly planned project guidelines and specifications for the needed software, an IT system can get complicated and confusing quickly.

Evaluating Your Systems after SOX

IT professionals have a role in assuring that records are maintained accurately and in accordance with Generally Accepted Accounting Principles (GAAP). A company's IT systems and their methods of generating records, as well as the company's policies and use of the systems, need to be evaluated. In today's post-SOX environment, IT should be the first "internal control" cop on the beat.

Organizing company data

Contrary to popular belief, spreadsheets are *not* always an acceptable way to organize or store critical data. Why? They're prone to human error, and they can be manipulated easily without a paper trail noting who changed what. In other words, they allow for possible fraud.

On the other hand, centralized database software that can verify data, prevent human error, and track the flow and manipulation of crucial financial data is the key to IT compliance. This type of IT setup helps ensure that there is control over the data and that it's accurate and fraud-resistant.

Having data centralized into a single, encompassing system eases the process of documenting the system and ensuring that reports are accurate. Companies should also create a clear system of policies that directs the use of the IT systems and restricts unauthorized users.

Enterprise resource planning (ERP) is a concept within the IT profession that describes computer systems that integrate all the accounting practices of a company into one single system. ERP involves combining and integrating data systems, such as payroll systems and accounting systems, and reduces the overall complexity and redundancy of having multiple programs. Because the majority of companies use ERP software suites, they're usually well documented, heavily tested, and incorporate SOX and GAAP concepts into their processes.

Getting into the GAAP

Here's an example of the kinds of GAAP-related issues that SOX is in place to prevent: In one company (which shall remain anonymous), the IT department discovered a serious error in one of the company's computer programs. The program had originally been written in the 1970s (on old-fashioned punch cards) and periodically updated. This particular program was used daily to record accounts receivable and billing transactions.

One data variable in the program was only six digits long, which most of the time wasn't a problem, especially in the 1970s, because rarely did the company bill or receive more than a million dollars in one transaction.

However, in some instances where the numbers went into the millions, the front-most digit of the entry would get cut off. So, for example, $1,234,567 would get recorded in the company's system as billed and received at $234,567. The auditors caught the error when the company's books were a few million off.

Preventing Control Problems before They Happen

SOX requires that there be reasonable assurance regarding the prevention or timely detection of security breaches that allow access to company financial data. Theoretically, under SOX, a security hole such as the one that occurred at TJX Companies (see the earlier section "Examining the case of TJX"), should be identified through a company's process of evaluating their IT systems and controls.

Implementing a strong program of security that prevents unauthorized access and fraud is key to ensuring the accuracy of financial reports and can't be overlooked when planning SOX compliance strategies. As an added bonus, security measures undertaken for SOX can help protect against a catastrophic event like the loss of millions of credit card numbers.

Spelling out security

Role-based security is a system of policies and procedures that ensures that only users who need access to specific data are allowed that access. With most systems, this security is accomplished using user sign-ons and passwords as well as program restrictions. Role-based security helps provide assurance that unauthorized access or manipulation of financial records won't occur. It also helps minimize the occurrence of internal fraud.

For example, under role-based security, a human resources employee may have full access to payroll programs, partial access to purchasing/acquisition, and no access to accounts receivable. Similarly, a factory employee who uses the computer system for inventory tracking may not have access to any accounting programs except perhaps only to view his own payroll records.

Role-based computer security systems should be supplemented by policies that create clear guidelines regarding acceptable computer use. Besides being created, these policies must be strictly enforced, and violations should have clear consequences.

Logging it all in

Access logs, which are computer files that record information regarding what financial data or files that users accessed or changed and when, are important to tracking fraud. They can be electronically monitored for unusual activity, and they can be programmed to alert companies early to issues of intrusion or fraud. Well-implemented accounting software should keep accurate, current, and historical access logs and should have a policy or programs to monitor such logs.

Had such a system been in place at TJX Companies (see the earlier section "Examining the case of TJX"), the intrusion and loss of information may have been caught years sooner.

Falling Back on COBIT

COBIT is an IT governance framework that has been around since 1996. Because it's extremely helpful for implementing IT internal controls, COBIT is a particularly useful toolset for IT professionals grappling with SOX issues.

COBIT standards were first published in April 1996 by two professional organizations: the Information Systems Audit and Control Association (ISACA) and the IT Governance Institute (ITGI). Since its publication, COBIT has been primarily used by IT professionals and has been accepted as the international standard for IT governance. Some companies choose to adopt parts of the framework for benefits that go beyond SOX compliance.

The COBIT framework identifies the following IT stages that need to be managed:

✔ **Planning and organization:** IT professionals must first come up with an information infrastructure that's organized to meet the business needs of the company. The IT systems are then analyzed to determine whether they meet the objectives and controls of the company.

- ✔ **Acquisition and implementation:** After IT strategies are identified, a company must develop technology to carry them out, and IT professionals acquire and implement the technology.

- ✔ **Delivery and support:** IT professionals must then train and support the actual users of the system and manage security, delivery/installation, and system maintenance.

- ✔ **Monitoring and evaluation:** The techies in the company must take responsibility for monitoring the systems to make sure that financial internal control objectives are consistently met.

You can access COBIT standards at `www.isaca.org/Template.cfm?Section=COBIT6&Template=/TaggedPage/TaggedPageDisplay.cfm&TPLID=55&ContentID=7981`. At this site, you can also find guidelines, best practices, and tips for implementing all the aspects of the framework described in this section.

Chapter 16

Surveying SOX Software

. . . .

. . . .

*T*horoughly testing your company's internal control under the Sarbanes-Oxley Act's Section 404 is expensive, but the right software tool can soften the blow. Rather than reinvent the wheel, your company can purchase a single software package to prioritize risks, identify key controls for testing, develop standardized forms, and create a system for entering and storing SOX Section 404 documentation. Many off-the-shelf products are available, which means your company may not have to engage expensive consultants to design a customized solution.

Selecting the right SOX software tool can be a pivotal decision for your company. This chapter addresses some SOX software packages on the market and looks at the ways companies can use them to streamline compliance with the dreaded SOX Section 404 (which is discussed in excruciating detail in Chapter 12). This chapter also examines the special COSO standards that were developed for companies to structure the testing of their internal financial control as well as the separately developed COBIT standards developed by information technology professionals.

Some SOX Software Trends

Software vendors are flocking to the SOX software market, offering products for all manner of companies and projects. As of this writing, it's estimated that more than 90 percent of Fortune 500 companies are using at least some SOX software products developed outside their companies. The market for Sarbanes-Oxley software is currently a multibillion-dollar-a-year industry.

This section provides you with some useful background information about the SOX software industry to help you evaluate the viability of the companies from which you may decide to purchase a product. (It is indeed a concern whether or not your software vendor will be around in a year or two when your company is considering a major financial commitment.)

Some of the significant market trends in the SOX software industry include the following:

- **Customized consulting for big firms:** Large accounting and IT consulting firms are being hired to create customized software for many of their clients.

- **Off-the-shelf software for the smaller firms:** Small firms and not-for-profits are optioning for off-the-shelf starter programs, such as SarbOxPro (discussed in Chapter 17), that help them document controls and procedures from scratch.

- **The lack of a dominant market leader:** Currently, no particular software vendor has a dominant share of the SOX market. With more than 60 companies offering products, consolidation of some companies and their client bases is inevitable. What this shifting market means is that some companies may go out of business, leaving their products unsupported. Or you may end up working with a vendor different from the one with whom you originally contracted.

- **No track records:** Because SOX is still relatively new, no company has a track record of multiple releases and a big beta trail. Bugs and flaws are to be expected, and the products will likely be debugged and improved based on user feedback and market data.

- **Costs of software are relatively small:** SOX-specific software products range anywhere from $2,500 to millions depending on whether the company opts for an off-the-shelf solution or a costly customization from a consulting firm. However, one cost characteristic is assured across the board: In every organization, the cost of the software is very small in relation to the costs of labor and training employees and consultants to use it.

- **Add-ons abound:** Some software vendors, such as Hyperion Solutions Corporation, are adding modules and capabilities for SOX compliance to existing financial management programs. Popular add-ons include audit-trail templates and components that document the flow of work within a company to help identify processes that must be monitored for Section 404 compliance.

- **Industry-specific programs find a niche:** Some industries, such as banking, are finding vendors with programs and add-ons designed especially for them. After the first-year crash compliance, many consulting firms are likely to offer specific software for the industries that they most frequently service.

In view of the market trends listed here, your company should carefully negotiate license terms for SOX software. Don't be shy about negotiating for extras like longer warranties and clauses that allow you to terminate the contract under circumstances such as disappointing software performance. Intense competition for market share among SOX software vendors should put your company in a strong negotiating position for favorable contract and service terms when purchasing SOX software products.

At this stage of the game, your company should carefully consider what functions your software must provide, and you should negotiate software contracts with a clear understanding of minimum performance standards.

Identifying the Types of Software on the Market

Many different types of SOX-related software products are on the market. They offer different features and have widely different price structures. When shopping for SOX software, make sure you're comparing apples to apples by keeping the following general categories in mind:

✔ **One-stop SOX for small companies:** Small companies find programs like SarbOxPro and ProCognis, the interfaces of which are illustrated in Figures 16-1 and 16-2, particularly helpful. (SarbOxPro is covered in more detail in Chapter 17.) For a relatively small investment, these programs can help a small company create a centralized database of controls and processes. The programs also track the testing done on key controls as well as several aspects of the company's control environment.

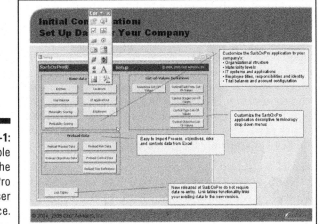

Figure 16-1:
A sample of the SarbOxPro user interface.

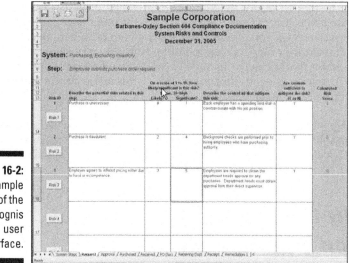

Software programs for small companies are designed to gather SOX-related information to document the company's overall compliance with SOX with a single interface. These programs also generate reports on processes, risks, controls, and compliance for management and process owners to assess their effectiveness. For a relatively small investment ($1,000–$2,500), these comprehensive off-the-shelf programs provide an overall framework of COSO compliance (see the section "The COSO Standards for Software" later in this chapter for more details).

✔ **Monitoring tools:** SOX has created a market for programs that provide enhanced monitoring of company assets or communications. These programs are useful for companies that have SOX-compliant structures in place but need to enhance the monitoring of those controls. An example of this type of program is Spector, which is available at www.spector soft.com.

✔ **Industry-specific programs:** Many software programs are designed to perform specific SOX-related tasks or are designed for specific industries. For instance, some programs monitor receivables and payables. Industries with special overlapping regulatory requirements, such as the mutual fund industry or the healthcare industry, may benefit from off-the-shelf software solutions tailored for these niche markets. For example, Physmark (www.physmark.com) is a SOX software compliance product designed especially for the healthcare industry.

✔ **Customized IT solutions:** Large accounting firms, such as KPMG, offer special consulting services to help design and write software for their clients. Generally, companies having gross revenues that exceed $75 million (known as *accelerated filers*) opt for customized solutions.

✔ **Task-specific software:** Some software is designed to perform specific tasks. For example, financial statement certification is designed to provide a process for management to sign off on the accuracy of the financial statements for Section 302. (For more on management certifications and Section 302, turn to Chapter 10.)

Although companies that use SOX software may switch products in subsequent years (or even in the current one), swapping software is likely to raise regulatory issues as well as logistic ones.

Shopping for SOX Software

Although most software vendors have Web sites and online brochures, SOX software products can be very difficult to compare. Product demonstrations generally take several hours, and generally it's difficult to get more than an overview of such a complex product during a demo.

The following is list of questions that management, IT committees, and process owners should ask vendors when evaluating SOX software products for purchase:

✔ **How versatile is the software?** Does it fulfill all the functions that our company needs for SOX compliance? Does it contain adequate functionality for identifying processes and controls and for document management?

✔ **What technology does the software require to run?** Exploring technology requirements ahead of time is particularly important for small companies that may run into additional unanticipated outlays as a result of being unprepared for the requirements of new software.

✔ **Does the product interface well with the company's existing systems?** What kind of customization is necessary for it to do so?

✔ **How is historical company information imported into the system?** Does this information require special customization or formatting?

✔ **What other companies have used the product?** What have been their experiences?

✔ **How large is the vendor's current customer base?** Does the vendor currently service a large customer base over which it can spread the costs of support and additional research?

✔ **What ongoing costs does the software carry?** What's the initial investment, and what are the maintenance fees? What upgrades are expected? Does the vendor have a strategy for upgrading and developing the program?

REMEMBER

✔ **What are the software's security and validation procedures?** How is the system protected from tampering and unauthorized access?

Software that's maintained by an application service provider and hosted on the company's network should have encrypted data transmission over the Internet and regular backups.

✔ **What type of training is offered by the vendor?** Do the documenters, auditors, and other personnel perceive the interface as easy to learn?

✔ **What types of reports can be generated with the product?** What type of data is captured and included in the reports? Can sample reports be viewed?

✔ **Does the vendor have a sample database for demonstration purposes?** Can company representatives experiment by entering data into a demonstration version of the program?

✔ **Does the program facilitate document management and workflow?** How are relevant documents (such as flowcharts and prior reports) imported, viewed, and referenced in the program so that those documents can be referenced for documenting processes and controls?

✔ **Does the vendor have adequate staff and funding to support the product?** Is the vendor financially stable and well managed?

✔ **Does the program offer standardized libraries of processes and controls or other embedded content that can save the company time in the initial years of compliance?**

✔ **Can the software be conveniently accessed from all company locations?** Can it be used by everyone responsible for testing and documenting, or does it require specialized skills?

✔ **Does the software offer any benefits beyond SOX compliance?** Does it have features that can help the company save money?

SOX Meets Cousin IT

Financial statements filed with the SEC are compiled from data gathered from dozens, if not hundreds, of financial pulse points within a company. At most companies, the accuracy and timeliness of financial reporting depend on the *information technology,* or IT, environment. SOX Section 404 doesn't explicitly spell out requirements for corporate IT systems or procedures for gathering information within a company to document internal control. So, if a company wanted to, it could theoretically document and test all its processes using pen and paper. However, this method wouldn't be very efficient and probably wouldn't inspire the confidence of the CEO or CFO who would be forced to flip through thousands of pages each quarter. For these reasons, IT plays a critical role in the overall compliance process.

IT and SOX compliance will always go hand in hand. In fact, many experts have indicated that the heads of IT departments (usually called *chief information officers,* or CIOs) should be required to certify the financials for companies along with CEOs and CFOs.

SOX requires senior management to include within the company's annual 10-K report (which must be filed with the SEC) a separate *internal control report* to evaluate processes for collecting, securing, retaining, and reporting financial information. Companies also have to provide quarterly evaluations of changes that materially impact internal control over financial reporting or that could do so in the future.

Collecting scattered company data

Most companies already have considerable technology in place for SOX compliance. However, the information gathered is likely to be in lots of places, spread across databases maintained by many departments and locations. Each department is likely to have its own standards and policies for gathering the type of information it needs to conduct its operations and report its results to management.

Many companies rely on SOX software to collect Section 404 data that's scattered throughout the company. Because everyone uses a single data entry system, the software can standardize Section 404 documentation throughout the company. A software system endorsed by management and used by the company as a whole links the people gathering the documentation in different departments, such as IT, accounting, and operations. The software also connects personnel in different geographical locations and can coordinate the compliance efforts of every subsidiary and division of a single company.

Evaluating your company's existing IT systems

Not every company needs to overhaul its existing IT systems to comply with SOX. Some companies that have good internal controls and high levels of standardization for testing and documentation may get by with relatively minimal software upgrades and changes. Either way, the following sections explain how to evaluate your company's IT systems.

Taking care of SOX-specific tasks

A public company's IT systems must be able to perform certain SOX-related tasks to ensure its ability to comply with Section 404. For instance, your company's IT systems must have capabilities to:

✓ **Report transactions and collect data:** Most companies currently collect data on many financial transactions, including receivables, payables, and collections. Thus, IT systems may already be in place to document processes and controls as required by SOX.

✓ **Investigate whistle-blower complaints:** If an employee files a complaint under the SOX whistle-blower provision (covered in Chapter 18), the company must be able to locate the necessary data to investigate the basis of the complaint. So a company must have IT systems that allow access to records that substantiate a culture of corporate compliance.

✓ **Identify processes and control environments:** Does the company currently document its processes? Does each department document them using relatively uniform tools and output? If not, the company may benefit from a software product that assists in creating a database of processes and documenting workflow. The flowchart in Figure 16-3 illustrates how one such software product from ProCognis (available at www.pro cognis.com) is structured to document the processes and control environments of a company.

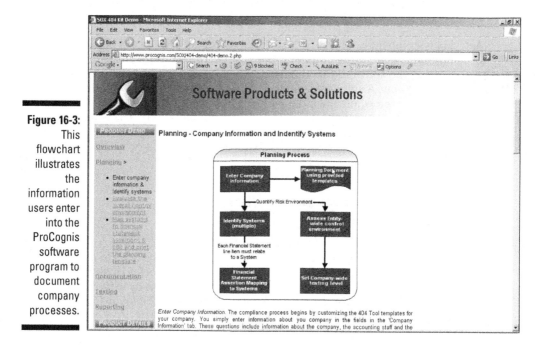

Figure 16-3: This flowchart illustrates the information users enter into the ProCognis software program to document company processes.

✔ **Document existing controls:** If the company doesn't maintain a centralized database documenting its controls on various processes, a product that offers an existing library of controls and tools for creating this type of database may be a critical component of the company's Section 404 compliance.

✔ **Identify key controls:** When a company takes an inventory of its internal controls, it needs to be able to determine which controls are the most significant in terms of the risks that they're intended to prevent. Software tools can identify the areas in which material risks are likely to occur as well as the key controls for preventing those risks. For example, a software program may identify key controls based on factors such as the dollar amounts involved or the volume of transactions.

✔ **Create reliable reports:** SOX requires management to know what's happening within the entire company to the extent necessary to certify its internal controls. A company's existing IT systems should have the ability to summarize information in readable report formats that can be reviewed by the *process owners* (the people responsible for ensuring the accurate completion of the process within the company) and by management to fulfill both the requirements of Section 404 and the objectives of Section 302.

✔ **Perform accurate record retention:** Records must be retained and tracked as part of the company's overall internal control and workflow management. Document management software products and modules designed specifically for this purpose are on the market.

✔ **Track costs:** SOX compliance is costly, but companies can save money by planning individual SOX projects and tracking the costs associated with them. If the company currently doesn't have the IT infrastructure to do these tasks, it should investigate software tools on the market for doing so.

✔ **Secure information:** An important aspect of financial control within a company is the ability to secure financial information so that only appropriate persons have access to it and so that it can't be improperly altered. Most IT systems have security components in place that can be adapted for an overall SOX-compliant system.

✔ **Report events:** Many software products on the market offer monitoring capabilities to enhance a company's existing internal controls. These products monitor events, such as unauthorized transactions or distribution of information, and, in some cases, report such events to management in real time.

Deciding how to proceed

Although many necessary technology components may be present to some extent in a company's existing IT framework, every company must decide whether to:

- ✔ Refocus existing IT systems for SOX compliance

- ✔ Hire independent consultants to design customized systems

- ✔ Purchase products and modules already designed for SOX compliance and train staff on using them

The COSO Standards for Software

Because SOX is silent as to the types of documentation that satisfy Section 404, the SEC provides some guidance to companies by directing them to a set of standards developed by the Committee of Sponsoring Organizations of the Treadway Commission (COSO). Most SOX software is designed to comply with the COSO standards.

The COSO standards provide welcome guidance to companies that are deciding how to organize their documentation. Many software tools have interfaces and formats designed to reflect compliance with COSO, using key terminology from the COSO standards to identify the software functions.

The SEC directs companies to look for established, well-recognized standards to use in documenting internal controls and processes. It identifies the COSO Internal Control Framework as its preferred set of standards (and has yet to identify any other set of standards).

The COSO framework provides five components that every software program should address:

- ✔ **Control environment:** COSO requires every company to establish the foundation for an internal control system by demonstrating that discipline and structure exist within the organization and that they set the tone for compliance. Having good software systems or well-designed IT components in place can help document the existence of a strong control environment and provide visibility of compliance processes.

- ✔ **Risk assessment:** Software applications can help management identify risk factors by assisting in the compilation of data from surveys, by comparing practices of the company to a statistical standard, and by alerting management to critical events and discrepancies (called *exceptions*).

✓ **Control activities:** COSO requires that companies evaluate the specific policies and procedures that they have in place to ensure that management's directives are carried out. Companies have to document key processes and identify the controls used to ensure the accuracy of those processes. Software programs can help streamline this COSO component by providing libraries of procedures and controls and user-friendly interfaces that allow employees documenting the controls to store the information in a standardized format that can be retrieved by other employees in the organization.

SarbOxPro (available at `www.sarboxpro.com`) is a program that offers both standard libraries and an interface for adding specific company controls to the standard library. Figure 16-4 shows how controls input into the SarbOxPro program are saved to a standard library. (For more information about SarbOxPro, check out Chapter 17.)

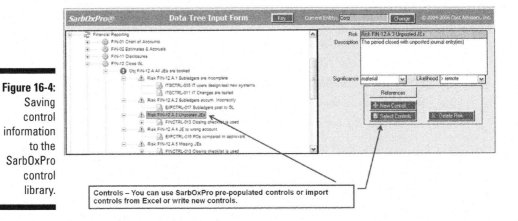

Figure 16-4:
Saving
control
information
to the
SarbOxPro
control
library.

Conforming to the COSO standards

COSO was originally formed in 1985 as an independent private-sector initiative to study factors that can lead to fraudulent financial reporting; it developed recommendations for public companies and independent auditors.

The commission was jointly sponsored by five major professional associations: the American Accounting Association, the American Institute of Certified Public Accountants, Financial Executives International, The Institute of Internal Auditors, and the National Association of Accountants (now the Institute of Management Accountants). The commission also had representatives from industry, public accounting, investment firms, and the New York Stock Exchange.

✔ **Information and communication:** An important component of the COSO framework is the premise that internal controls can't be properly implemented unless the company has procedures for communicating the controls to the people who are supposed to carry them out on every level. Usually these procedures are carried out with software and information technology.

✔ **Monitoring:** The quality of the internal controls must be assessed to determine how effectively they detect irregularities. Monitoring also assesses how well people within the organization implement the control. Software programs and IT systems within the company should make data available to assess both of these aspects of the control's effectiveness. Some programs provide continuous monitoring, and others track data that can be analyzed by process owners and management at regular intervals.

Most companies in the United States use the previous COSO criteria when designing their IT systems. For example, Figure 16-5 shows the model used by the ProCognis software tool, which is a COSO-based design. (You can find more information on this product at www.procognis.com.)

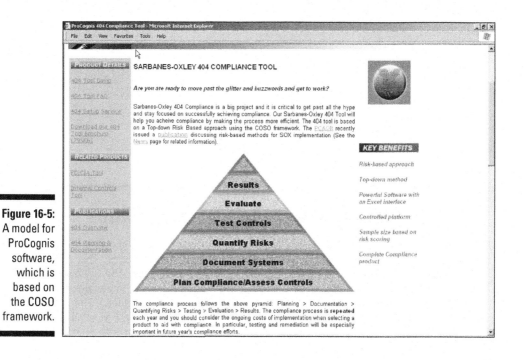

Figure 16-5: A model for ProCognis software, which is based on the COSO framework.

Will SOX software pay for itself?

SOX requires detailed documentation and analysis of business processes related to financial reporting and disclosures. The right software tools can yield a wealth of data for implanting process improvements. For example, organizations may find duplicate expenditures, redundant processes, and opportunities to standardize processes among divisions and subsidiaries that may offset the cost of complying with SOX.

It's worth noting that in a poll by a research organization called the Meta Group, 39 percent of firms surveyed said that SOX will eventually make them more competitive.

Complying with COBIT

A separate but equally important set of standards with respect to SOX software is the Control Objectives for Information and Related Technology, or COBIT, developed by the IT Governance Institute (ITGI). The purpose of the ITGI (www.isaca.org) is to set standards for measuring performance and risk in information technology professions.

COBIT is a generally applicable and accepted standard for good information technology security and control practices. These standards are intended to provide "a reference framework for management, users, and IS audit, control and security practitioners."

The COBIT standards can be downloaded for free at www.isaca.org/ Template.cfm?Section=COBIT6&Template=/TaggedPage/TaggedPage Display.cfm&TPLID=55&ContentID=7981. In 2003, the ITGI published a document called, "IT Control Objectives for Sarbanes-Oxley," which adapts the COBIT standards specifically for SOX. Of COBIT's usual 34 IT processes and 318 detailed control objectives for IT professionals, the SOX adaptation identifies 27 IT processes and 136 detailed control objectives as critical to SOX compliance.

Chapter 17

Working with Some Actual SOX Software

Sarbanes-Oxley (SOX) software can be costly, but if yours is a small business, you have plenty of options that won't strain your petite IT budget. In fact, the three off-the-shelf software solutions programs that I discuss in this chapter are available for only a few thousand dollars. Each of these surprisingly versatile programs offers a comprehensive framework for SOX Section 404 compliance and is designed to minimize training time.

In this chapter, I focus on some simple examples of SOX-compliant software used primarily in smaller companies. As a good representative of the off-the-shelf software solutions available, I've chosen to look at several sample products, including SarbOxPro.

If your company has already worked with costly consultants and implemented an IT solution, this chapter can still be useful to you as an aerial view of how software and information technology go hand in hand with SOX compliance.

Doing Your Research before a Software Installation

It's never a good idea to throw money at a solution before you analyze the problem. SOX software is a great tool for streamlining documentation — but only if you lay the groundwork for implementing it. This section gives you a sense of how to evaluate the flow of financial information in your company prior to implementing a software solution, and it also introduces you to the important accounting concept of the trial balance.

Cost Advisors, Inc., the makers of SarbOxPro, has put together a terrific project guide explaining the relationship of SOX and software. You can request a free copy of this guide from the SarbOxPro Web site located at www.sarbox pro.com/freetrial.aspx.

Tracking the flow of information in your company

The flow of financial information within every company is unique; it's based on both the structure of the company and its subsidiaries and on the cycles of the company's business. According to Bill Douglas, CEO of Cost Advisors, Inc., "It is important to start with a firm understanding of the big picture (framework) around Sarbanes-Oxley Section 404. . . . There can be many entities within a single consolidated company and many [business] cycles within each entity." The flowchart shown in Figure 17-1 illustrates some of the key terms you'll come across in a Sarbanes-Oxley project. These terms describe the flow of information within a company.

SOX is primarily concerned with risks, controls, and tests — the bottom three boxes to the bottom right of the diagram in Figure 17-1 — but the rest of the information illustrated must be known about the company before risks, controls, and tests can be gathered.

Some of the terms in Figure 17-1 stem from the SOX statute, Securities Exchange Commission (SEC) rules, and COSO and COBIT standards (discussed in Chapter 14). Others are rooted in the vernacular that IT professionals have used for years in talking about the flow of information to be documented within a company. Moving from left to right on the diagram, each box represents increasingly specific information about a company. In order to comply with SOX, you must proceed down the hierarchy in this logical manner, generating increasingly specific information about your company.

A documenter must identify a company and all its subsidiaries (entities) and locations before proceeding to collect information about the cycles (sequences of transactions) that occur within the company. After the documenter knows about the business cycles (for example, a sales cycle moving from order to final payment), he can begin to document the processes within that cycle. In turn, after he knows the processes, he can move on to the controls and tests for those processes using a reliable software product. Figure 17-2 illustrates a sample business cycle for a customer sale.

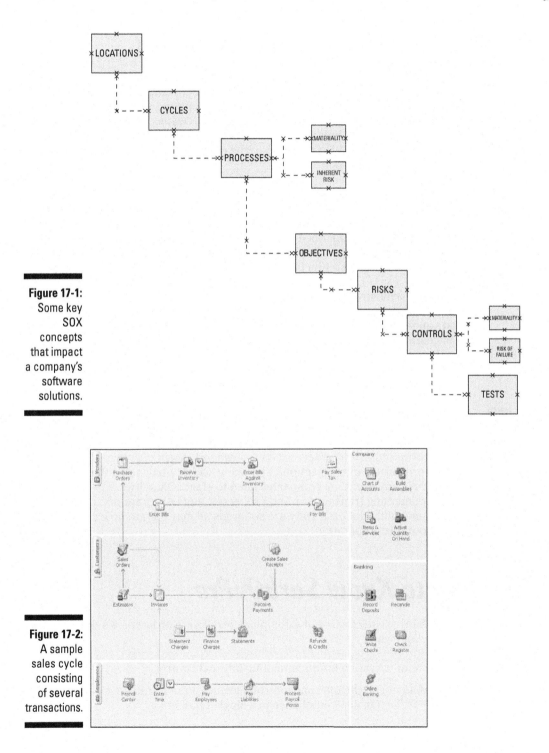

Figure 17-1:
Some key
SOX
concepts
that impact
a company's
software
solutions.

Figure 17-2:
A sample
sales cycle
consisting
of several
transactions.

Following the trial balance trail

Traditionally, a *trial balance* is a document that adds up all the debits and credits for transactions within a company so that mistakes can be traced if debits don't equal credits. Most of today's accounting software adds debits and credits correctly, so companies create *trial balance reports* as summaries of all the company's individual transactions. Because the trial balance report tracks transactions, it's a valuable cache of information for SOX Section 404 purposes.

The trial balance identifies all the income and asset accounts maintained by the company from the date that the beginning balances were calculated to the date the trial balance was "closed." The trial balance effectively combines the information summarized on both the balance sheet and the income statement. If all transactions and account adjustments have been recorded properly, the debits and credits balance.

Figure 17-3 illustrates a simple trial balance. By looking at all the accounts in the trial balance, you can identify the most significant ones on a strictly dollars-and-cents basis. The more significant the account, the greater the risk of inaccuracy on the financial statement if the account is misstated. Several SOX software programs, including SarbOxPro, depend on analysis of a trial balance (or a similar report) as the starting point for statistically identifying a company's most significant risks and key controls.

A trial balance is just one type of report used by a company to document its transactions. In fact, not all companies will work with a trial balance to identify transactions and processes. Another type of report commonly used to glean transaction and process data is a *general ledger,* which companies use to record entries of transactions that occur without balancing the debits and credits. In any event, all companies need to start SOX software preparations by documenting transactions and processes, and corporate policies, structures, and individualized software solutions all may dictate how companies go about this preparation.

Getting to Know SarbOxPro

SarbOxPro is an example of a compliance software program. It's designed to do the following:

- ✔ Create a system for documenting internal control
- ✔ Maintain all the internal control information required for a company's SOX Section 404 compliance in a single repository

Figure 17-3:
A very
simple trial
balance
for a small
company.

4:11 PM

12/15/07

Accrual Basis

Rock Castle Construction
Trial Balance
As of November 30, 2007

	Nov 30, 07	
	Debit	Credit
Checking		101,166.95
Savings	49,368.42	
Accounts Receivable	38,446.76	
Tools & Equipment	5,000.00	
Inventory Asset	7,930.29	
Retainage	4,176.80	
Undeposited Funds	52,704.40	
Land	90,000.00	
Buildings	325,000.00	
Trucks	78,352.91	
Trucks:Depreciation	0.00	
Computers	28,501.00	
Furniture	7,325.00	
Accumulated Depreciation		121,887.78
Pre-paid Insurance	1,716.85	
Accounts Payable		70,996.41
QuickBooks Credit Card		70.00
CalOil Card		5,111.80
Payroll Liabilities		7,100.58
Sales Tax Payable		5,596.19
Bank of Anycity Loan		19,932.65
Equipment Loan		3,911.32
Note Payable		18,440.83
Truck Loan		50,662.77
Opening Bal Equity		402,081.82
Owner's Equity:Owner's Contribution		25,000.00
Owner's Equity:Owner's Draw	6,000.00	
Retained Earnings	131,898.50	
Construction:Labor		22,703.25
Construction:Materials		38,341.50
Construction:Miscellaneous		2,328.52
Construction:Subcontractors		35,085.00
Cost of Goods Sold	3,871.59	
Automobile:Insurance	712.56	
Automobile:Fuel	160.08	
Bank Service Charges	37.50	
Freight & Delivery	35.00	
Insurance	297.66	
Insurance:Disability Insurance	150.00	
Insurance:Liability Insurance	1,050.00	
Insurance:Work Comp	825.00	
Interest Expense	619.19	
Interest Expense:Loan Interest	288.05	
Job Expenses:Equipment Rental	300.00	
Job Expenses:Job Materials	35,924.99	
Job Expenses:Permits and Licenses	525.00	
Job Expenses:Subcontractors	38,829.00	
Payroll Expenses	19,764.78	
Rent	0.00	
Repairs:Computer Repairs	45.00	
Repairs:Equipment Repairs	0.00	
Tools and Machinery	350.00	
Utilities:Gas and Electric	154.40	
Utilities:Telephone	100.71	
Utilities:Water	61.85	
Interest Income		93.42
Other Income		12.50
TOTAL	**930,523.29**	**930,523.29**

SarbOxPro is a relatively simple software program that uses the information in your company's trial balance to help identify both the greatest risks to your company and the key controls in place to mitigate the most significant risks. As of this writing, SarbOxPro costs less than $3,000. Users also can purchase an optional maintenance plan for $995 a year. You can get more information at www.sarboxpro.com.

Seeing as how SOX has management at many companies wondering where to start, a product like SarbOxPro can really help a company get its arms around an elephant like SOX. If your company meets any of the following characteristics, you may consider using SarbOxPro:

✔ Small to medium-size public companies

✔ Nonpublic companies (including not-for-profit companies) that opt to become SOX compliant

✔ Companies with limited budgets

✔ Companies that use Microsoft Office products

The SarbOxPro checklist

Cost Advisors, Inc., the makers of SarbOxPro software, has created a checklist of items to consider before going ahead with software implementation. This checklist, shown in Figure 17-4, reflects the steps that every company should complete for its SOX software evaluation. These steps both save the company money and help it comply with the law.

✓ Examine the Costs

✓ Sell the Project Internally

✓ Strategize Documentation Labor

✓ Understand the Documentation Hierarchy

✓ Define the Scope

✓ Establish Process Teams

✓ Structure the Documentation Format and Assessment Techniques

✓ Conduct Process Team Meetings

✓ Evaluate Controls at Third-Party Vendors

✓ Implement Quality Control

✓ Perform Testing

✓ Document the Control Environment

✓ Make Improvements in the Process

✓ Choose a Software Tool

Figure 17-4:
A software implementation checklist from the makers of SarbOxPro software.

The SarbOxPro data tree

For anyone familiar with Windows Explorer and its data tree structure of folders and documents, SarbOxPro is an intuitive program. The SarbOxPro data tree looks a lot like Windows Explorer's, as you can see in Figure 17-5; in SarbOxPro, you can directly create, modify, or remove elements in the data tree, such as cycles, processes, objectives, risks, or controls.

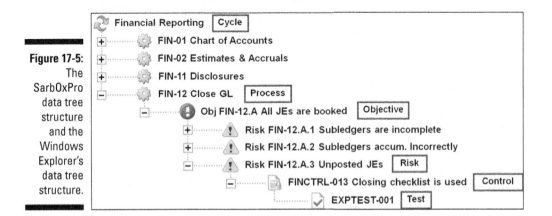

Figure 17-5: The SarbOxPro data tree structure and the Windows Explorer's data tree structure.

SarbOxPro's data tree breaks down like so:

- A **cycle** can have multiple **processes** under it.
- A **process** can have one or more **objectives** listed under it.
- An **objective** can have one or more **risks under it.**
- A **risk** can have one or more **controls** under it.
- A **control** usually has only one **test** under it.

SarbOxPro stages

The process of documenting Section 404 compliance involves three main task categories, which are represented on the main SarbOxPro screen shown in Figure 17-6. (From this main screen, documenters can access other areas of the program.) These three main task categories are:

- **Initial Configuration:** In this area of the program, documenters add information about the company and its accounts. Users input information about the entities and locations being reported on, they import the company's trial balance and employee list, and they identify the IT applications, the inherent process risk, and the level of materiality (importance) used for their project. Users can also customize the assertions, control stages, control types, control objectives, and test frequencies to be used within the program.

✓ **Data Input:** In this area, documenters identify cycle, process, objective, risk, control, and test data gathered during the course of the Section 404 compliance process.

✓ **Reports:** This section of the program allows management and other users to view summaries of data gathered as a result of SOX Section 404 compliance testing. These users can also interpret the data to make decisions about certifications and changes in the company's controls.

Each of these task categories is discussed in more detail in the following sections.

Figure 17-6:
This SarbOxPro screen allows you to access the three main areas of the Section 404 documentation program.

Main Menu
Sarb\OxPro®
INTERNAL CONTROLS MANAGEMENT TOOL
Version 3.05 · About
Data backup None · Backup
Initial Configuration · Data Input · Reports
Cost Advisors downloadable software for financial risk management · Help · Quit

Setting up the initial configuration

The makers of SarbOxPro recognize that it's impossible for an organization to test every single process and control. The designers also know that in order for companies to figure out which processes to test, they need some standards for deciding the importance (materiality) of the processes.

 REMEMBER

At a minimum, software should initially be configured to document the following:

✓ The most significant entities (parents, subsidiaries, branches, and so on) where the company's business is transacted

✓ The processes within each entity that cause financial transactions to be recorded in the trial balance

✓ The risks in each process

✔ The controls that prevent the risks from happening

✔ The tests to ensure that the controls are in place

Figure 17-7 shows the main screen of the SarbOxPro software program. It's designed to help company employees (rather than costly outside consultants) compile the following data:

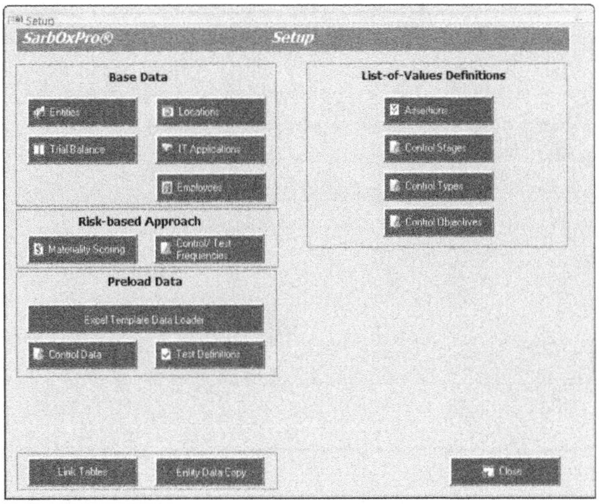

Figure 17-7: An intuitive interface for aggregating information about the company.

✔ **Entities and locations:** SarbOxPro allows users to identify different company entities and locations using the screens like the one shown in Figure 17-8.

SarbOxPro lets you create the equivalent of a standardized template for controls that are constant from location to location. This action simplifies the process of documenting controls at each location.

✔ **Trial balance:** Users can import an entire trial balance or trial balance groupings into SarbOxPro from Microsoft Excel.

✔ **IT applications:** SarbOxPro helps users document all the different IT applications used in their organization that relate to their processes. The program makes maintaining a centralized listing easy.

✔ **Risk-based approach and materiality scoring:** SarbOxPro allows management and process owners to specify percentages to use to determine the inherent process risk and the risk of control failure and decide whether an account or test result is considered "insignificant," "material," or "critical" (with a few levels in between those criteria) as shown in Figure 17-9.

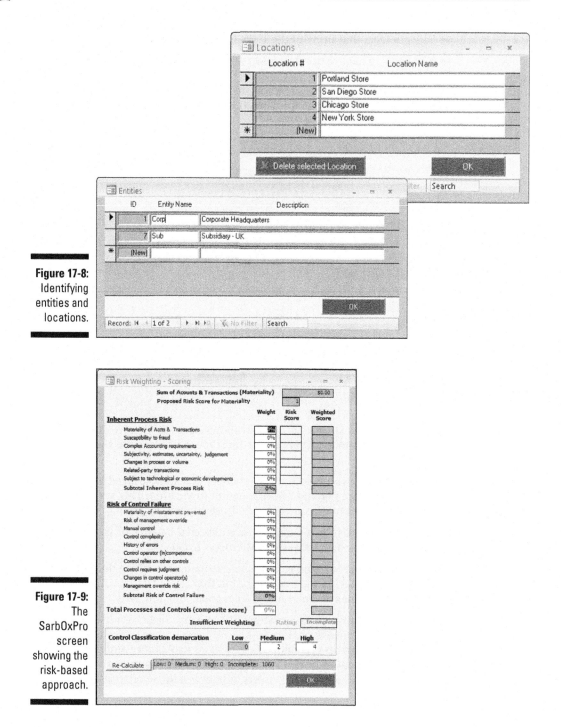

Figure 17-8:
Identifying
entities and
locations.

Figure 17-9:
The
SarbOxPro
screen
showing the
risk-based
approach.

✔ **Employees:** In case questions arise later, it's important to know which employees are involved in carrying out process testing. SarbOxPro helps with this information gathering by maintaining a database of employee information.

✔ **Processes:** SarbOxPro runs on Microsoft Access and is designed to ensure that processes are named using consistent conventions so that they aren't mistakenly listed and tested more than once or overlooked by all the documenters who are spread across all the locations in a typical SOX Section 404 project.

✔ **Controls:** As with processes, SarbOxPro ensures that controls are named using consistent conventions to prevent them from being tested repeatedly or overlooked. The program also has a rich library of identified control types that can be selected and correlated to the company's processes, as shown in Figure 17-10.

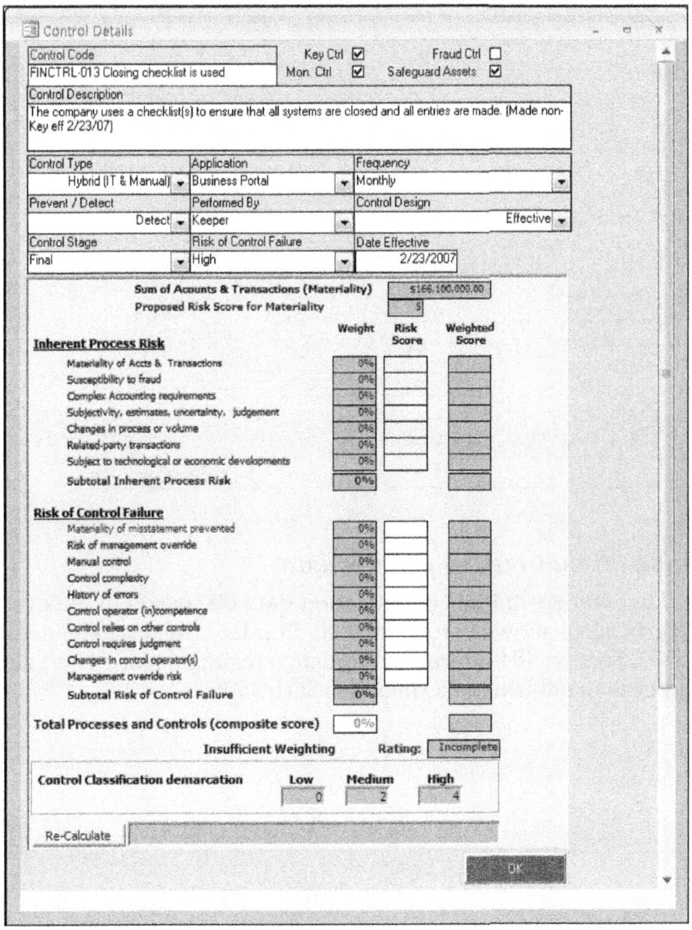

Figure 17-10:
The SarbOxPro control library.

✔ **Assertions:** *Assertions* are representations on the financial statements that must be tested to determine whether they're true. SarbOxPro allows users to map assertions to the trial balance accounts in the initial configuration.

✔ **Control stages:** Control testing is an ongoing process that's completed in stages. SarbOxPro continuously documents the status of the testing. It also visually alerts users in the data tree when a control needs to be tested and when the last conducted test failed.

✔ **Frequency of controls:** SarbOxPro allows you to document how often your company tests its controls, as shown in Figure 17-11.

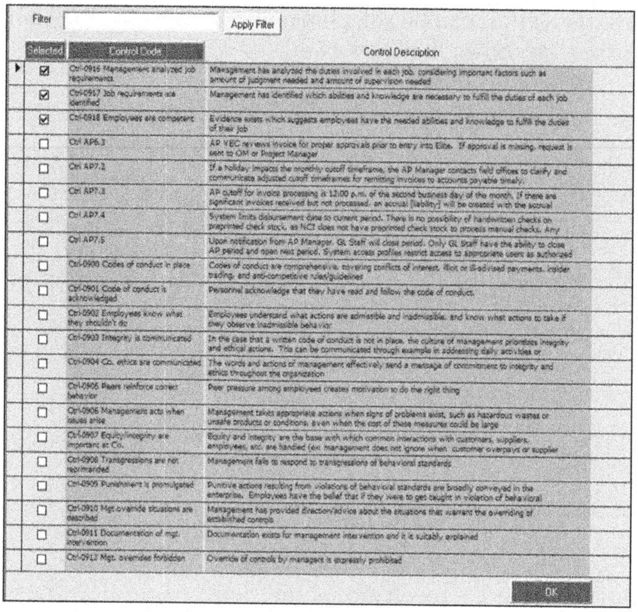

Figure 17-11: Tracking the frequency of control tests.

Entering all that testing process data

After you enter the initial configuration data discussed in the preceding section, SarbOxPro allows you to enter and update the data you gather from your SOX Section 404 internal compliance testing. Figure 17-12 illustrates the process of entering test data into SarbOxPro.

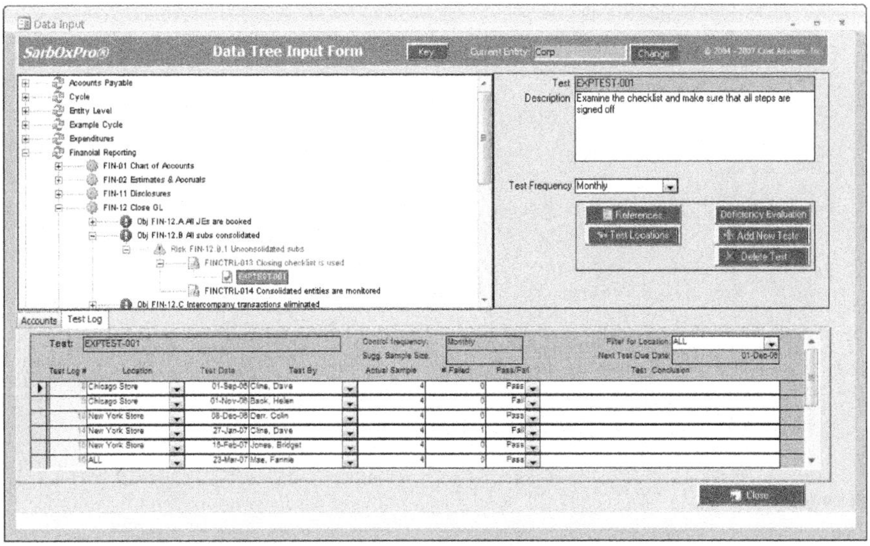

Figure 17-12: Entering the Section 404 test data with SarbOxPro.

Creating reports

The best feature of a program like SarbOxPro is that it allows you to get reports about test results at any time during the SOX Section 404 audit using a variety of filtering criteria, as shown in Figure 17-13. You can export data to Excel to create your own reports or use the preformatted reports offered by the SarbOxPro program.

TIP

With purchase of the maintenance plan, SarbOxPro also offers users a robust pivot table tool that reads the live data from SarbOxPro and allows users to drill down into their data even further using Excel, as shown in Figure 17-14.

REMEMBER

Reports are a critical management tool because they summarize the data on which management relies to personally certify the company's financial statements under Sections 302 and 906 (discussed in Chapter 10).

Opting for Other Types of Software Solutions

Small companies looking for something even simpler than the popular SarbOxPro program may opt for a general information management system used to gather information other than that which is required by SOX. Web-based solutions are also available. This section explains these types of products and examines a couple representative examples.

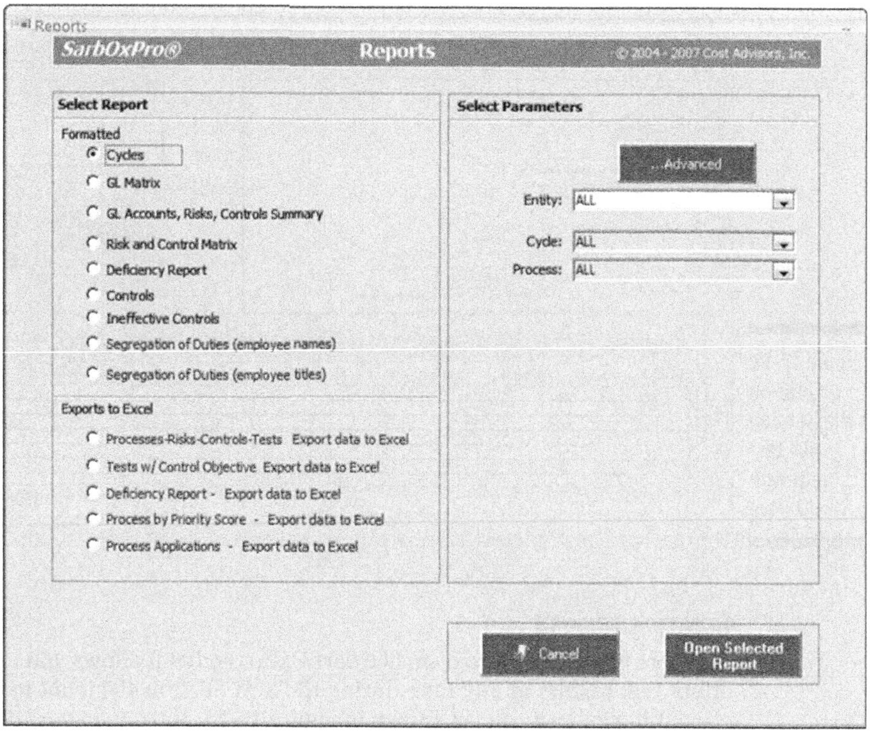

Figure 17-13:
Filtering
Section 404
test data to
create
reports.

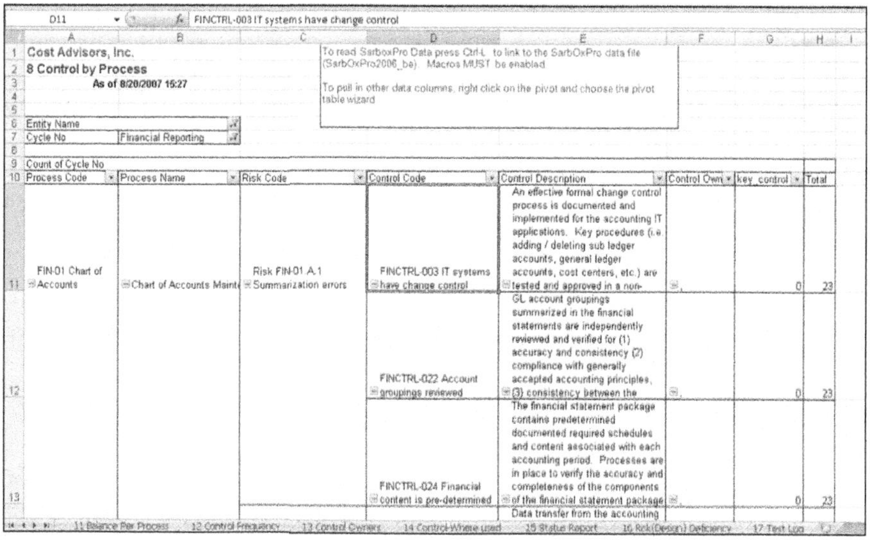

Figure 17-14:
Using Excel
to examine
data.

Web-based SOX products can be a particularly easy-to-implement solution for small companies. An example of such a product is Complyant (www.comply ant.com). Complyant provides content databases and Web-based templates (such as the one shown in Figure 17-15) for entering information. Behind the templates is a relational database that allows the company to create reports on information entered.

Complyant runs on the user's browser software and on a .net framework and SQL server database. All users within must have IDs and passwords in order to access the company's Complyant system.

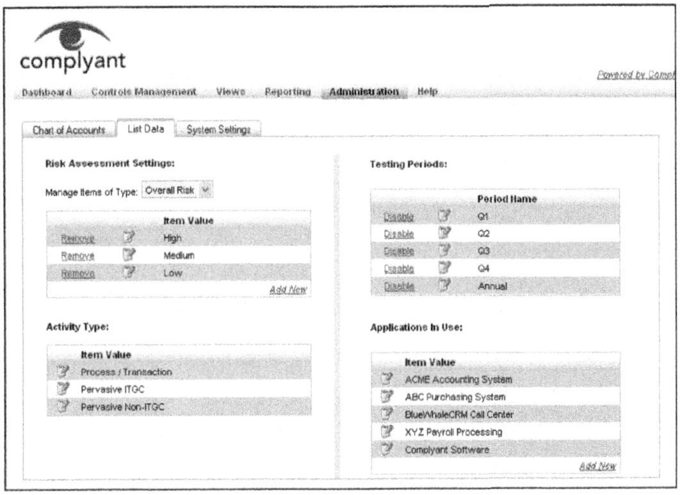

Figure 17-15:
A sample
Complyant
template
for SOX
Section 404
documen-
tation.

Web-based SOX solutions like Complyant offer a number of advantages to users:

- ✔ **Compatibility with existing desktop applications:** Complyant is designed so that everyone in the company can access the tool from their desktops.

- ✔ **Less paperwork:** With a Web-based tool, employees have fewer documents and databases to manage internally.

- ✔ **Ease of updating:** These types of systems require no downloads or upgrades; updating is all done by the company offering the Web-based tool.

Part V
To SOX-finity and Beyond

The 5th Wave   By Rich Tennant

"Cooked books? Let me just say you could
serve this profit and loss statement with
a fruity Zinfandel and not be out of place."

In this part . . .

This section looks at the future of SOX — from who's getting sued under SOX and how you can keep your company (and yourself) clear of the courtroom to how its effects extend beyond large, publicly traded companies. After examining the legal side of executive perks and whistle-blowers, this part looks at governance trends for not-for-profit and privately held companies. It also discusses the compliance requirements for outsourced services.

Chapter 18

Lawsuits under SOX

* *

In This Chapter

▶ Looking at the first major trial after SOX

▶ Examining the Enron litigation

▶ Understanding how the Arthur Andersen precedent threatens big accounting firms

▶ Explaining why private individuals can't sue under SOX

▶ Understanding whistle-blower lawsuits

* *

Some companies are motivated to comply with the Sarbanes-Oxley Act (SOX) out of a sense of social responsibility and a belief that it will increase company profits. However, at least initially, many companies comply mostly to avoid being sanctioned, sued, or even criminally prosecuted. In the first several years following its enactment, it appears that SOX hasn't been the boon for securities litigators that it has been for auditors. However, the act is having an impact on the litigation process. According to the National Economic Research Association (NERA), since the passage of SOX, at least nine settlements of major securities lawsuits have incorporated SOX reforms, including cases involving HCA Inc. and Sprint.

This chapter examines some of the criminal and civil trials played out in the media after SOX. I update you on the aftermath of the Arthur Andersen criminal case, and then I explain how recent case law limits the rights of private individuals to bring their own civil suits under SOX. Finally, I look at how SOX's whistle-blower provisions are impacting the nation's workplaces. As of this writing, the big winners in the courtroom and in the media are one high-profile CEO, the four big accounting firms, and a few assorted whistle-blowers.

The Smoking Gun: Knowledge

The most unnerving potential work scenario for any chief executive or financial officers (CEOs and CFOs) of a corporation is the prospect of being sued as an individual. After SOX, corporate America has seen criminal trials against former powerful top management figures as a result of the SOX requirements stating that management must personally certify the accuracy of the company's financial statements. SOX Sections 302 and 906, which contain these requirements, are discussed in detail in Chapter 10.

Enron, WorldCom, and Tyco management have received decades-long prison sentences and massive fines as they attempt to defend their roles in massive corporate collapses. Only one, CEO Richard Scrushy of HealthSouth Corporation, discussed later in this chapter, has been acquitted so far.

SOX Sections 302 and 906 both attempt to create a legal link between CEOs and CFOs and the financial statements put out by their companies. They do so by requiring that CEOs and CFOs personally certify their companies' financial statements. Both sections impose harsh penalties:

- ✔ SOX Section 906 authorizes a prison term of up to ten years and a fine of up to $1 million for any executive who "knowingly" certifies a regulatory filing that doesn't "fairly present, in all material respects, the financial condition and results" of the company. Any executive who "willfully" certifies a false filing faces up to 20 years in prison and a $5 million fine. (*Willfully* is a legal standard predicated on deliberate conduct.)

- ✔ Section 302 contains civil penalties for signing false reports. It provides that the signing officer must certify that he or she has reviewed the report and that, based on his or her knowledge, the financial statements fairly represent the company's operations.

Harsh as the requirement may have sounded when the law was first passed, liability under both sections is predicated on what the CEOs and CFOs actually know. This legal standard means that at least one CEO (Richard Scrushy, as discussed later) was able to successfully defend against criminal charges by claiming that his subordinates pulled the wool over his eyes.

It's a demoralizing prospect to prosecutors that high-level management may walk out of criminal courtrooms as free men and women while employees who claimed to have taken direction from them are convicted. Accordingly, the prosecutors are likely to revamp their strategies and attempt to shift the courtroom focus from what CEOs and CFOs actually knew to what they *should* have known.

The First Big SOX Trial: Richard Scrushy

Top executives across the country were riveted in 2005 by coverage of the trial of Richard Scrushy, one of the first CEOs to be prosecuted under SOX. Under SOX Section 906, the prosecution had to prove that Scrushy acted willfully in order to convict him. Legal analysts are still debating exactly what *willfully* means under Section 906, but most lawyers seem to concur that it requires clearly knowing what was happening and either participating or deliberately not preventing it.

The squishy Scrushy facts

In early 2005, Richard Scrushy, the former CEO of HealthSouth Corporation, was prosecuted for SOX-related violations tied to HealthSouth's downfall. Scrushy was indicted on 36 criminal counts, including charges of criminal conspiracy, securities fraud, wire and mail fraud, false statements, false certi-fication under SOX Section 906, and money laundering.

Scrushy was a former respiratory therapist who cofounded HealthSouth in 1984 and built it into a national chain of rehabilitation and outpatient surgery hospitals. At issue in the lawsuit was an alleged scheme to inflate Health-South's earnings by $2.7 billion from 1996 to 2002. Prosecutors contended Scrushy personally amassed more than $200 million as the price of HealthSouth's stock rose based on fraudulent financial reports. They argued that HealthSouth was precisely the Enron-type scenario that SOX was created to prevent.

The prosecution had persuasive evidence against Scrushy as compared to the cases against former top executives at WorldCom, Adelphia Communications, and Tyco International. The case was viewed as strong for the following reasons:

- ✔ Five former company CFOs pleaded guilty to fraud and implicated their former boss.
- ✔ The jury heard recorded conversations between Scrushy and a CFO in which they discussed balance-sheet problems. (During the conversation, Scrushy asked, "You're not wired, are you?")
- ✔ Aaron Beam, the former CFO at HealthSouth, claimed Scrushy had direct knowledge of accounting fraud at the company.

The Scrushy trial lasted four months and centered on testimony of the five former CFOs who cooperated with the government by pointing fingers at Scrushy and who pled guilty to various charges. As in other CEO trials, lawyers argued that Scrushy was a victim of a conspiracy by his subordinates and was unaware that fraud was perpetuated by those beneath him.

The judge in the case carefully instructed the jury not to assume that Scrushy was responsible for the fraud just because he was the CEO. However, she also instructed the jury that they could find Scrushy guilty if he "deliberately closed his eyes" to wrongdoing. Ultimately, on July 1, 2005, Scrushy was acquitted of all 36 charges that he signed false financial filings. One juror observed after the trial, "As for evidence, I wanted something in black and white, something like fingerprints. That wasn't there."

The prosecutors' post-game recap

After Enron and the wave of corporate scandals that followed it, Congress intended that the SOX certification requirement would make it easier to prosecute white-collar crimes. Even if other elements of a fraud weren't linked to the executive, the signing of a false affidavit would serve as a smoking gun. But that's not quite how things have worked out. However, as the Scrushy trial indicates, convicting an executive of knowingly violating the certification requirement involves proving the same facts necessary to support other criminal charges that were on the books long before SOX. In the end, all that appears certain is that SOX increases possible prison time.

The crucial element of SOX Section 906 is knowledge. Proving what an executive knew or didn't know of a fraud in a large, publicly traded company with thousands of employees is a huge prosecutorial undertaking.

In addition to charging Richard Scrushy under SOX Section 906, prosecutors brought charges against him for securities fraud and conspiracy. In post-trial interviews, jurors revealed that after they failed to find Scrushy guilty of the non-SOX charges, the SOX-related counts fell like dominoes. A prominent securities attorney quoted in *The New York Times* surmised, "I can't imagine a case where you couldn't prove that the person had engaged in fraud, so you found them not guilty on that count, but then found him guilty for certifying false filings [under SOX]."

Of the failure to get a conviction against Scrushy, the lead prosecutor in the case said, "I don't think it says anything on the strength of the Sarbanes-Oxley Act." She observed that SOX "was just one of several federal statutes that was used. It will be tested again."

Questions raised by the Scrushy trial regarding executives' behavior include the following:

- Is recklessly disregarding information the same as "knowing"?
- Do company executives have a duty to inquire about all ongoing financial matters?
- To what extent do executives have a duty to supervise subordinates and verify their actions?

In the end, many lawyers have concluded that the liability that top executives face under SOX may not be all that different from that which they faced under criminal and securities laws prior to SOX.

The Scrushy epilogue: Civil suits, a tax refund, and a new trial

Although he was acquitted on all 36 criminal charges, Scrushy faced civil suits from HealthSouth's shareholders. (The shares reached a high of just above $30 in April 1998 only to plummet to 10 cents a share after the fraud became public in March 2003.)

HealthSouth predictably sought to distance itself from its embattled CEO. "The new board and new management team remain appalled by the multibillion-dollar fraud that took place under Mr. Scrushy's management and environment under which such fraud could occur," HealthSouth officials said in a public statement. "Under no circumstances will Mr. Scrushy be offered any position within the company by this management team or by this board of directors."

In 2007, HealthSouth Corp. announced that it received a $440 million income tax refund from the IRS for overpayments made on inflated profits reported by Scrushy and his management team. HealthSouth's new management said that it will use the money from the tax refund to pay off about $1 billion in debt this year. Investors were cheered by news of the refund. HealthSouth shares rose 5.6 percent after the announcement.

Although Scrushy was acquitted on all counts during his 2005 SOX/fraud trial, he was convicted on an unrelated matter two years later. In June 2007, Scrushy was sentenced to nearly seven years in federal prison for bribing former Governor Don Siegelman (who was also sentenced to seven years in prison).

Another Test of the "Ignorance" Defense: Kenneth Lay

In the fall of 2005, the Justice Department and Securities Exchange Commission (SEC) finally brought charges against Enron's former CEO, Kenneth Lay. Many Enron officials (including Lea Fastow, one official's wife) had already been tried and sentenced and had begun serving time for their roles in Enron's collapse. Still, government agencies continued to ponder whether to indict Lay.

The delay, it appears, was attributable to that tricky issue of knowledge: What did he know — or not know — about the fraud being perpetrated at Enron while he was at the helm? The Justice Department, after consternating for years, finally opted to indict Lay for covering up Enron's fraud (beginning in 2001). The SEC filed a corresponding civil suit.

Both government agencies appeared convinced: Lay didn't initially know of the fraud that brought his company down. Neither agency indicted Lay for organizing the fraud or even knowing that the books were being cooked in 1999 and 2000. However, these are the factors that *did* persuade the Justice Department to finally indict Lay:

✔ **As he was reassuring Enron employees that the company would be saved, he was secretly selling off his own shares of company stock.** He used what's now known as the *Lay loophole* in federal securities, which provided that stock transactions between an executive and the company itself didn't have to be disclosed until the following year.

SOX slams the Lay loophole closed by requiring that all insider transactions be disclosed within days of their taking place.

✔ **He repeatedly borrowed $4 million from the company and then satisfied the loan by tendering stock to the company.**

SOX now prohibits corporations from making loans to their executives.

In the civil suit filed by the SEC, the agency alleged that Lay violated insider-trading laws by selling stock when he knew of the fraud in 2001 but not prior to that. In fact, the only crime that Lay was alleged to have committed prior to 2001 was failing to disclose to lending banks that money he was borrowing would be used to purchase Enron shares.

Oh Kenny Boy . . .

The following ballad is sung to the tune of "Danny Boy":

Oh Kenny Boy, the jails, the jails are calling,
From state to state, and through the world so wide.
The money's gone, and all the chips are falling,
'Tis you, 'tis you must go and you must hide.

But come ye back when lawmen stop their yam'ring,
Or when Congress is hushed and Dems are eating crow. 'Tis I'll be there in office or in Crawford,
Oh Kenny Boy, oh Kenny Boy, I love you so.

But if you're jailed, and I am in the Oval,
If I'm still Prez, as Prez I expect to be,

Don't come and ask for favors or a pardon,
Don't kneel and say a rescue plea to me.

For I shan't hear, tho' loud you beg before me,
Though all I craved you gladly gave to me.
You'll have to fend without me if you love me,
And you will keep your peace, so I stay Prez and free.

I found this tune on the Web site of humorist Madeline Begun Kane located a www.mad kane.com/bushkennyboy.html. Kane sings and writes poetic tributes to Bush, DeLay, and Supreme Court nominees and justices, and she pokes fun at the legal profession and even at feminism. Check out her latest: *Ode to Tom DeLay.*

Some observers speculated that the delay in indicting Lay signaled a weak case. They inferred that because Lay was the face of Enron, the prosecutors' goal was to get any indictment.

President Bush once publicly called Kenneth Lay "Kenny Boy." The media seized upon this to assert Lay's supposed connections to the Bush administration, inspiring political jibes like the ballad *Oh Kenny Boy,* reprinted in the nearby sidebar "Oh Kenny Boy . . ."

Ken Lay was found guilty and then died before sentencing.

The inescapable conclusion of this case is that it's difficult to prove what a CEO knew and didn't know at the time fraud occurred. The question of knowledge will continue to be the critical burden of proof under SOX Sections 302 and 906, which now require CEOs and CFOs to personally sign off on their companies' financial statements — something Lay wasn't required to do prior to SOX. (Turn to Chapter 10 for more on these SOX sections.)

Timing Is Everything: Andersen, Ernst, and KPMG Litigation Outcomes

In 2001, Arthur Andersen was the largest accounting firm in the world with 28,000 employees in the United States alone. By 2002, it had collapsed under a criminal indictment. Prior to Andersen's demise, there were only five major firms (the "Big Five") that had the capability to audit the largest U.S. firms. The availability of sophisticated audit service providers for large firms was suddenly constricted. Concerns surfaced about the future quality of accounting professionals in the workplace since Arthur Andersen had been the training ground for the CPA profession. Thousands lost their jobs.

In 2005, KPMG, one of the remaining the "Big Four" audit firms, came very close to suffering the same fate as Arthur Andersen for peddling illegal tax shelters. However, with KPMG, the Justice Department proceeded carefully; it didn't want its indictment to put the KPMG under and shrink the number of major accounting firms to the "Big Three."

William McDonough, head of the Public Company Accounting Oversight Board (PCAOB), publicly expressed relief in September 2005 that the Department of Justice had reached a settlement with KPMG over its past sales of tax avoidance schemes to clients. As of this writing, the remaining Big Four firms are

- ✔ Deloitte & Touché
- ✔ Ernst & Young

- ✔ KPMG
- ✔ PricewaterhouseCoopers

The public has a sense that all of the Big Four remain vulnerable in the marketplace to scandal and litigation at any time.

PCAOB Chairman McDonough has warned that the solution to the problem of audit concentration can't be solved by a merger of smaller accounting firms. Even if the firms ranked five through eight were all merged into one, the resulting company would still be far smaller and less capable of doing large-scale audits than any of the Big Four.

"None of us has a clue what to do if one of the Big Four failed," McDonough told the press in 2005. He explained that if even one of the Big Four accounting firms was to collapse, the best accountants would likely flee from the profession to seek better opportunities in other fields.

Other experts point out that competition in the industry would be severely diminished, and fees for public companies already socked by SOX compliance costs would skyrocket. Moreover, the possibility of losing a major accounting firm raises a question of whether enough high-quality, experienced firms would be available to perform the complex public company audits that the U.S. economy and the investing public depend on.

Arthur Andersen's victory: Three years too late

In June 2002, Arthur Andersen was convicted of a single count of obstruction of justice, which was enough to precipitate the accounting giant's downfall. The count alleged that Andersen deliberately shredded Enron documents in order to thwart a pending investigation.

Document shredding was only one of the many misdeeds that came to light after the collapse of Enron, as discussed in Chapter 2. A member of the firm sent a memo allegedly advocating shredding as part of the firm's "document retention policy." Those involved in the Enron audit were all too eager to comply. The company defended its document retention policy as necessary financial housekeeping and denied the shredding was intended to block a future investigation.

On May 31, 2005, the U.S. Supreme Court overturned Arthur Andersen's conviction; in a unanimous opinion, the nine justices on the high court concluded the "jury instructions at issue simply failed to convey the requisite consciousness of wrongdoing." Chief Justice William Rehnquist admonished, "Indeed, it is striking how little culpability the instructions required."

Unfortunately, at the time that the Supreme Court overturned its conviction, Arthur Andersen was nearly defunct, with only about 200 employees left (most of whom handled its ongoing legal matters). Its downfall had an economic ripple effect. Not only were about 28,000 Andersen employees thrown out of work, but substantial jobs were lost in companies that provided goods and services to Andersen. The Andersen downfall also served to restrict competition and drive up audit fees just as most public companies were experiencing the initial sticker shock of SOX compliance.

An Ernst error

In the fall of 2005, SEC Chief Administrative Law Judge Brenda Murray ruled that the accounting firm Ernst & Young acted improperly by auditing PeopleSoft Inc., a huge public company with which the firm had a profitable relationship in other business areas. Because of the SEC's contention that Ernst had violated rules on auditor independence, Judge Murray entered an unusual order barring Ernst from accepting new audit clients in the United States for six months. She also fined the firm $1.7 million.

The SEC contended Ernst had violated rules on auditor independence because of its profitable relationship with PeopleSoft Inc. in other business areas. Ernst's consulting and tax practices used PeopleSoft software in their business, and the two companies collaborated in promoting some of their joint business activities. The evidence in the SEC's case revealed that

- ✔ Ernst had billed itself in marketing materials as an "implementation partner" of PeopleSoft.
- ✔ Ernst had earned $500 million over five years from installing PeopleSoft programs at other companies.

SEC officials said the decision against Ernst & Young would send a message to other firms that, "auditor independence is one of the centerpieces of ensuring the integrity of the audit process."

Ernst & Young ties with its competitor, KPMG, for receiving the longest suspension of signing new clients ever imposed by the SEC. In 1975, Peat Marwick, a predecessor of KPMG, received a similar six-month suspension for failing to audit five companies, one of which was Penn Central, a railroad that subsequently went bankrupt.

Kid gloves for KPMG?

In 2005, in a case described as the largest tax evasion scheme in U.S. history, the Justice Department criminally charged eight former executives of the major accounting firm KPMG with conspiracy to sell fraudulent tax shelters that shorted the IRS at least $2.5 billion.

According to prosecutors, the firm earned around $115 million in fees for selling illegal tax shelters over a seven-year period. Court documents described the shelters "as a means for wealthy individuals with taxable income or gains generally in excess of $10 million in 1996 and of $20 million in 1998–2000 fraudulently to eliminate or reduce the tax paid to the IRS on that income or gain." KPMG received a $456 million fine to settle the federal investigation of its marketing of the illegal tax shelters.

Although KPMG as an entity was charged with conspiracy in a criminal complaint, the firm was granted something referred to as *deferred prosecution*. Basically, deferred prosecution means that the Justice Department made a decision not to prosecute the firm; it allowed KPMG to avoid a grand jury criminal indictment by paying the penalty, submitting to some independent monitoring, and continuing to cooperate with the Justice Department investigation.

Attorney General Alberto Gonzales defended the government's decision to defer prosecution, but in the minds of many, the decision sent a message that prosecution is risky because there are simply too few big accounting firms, and the Justice Department didn't want to set in motion an Andersen-esque demise for KMPG.

Gonzalez publicly stated: "I want to be clear. No company is too big to be prosecuted. We have zero tolerance for corporate fraud, but we also recognize the importance of avoiding collateral consequences whenever possible." Gonzales also pointed out the range of potential economic victims from the possible fallout of a KPMG downfall; Gonzalez explained that the Justice Department's decision reflected "the reality that the conviction of an organization can affect innocent workers and others associated with the organization, and can even have an impact on the national economy."

While deferring to prosecute KPMG, federal prosecutors had no such reservations indicting individuals associated with the scandal. In August 2005, the Justice Department indicted eight former KPMG officials and a lawyer accused of helping wealthy clients evade billions of dollars in taxes. It's the largest criminal tax fraud case in history.

The Gemstar Case: Interpreting Section 1103

SOX Section 1103 is a provision directed at recouping big bonuses paid to fraudulent executives. The statute kicks into effect if a company is being investigated for a possible violation of federal securities laws and it appears to the SEC "likely" that the company will make "extraordinary payments (whether compensation or otherwise)." Under the statute, the SEC may ask a federal district court for a temporary order requiring the issuer to hold the fund in a special interest-bearing account (called an *escrow account*) for 45 days. If the individual slated to receive the supposed "extraordinary payments" actually is charged with a securities violation in a civil proceeding, a court can withhold the payments until the end of the trial.

Because neither SOX Section 1103 nor any SEC rule defines an "extraordinary payment," courts have begun to look at this issue. For example, in May 2005, a three-judge panel ruled that multimillion dollar termination fees to be paid to two executives of Gemstar after the company discovered that it had overstated its revenue by millions of dollars were not extraordinary. The panel in this case noted the lack of "evidence as to what would be an ordinary payment under comparable circumstances."

In the Gemstar case, the district court had placed the funds in escrow, but its logic was vague in that it had relied, in part, on the fact that the payments at issue had been negotiated over a long period of time by many different people in the company. The district court called this process extraordinary, but the appeals court said the circumstances didn't constitute that label and complained it hadn't received enough evidence from the lower (district) court to review the case on appeal and had no choice but to reverse the district court's ruling.

Suing under SOX Section 304

SOX Section 304 calls for *disgorgement* of profits and bonuses from top corporate executives in the wake of an alleged accounting scandal. (Disgorgement is an odd word choice that simply means they have to give it back.)

Who can sue officers and directors to disgorge their bonuses? According to a recent federal district court case, only the SEC can. In *Neer v. Pelino,* the court held that SOX doesn't provide a private right of action for shareholders to file a suit on their own behalf. (This type of lawsuit is known as a *shareholders' derivative suit.*)

The Court held that Congress intended for Section 304 to be enforced only by the SEC, and not by shareholders in private lawsuits. The judge reasoned that Congress "explicitly created a private right of action in only one place, and that is in Section 306" — a provision that prohibits corporate officers from buying or selling securities during a pension fund blackout period. (Blackout periods are covered in Chapter 11.)

Suing under Section 806: The Whistle-Blower Provision

SOX Section 806 confers public company employees who report suspected violations of a range of federal offenses the right to sue both the company and its employees and agents for reinstatement and back pay.

Blowing the whistle before and after SOX

Whistle-blowers, employees who lawfully disclose private employer information, have been the heart and soul of many federal fraud cases against many well-known companies.

Prior to SOX, most of these types of complaints were brought under the False Claims Act, which encourages whistle-blowers to come forward by promising them up to 25 percent of the money recovered by the government as a result of the shared information. The act was first passed during the Civil War but was resurrected and amended in 1985. Since then, it has generated $12 billion for the federal treasury (and more than $1 billion for hundreds of whistle-blowers).

SOX offers additional whistle-blower protections to those who help uncover fraud against publicly traded companies. Specifically, SOX

- ✓ Protects whistle-blowers from being fired.
- ✓ Provides remedies for whistle-blower reinstatement.

Windfalls for whistle-blowers

Several years before SOX, hospital CFO Jim Alderson refused to go along with his employer's phony billing practices and was let go. Alderson sued for wrongful discharge and alerted the government to the fact that it was being cheated out of $1.7 billion in Medicare funds by the nation's largest commercial hospital chain. Under the False Claims Act, Alderson received a 10-percent share of the money recovered by the government.

What happens when the whistle blows?

Under SOX, a whistle-blower is an employee who provides information to a federal regulatory or law enforcement agency, to a member or committee of Congress, or to a person with supervisory authority over the employee about conduct that the employee reasonably believes constitutes a violation of the following:

- ✔ Any rule or regulation of the SEC
- ✔ Federal criminal provisions relating to securities
- ✔ Bank, mail, or wire fraud
- ✔ Any other federal law relating to fraud against a company's shareholders

SOX Section 806, which is enforced by the federal Occupational Health and Safety Administration (OSHA), declares that officers, employees, contractors, subcontractors, and agents of the company are forbidden to engage in any retaliation against a whistle-blower.

According to OSHA, the protection of Section 806 extends not only to employees, but also to the employees of contractors, subcontractors, and agents of public companies.

Filing the complaint

If an employee believes he or she has been fired, demoted, suspended, threatened, harassed, coerced, or put on any sort of blacklist because of whistle-blowing, he or she can file a complaint with OSHA within 90 days of the alleged discriminatory treatment. After OSHA receives the complaint, the agency notifies the employer of the allegations and evidence and gives it an opportunity to respond. The Secretary of Labor issues its decision within 180 days of the filing of the complaint.

OSHA's review of the complaint

OSHA conducts an initial review of each SOX-related whistle-blower complaint and decides whether the employee filing the complaint makes the required basic case (called a *prima facie case*) against the employer. The required elements for a prima facie case are:

✔ **Protected activity:** The employee engaged in conduct or an activity that was protected by SOX or another law.

✔ **Employer knowledge:** Either actually or constructively, the employer knew or suspected that the employee engaged in the protected activity.

✔ **Unfavorable action by employer:** The employee suffered an unfavorable personnel action, such as termination, demotion, or suspension.

✔ **Sufficient circumstances:** The circumstances must raise the inference that the protected activity was a contributing factor in the unfavorable action.

Whether the employer actually violated the specified SOX laws and regulations isn't important. All that's required for a valid Section 806 complaint is an objectively reasonable belief that the employer's conduct constitutes such a violation for the employee to be protected under Section 806.

OSHA's investigation

If OSHA finds that the complainant has the elements for a prima facie case (as explained in the preceding section), the employer is given 20 days to respond after it receives notice of the complaint filing. The employer can respond in writing or request a personal meeting with OSHA; it's required to demonstrate by clear and convincing evidence that it would have taken the same personnel action even in the absence of the employee's whistle-blowing activity. If OSHA finds that the employer has met this burden, it dismisses the complaint. Otherwise, OSHA must conduct a formal investigation into the merits of the complaint.

OSHA takes the position that an employer's company counsel doesn't have the right to be present during interviews of nonmanagement and nonsupervisory personnel. In fact, as a matter of practice, OSHA often doesn't notify the company or its lawyers when such employees are contacted in the course of an investigation. OSHA also redacts witness statements or summarizes them to protect employees who ask to remain anonymous.

After OSHA finishes its investigation, it decides whether there's reasonable cause to believe the company violated Section 806 by discriminating against the whistle-blower. If it sides with the employee, OSHA's order may include reinstatement or coverage of lost pay. The employer has an opportunity to submit a written response or to meet with the investigators to interview more witnesses and submit evidence within ten business days of OSHA's notification to the employer.

Dealing with appeals

If either party disagrees with OSHA's findings, it may file an appeal with the Chief Administrative Law Judge in the Department of Labor. If neither party appeals within 30 days of receiving OSHA's findings, the preliminary order becomes the final decision of the Secretary of Labor, and no further judicial review is allowed.

If an appeal crops up within 30 days, an administrative law judge conducts a new hearing on the complaint. The administrative law judge's order may be appealed to the Department of Labor's Administrative Review Board. A petition for review must be filed within ten business days of the administrative law judge's decision, and review by the board is discretionary. Unless the board accepts the case within 30 days of the filing of the petition for review, the administrative law judge's decision becomes final. It may be appealed to the U.S. Court of Appeals.

As of this writing, the Department of Labor has reported approximately five dozen cases that have been appealed or considered by administrative law judges. Most have been dismissed for untimely filing or withdrawn, signaling settlement without reaching a decision on the legal merits of the case.

Tips for defending against whistle-blower suits

Whistle-blower complaints in the post-SOX era require more attention and certainly more paperwork than before. No matter how unfounded the complaint may seem, your company can practice safe SOX by doing the following:

- ✔ **Take all complaints seriously.** Make sure that all complaints brought by employees are fully investigated and documented. Employees should be instructed on procedures for processing complaints and directed never to make a determination that the complaint is trivial or frivolous.

- ✔ **Track the timing.** If an employee is contentious and requires discipline, try to delay taking any action until his or her complaint is investigated. The mere coincidence of timing may lead to an inference that the company fired the employee in retaliation for the whistle-blower complaint.

- ✔ **Document every phase of the investigation.** Document the complaint itself, everyone who is made aware of it, information gathered that's relevant to the outcome of the complaint, action taken in response to the complaint (if any), and how the matter is concluded.

Chapter 19

The Surprising Scope of SOX

*T*his chapter explores the outer limits of the Sarbanes-Oxley Act (SOX), taking a look at its surprisingly broad scope. Congress probably didn't consider the impact that SOX would have on outsourced services, not-for-profit organizations, and foreign corporations. Nevertheless, these types of entities are being impacted by the pervasive standards introduced by SOX.

In this chapter, I examine a company's obligations with respect to the work it sends out beyond its four walls. I also look at the guidance SOX offers to not-for-profits as they struggle with their own governance issues. Finally, I take you across the ocean to understand how SOX impacts European companies that list their stock on U.S. exchanges.

Outsourcing under SOX

SOX Section 404 requires companies to assess and audit the effectiveness of their internal control and how they impact the companies' financial statements. (Internal control is discussed in Chapter 12.) This requirement extends to *all* aspects of a company's financial operations — even if some of them happen to occur outside the company.

If your company relies on outside companies to process financial information, it must make sure adequate internal controls are in place just as if the company had done the work in-house. SOX requires companies to monitor control conditions at facilities where they outsource services and at hosting sites where they may store sensitive company data.

The responsibility for monitoring internal control for outsourced services arises from *SAS 70,* an auditing standard developed by the American Institute of Certified Public Accountants, or AICPA. This document contains audit requirements for the control activities a company puts in place at a service organization or outsourcing firm.

Summarizing SAS 70

Under SAS 70, an audit of internal control for outsourced services can be performed by the service provider's auditors or by the company relying on its work. SAS 70 identifies two types of audit approaches:

- ✓ **Type 1 audit:** Focuses on general controls at one point in time. This type of audit is a "snapshot" approach that doesn't involve audit testing.

- ✓ **Type 2 audit:** Looks at control conditions over a designated period of time. Auditors conduct tests that span this time period and perform testing to verify the effectiveness of controls at service organizations.

Regardless of the type of audit approach chosen by the audit firm, the company's audit committee must work with the audit committee to make sure that the SAS 70 report generated is adequate to address the requirements of Section 404 (discussed in Chapter 12). The issues that must be addressed include the following:

- ✓ **Scope:** It's up to the company and the service provider to determine the scope of the audit and what will be tested. Ultimately, the company's outside auditors are required to include an evaluation of this testing within their overall Section 404 audit of the company.

- ✓ **Lead time:** Many service providers are just getting up to speed with SOX. Smaller service providers who have until July 15, 2007, to comply with SOX may need extra lead time to comply with SAS 70 requests. (For details on the SEC compliance deadlines, turn to Chapter 12.)

- ✓ **Standardized certifications:** Companies that provide outsourced service may be able to save money and better serve their clients by asking their own outside audit firms to develop SAS 70 certifications that they can provide to companies. Doing so meets the needs of their customers in a proactive manner and helps the service provider avoid having to reinvent the wheel each time a customer requests an SAS 70 certification. (A sample SAS certification report is included in Appendix E.)

- ✓ **Additional testing:** After the SAS audit results come back, additional testing may be required. Ultimately, the customer is responsible for the testing.

Sidestepping SAS 70

Not all outsourced functions require SAS audits. Sensitive services, such as payroll, may require your company to secure an SAS 70 audit. However, your company may *not* need an SAS 70 from the following types of services providers:

- ✔ **Staffing:** If you use a temporary agency to help staff your company's IT or accounting departments, you probably don't need an SAS audit because the sensitive services are performed internally.

- ✔ **Software development:** You probably don't need an SAS 70 from a company to which you outsource application development activities if controls are already in place within your company to monitor the quality of the work.

- ✔ **Law firms and other outside consultants:** As with software development, the quality of these services is monitored within your company, so an SAS 70 certification probably isn't required.

Extending SOX Principles to Not-for-Profits

Although SOX applies to publicly traded companies, *not-for-profit companies* (NFPs) are becoming increasingly concerned about being sued and held to judicially created standards akin to those found in SOX. For this reason, SOX considerations are starting to surface in some unexpected places — school boards, charities, and other tax-exempt organizations are seeking some level of reform and accountability.

Not-for-profits must be prepared to demonstrate a commitment to good governance and internal control. Not-for-profits, as a rule, depend on public good will and their reputations to attract funds. Despite the most altruistic motives, a financial scandal can permanently undermine an organization's ability to attract contributions. Thus, words such as "accountability," "ethics," "transparency," "duty," "full-disclosure," and "social responsibility" have always been part of the vernacular of NFP governance — from the smallest NFPs to the largest.

Although SOX doesn't legally apply to NFPs, the statute has increased public awareness as to how companies of all types govern themselves. NFPs are likely to look to SOX for guidance in developing their own governance standards. Audit committees, compensation committees, written codes of ethics, and governance guidelines are all likely to find their way into NFPs.

Since SOX was proposed, several bills have been introduced in both federal and state legislatures to make nonprofit corporations, municipal agencies, and charitable groups more accountable. While this type of legislation is still years away, SOX-type standards for NFPs are inevitable.

Proponents of holding not-for-profits to SOX standards cite scandals in school districts, public colleges, and charities across the country. The IRS has already contacted 2,000 tax-exempt organizations across the country to inquire about their executive compensation.

NFPs aren't immune to lawsuits, and it's likely no NFP will want to risk being sued without certain safeguards in place. Many SOX-sensitive attorneys and accountants working for NFPs recommend that every NFP adopt most, if not all, of the following SOX-type standards:

- **Audit committee:** The NFP should create an audit committee and separate the function of that committee from the finance committee. As in the private sector, the NFP's audit committee should be composed of board members who aren't compensated for serving on the committee and don't have a financial interest or other conflict of interest with any company or person doing business with the NFP.

- **Outside consultants for the audit committee:** Most nonprofit organizations have volunteer board members who may or may not be trained in business and accounting principles. Therefore, it's important that independent, outside consultants, or other advisors be available to work with the audit committee. (SOX mandates that audit committees be permitted to hire outside consultants and that their companies be required to pay for the consulting services.)

- **Procedures for adopting the auditor's report:** The NFP audit committee should meet with the outside audit firm and recommend to the full board of directors whether the audit report should be approved or modified. The full board should formally accept or reject the committee's report.

- **Auditor independence:** SOX contains a number of requirements to ensure the independence of outside auditors. For example, SOX requires that audit firms rotate the lead partner every five years.

- **Prohibited services:** SOX prohibits the audit firm from providing certain nonaudit services. Prohibited services include bookkeeping, financial information systems, and other services (see Chapter 6 for a more complete list). NFPs may be used to receiving these services from audit firms. Consistent with the standards in SOX, an NFP's audit committee may, however, preapprove certain types of nonaudit services outside these categories, such as tax preparation. Additionally, auditors may be allowed to prepare Form 990 or 990-PF (for private foundations) if such services are preapproved.

✔ **CEO/CFO certification:** Like their counterparts in the private sector, the NFP should consider having CEOs and CFOs certify both the appropriateness of financial statements and the officers' fair presentations of the financial conditions and operations of their companies.

SOX and Foreign Companies

Under current law a company that wants to sell securities to the public in the United States, listing those securities either on the New York Stock Exchange (NYSE) or the NASDAQ, must reconcile its financial statements to U.S. accounting rules and comply with American securities laws, including SOX.

Legislators are looking at nonprofit governance standards

In September 2004, Senate Finance Committee Chairman Charles Grassley contacted the president of a group called the Independent Sector and asked it to convene an independent national panel to make recommendations on issues of governance, ethical practice, and accountability for the nonprofit sector. As a result, the national Panel on the Nonprofit Sector was named.

The panel made recommendations in 15 major areas for actions to be taken by the nonprofits themselves, by the IRS, and by Congress. At a minimum, the panel recommended that all nonprofit organizations voluntarily:

✔ Adopt and implement a policy regulating conflicts of interest.

✔ Include on their boards of directors individuals with financial literacy skills (that is, with experience reading and interpreting financial statements and information).

✔ Develop policies regarding whistle-blowers (people who report fraud and mismanagement within an organization). The whistle-blower provisions of SOX are discussed in Chapter 18.

The panel also recommended that Congress and the IRS take the following actions:

✔ Create rules to suspend the tax-exempt status of any organization that fails to file required annual Form 990 series returns with the IRS for two or more consecutive years after notice from the IRS.

✔ Require that CEOs (or other top management) certify that their IRS Form 990 returns are correct and complete.

✔ Require charitable organizations to conduct an independent audit of their finances if they must file a Form 990 return with the IRS each year and have total annual revenues of $2 million or more.

✔ Require that charities with $25,000 in annual revenues complete an annual notice supplying basic information.

You can locate the full text of the panel's final report and recommendations at `www.non profitpanel.org/final/`.

European companies that do business in the United States are becoming increasingly worried about the costs and restrictions of complying with SOX. Like U.S. companies, European companies have found the Section 404 provisions requiring attestation of internal controls to be the most burdensome, driving up their costs and audit fees. The European companies also express concern about SOX's ban on company loans to executives. As a result, they're mounting overseas efforts to make it easier for them to flat out quit complying with U.S. securities laws. Among these efforts, in 2005, 11 organizations representing 100,000 European companies sent a letter to the SEC chairman asking for changes that would allow them to simply stop registering with the SEC.

A European company can *delist* from the U.S. exchanges, meaning that its stock is no longer traded on the exchange (as discussed in Chapter 3). However, the company is still subject to securities laws unless it proves it has fewer than 300 American investors. If the company is able to do this, it may have to resume compliance with U.S. rules in the future if its American investor count passes the 300 mark.

According to a December 2004 article, which appeared in BusinessWeek Online, "the London Stock Exchange (LSE) is in discussions with a number of companies from China and Russia seeking refuge from U.S. regulation." The BusinessWeek Online article also reported that the "British online-travel group Lastminute and German software company Lion Bioscience already have initiated the process to withdraw from U.S. stock exchanges."

European companies have proposed that they be exempted from SEC registration if they delist and show that less than 5 percent of their total share volumes are in the United States. This proposal is likely to run into some opposition from the SEC, however, for the following reasons:

- ✔ The arrangement could be considered akin to accepting lower international standards in lieu of SOX.

- ✔ Foregoing SOX requirements for foreign companies could place U.S. companies at a competitive disadvantage because of their relatively higher compliance costs.

- ✔ Many American institutional investors would likely buy shares of companies that aren't listed on U.S. exchanges from overseas exchanges.

Part VI
The Part of Tens

The 5th Wave   By Rich Tennant

"Isn't that our bookkeeper?"

In this part . . .

In the grand *For Dummies* tradition, this part provides you with useful reminders and tips to help keep you from getting bogged down in the details of SOX. It provides you with bare-bones information about how to avoid getting sued, how your audit committee should proceed, how management can meet new obligations, and how auditors can and can't help your company. Finally, this part concludes with a list of resources for finding more information about SOX.

Chapter 20

Ten Ways to Avoid Getting Sued or Criminally Prosecuted Under SOX

In This Chapter

▶ Avoiding litigation and SEC investigations after SOX

▶ Implementing safe SOX practices and defensive measures

*W*ho is the SEC going to be looking at after Enron, WorldCom, Global TelLink, and HealthSouth? Why did Tyco's Dennis Kozlowski get 20 years under the old SEC rules while Richard Scrushy, the first CEO to face prosecution under the Sarbanes-Oxley Act (SOX), left the court room a free man? How could Scrushy walk while five of his subordinates pleaded guilty? How do you keep yourself, your department, and your company out of the SOX spotlight? Can you spend your bonus, or will you have to give it back if the company has a bad year?

You aren't the only one asking these questions and many more. In this chapter, I provide you with a few tips for keeping the litigators off your doorstep and for sleeping soundly after SOX.

Maintain an Active and Visible Audit Committee

Under SOX, every public company is required to have an audit committee that interfaces with the company's outside auditors. Many not-for-profit and private companies are opting to establish audit committees as well because they provide additional credibility for the audit process. Audit committees are responsible for giving good information to the auditors and for communicating audit issues to management. So this is one committee you want to make active, visible, and well funded in your company. (Flip to Chapter 8 for full audit committee details.)

Communicate about How to Communicate

In the first major case to go to trial after SOX, Richard Scrushy, the CEO of the teetering HealthSouth Corporation, was acquitted in July 2005 of 36 counts of signing false financial filings. Scrushy claimed he didn't know of the fraudulent activity that sent the five HealthSouth subordinates who reported to him to jail. (The Scrushy trial is recounted in Chapter 18.)

As the HealthSouth lawsuit makes clear, documented communication channels and visible networks can help you and your company maintain credibility in a SOX-related investigation. Documentation can help buttress testimony and jog memories.

Put policies in place to document how delegated work is supervised and how results and conclusions are communicated. Policies will vary for every company and may even be different within particular departments. And don't forget that employee titles don't always convey the actual level of supervisory responsibility that a position entails.

Combat Policy Paranoia and Section 404 Audit-Chondria

Communication is key under SOX (see the preceding section), but too much of it can also be a bad thing. Policies that micromanage workflow and audit minutiae can create their own red flags. For example, cynical attorneys may raise questions about why trivial policies were flexibly applied. Or future auditors may demand discussion about why nonmaterial discrepancies weren't further investigated or why items from last year's audit were dropped from this year's agenda. (For more information on surviving a Section 404 audit, turn to Chapter 13.)

Under SOX, a company's audit committee has the authority to hire independent advisors, such as attorneys, to help write good policies and determine how to handle audit issues. SOX-savvy attorneys can help the committee adopt policies that contain an appropriate level of detail. Attorneys also can act as good advocates when auditors propose resources reviewing potentially irrelevant or nonmaterial issues or when issues arise about the scope of sensitive SOX-related projects under Section 404.

Policies that have ill-conceived phrasing or extraneous detail create the risk that the employees can't literally comply with them and leave insufficient room for employees to exercise appropriate discretion in unforeseen circumstances.

Keep Bonuses within Bounds

During the Enron, WorldCom, and other corporate scandals, the media had a field day reporting on huge, questionable bonuses paid to executives of these failing corporations. In the post-SOX era, executive compensation has become a politically sensitive issue.

Document how and why executive bonuses were awarded. In the event that bonuses are challenged later, your company's compensation committee should have a market analysis on hand to support that the bonus amounts are in line with other companies. For instance, questions may be raised in a lean year as to why big bonuses were paid in a prior profitable one. (For a more detailed discussion of executive compensation, turn to Chapter 11.)

Separate the Whistle-Blowers from the Whiners

Whistle-blowers are employees who raise questions of fraud or noncompliance with accounting or governmental regulations in the workplace. So that a serious and valid complaint doesn't get glossed over and later return to cause major lawsuit trouble for the company, every whistle-blower complaint should be fully investigated, and its disposition should be documented. Make sure that levels of review are afforded to complaints based on their seriousness and credibility and that compliance with company policy is documented at every level to determine which complaints may have hidden merit.

Invest in IT Tools and Tricks

Buying and using a sensible SOX software product is an effective way to demonstrate that your company is committed to strong internal controls and that it's being systematic in its compliance. (Software solutions for companies of all sizes are discussed in Part IV.)

If the software tool generates good reports and summaries, it's easier to document what people in the company knew for certification purposes (which I discuss in Chapter 10).

Do Something with All That Data

Data gathered during a Section 404 audit should be evaluated according to a stated policy. It also should be shared with the audit committee, management, and board of directors as appropriate.

It's logical that many companies, having spent considerable resources to comply with Section 404, don't want to dedicate *more* resources to analyze that data. Understandably, companies want to get back on track developing core services and products. However, taking extra steps to parcel out the data to relevant decision makers can provide valuable databases of company-specific and current information on which to base future decisions affecting their departments.

Disclose Triggering Events on Time

Within four days of their occurrence (and sometimes less), SOX requires companies to disclose to the public (on Form 8-K) certain triggering events, such as the termination of major contracts, new financial obligations, write-offs, and financial restatements. Companies that don't disclose these events in a timely manner (as discussed in Chapter 3) risk both public sanctions and private litigation.

Document What's Delegated

Litigation under SOX has an increased focus on what management knew and what it was supposed to know. Under SOX, management is allowed to delegate authority and even outsource certain types of decisions. However, it isn't acceptable for management to take measures to insulate itself from information as to how that authority is being carried out.

Delegation of authority was a key issue in the HealthSouth scandal, when CEO Richard Scrushy walked free while five of his subordinates were convicted of fraud. After this incident, prosecutors and the public were determined not to let many more slippery CEOs escape liability under SOX by claiming they didn't know what their subordinates were doing.

Focus on Product and Service Delivery

SOX is legislation that's aimed at protecting the public from false financial reporting. If your company's credo is to focus on product and service delivery that generates real growth, rather than on plumping up paper profits, your company will more easily meet the objectives of SOX.

Chapter 21

Ten Tips for an Effective Audit Committee

In This Chapter

▶ Structuring your audit committee to be most effective

▶ Keeping your committee consistent with SOX

● ●

T he Sarbanes-Oxley Act (SOX) arms your company's audit committee with an arsenal of authority, including the ability to hire its own legal and accounting advisors. This critical committee is the linchpin of corporate accountability, serving as an essential interface between your company's management, auditors, employees, and board of directors. Because the audit committee is so important, this chapter offers ten tips on how to structure it to function most effectively.

Pick the Right Number of Members

Your company has plenty of leeway in deciding how many people should sit on its audit committee. The New York Stock Exchange (NYSE) rules provide that a committee must have a minimum of three members, but it doesn't place a limit on how large the committee can be. In fact, you can invite the entire board of directors to join (provided the members meet the financial independence and other requirements discussed in Chapter 9). However, do remember that each member of the audit committee must also sit on the company's board of directors.

As a practical matter, putting your entire board of directors on the audit committee probably isn't a good idea, nor is it a good idea to routinely limit membership to three members. A large audit committee can become bureaucratic and inefficient with respect to decision-making and review functions. On the other hand, a three-person committee can quickly become overwhelmed when it must manage an audit and several employee complaints simultaneously.

When determining the optimum number of audit committee members (which may depend on who's up to the task), ask the following questions:

- ✔ Is it more practical for a small committee to keep all board members informed of its activities or for all board members to be directly involved?

- ✔ Does the board believe that a larger committee will give shareholders a greater sense of accountability?

- ✔ How much responsibility are committee members willing to assume?

- ✔ To what extent are board members willing and able to devote the time necessary to serve on the committee, and will this commitment cause them to be diverted from other essential board functions?

- ✔ Will the logistics of coordinating a large committee make it inherently bureaucratic?

Set Up Subcommittees

SOX and Securities Exchange Commission (SEC) regulations permit an audit committee to delegate responsibility for matters under its direction to specific committee members, who make up what are called *subcommittees*. These subcommittees report back to the committee as a whole.

Subcommittees can be used effectively with regard to:

- ✔ **Handling specific complaints:** The audit committee can assign a subcommittee member to investigate specific complaints that it receives or issues that are brought to its attention; in most cases, the subcommittee member then makes informed recommendations to the entire committee. The committee can take advantage of particular members' areas of expertise in assigning matters for investigation.

- ✔ **Addressing specific reporting issues:** Issues may arise during the course of an audit that warrant additional research and analysis to determine how they're to be handled. These tasks can be delegated to a subcommittee for further recommendation.

- ✔ **Hiring and communicating with consultants:** SOX provides that audit committees must be permitted to hire consultants to assist in performing committee functions. A subcommittee can be assigned to select consultants and obtain and evaluate their recommendations.

- ✔ **Communication and report drafting:** Subcommittees can be used to prepare initial drafts of reports and communications for approval by the audit committee as a whole.

✔ **Dealing with certain segments of company operations:** Some committee members may be more familiar with particular operations or sectors of the company's operations and therefore can effectively make recommendations to the committee on related matters.

Find a Financial Expert

SOX provides that at least one member of the audit committee must be a *financial expert.* According to SEC regulations, a financial expert has expertise in Generally Accepted Accounting Principles (GAAP), audit procedures, and internal control.

Unfortunately, not every board of directors includes a former auditor, banker, or other financial expert who's willing to serve on the company's audit committee. However, failing to have a financial expert can cause a myriad of problems for your company. Because the NYSE and other major stock exchanges require an audit committee with a financial expert, you must find the requisite financial expertise to meet listing standards.

Your company can pursue several options when it finds itself without a financial expert. One option is to recruit another director for your board, one who qualifies as a financial expert. This approach, however, has at least one major drawback: The company may feel compelled to compromise its usual criteria and standards for selecting directors because it's under pressure to locate a specific type of person to serve a specific purpose.

Another solution is to hire an outside expert to advise the audit committee (SOX authorizes the audit committee to hire experts to assist in carrying out its functions). Hiring a financial expert rather than electing one to the board of directors is a strategy that offers the following advantages:

✔ An outside expert can be chosen solely on the basis of his or her expertise without regard to any other consideration.

✔ The board of directors may be more willing to defer to the judgment of an outside expert than to the audit committee (which is made up of board members).

✔ Most state and federal laws and corporate bylaws permit directors to rely in good faith on advice given by an outside expert.

✔ Differentiating the roles and responsibilities of audit committee members based on the fact that one or more members are financial experts is unnecessary.

When selecting an expert, inquire as to whether his or her professional liability insurance covers advising your committee. As a safeguard, your company should be able to recover from the expert's malpractice insurance carrier in the event that the expert provides incorrect advice that damages the company.

Create Questionnaires

SOX strives to ensure that both external audit firms and internal committee members have conflict-free consciences in every respect. To that end, auditors must be rotated after five years with a particular company and must be stacked two per audit. In addition, committee members and their immediate families must relinquish any financial ties to the company and its affiliates (other than receiving their directors' fees and ordinary dividends on stock). (For more information about the requirements that now apply to audit firms, see Chapter 6.)

Unexpected conflicts, however, creep into many scenarios. For example, a director may not realize that his adult child has taken a position with an affiliate; or an auditor may change jobs, and the new audit firm may not realize that she audited the new company two years ago when she worked for the prior company.

To avoid unpleasant surprises, audit committees should compile routine questionnaires designed to elicit all relevant information regarding potential conflicts of interest from potential committee members, consultants, and experts.

Adopt a Smart Charter

No company can trade on the NYSE or NASDAQ without a written audit committee charter. The exchanges each specify in their listing requirements what the charter must contain, but generally, contents include the committee's purpose, role within the company, and policies. Including these things will definitely make your charter smarter.

For more on audit committee charters, check out Chapter 8. Also, you can find a sample charter that meets the requirements of both exchanges in Appendix C.

Keep Track of Complaints

Congress and the SEC are serious about creating a safe environment for employees, accounting staff, and auditors to come forward with information that can impact audited financial statements. In this type of regulatory environment, no company can afford for its audit committee to treat any complaint as frivolous.

SOX requires an audit committee to have procedures in place for receiving and handling complaints about the company's "accounting, internal accounting controls or auditing matters, including procedures for submission of anonymous complaints by employees."

 Your company should keep careful records of how complaints are handled. And the audit committee should make sure that these records are complete, reasonably detailed, and consistent. Your committee should make sure that the records reflect that every complaint was handled without any bias or predisposition as to its merits.

Communicate Liberally

A recurring theme of the congressional hearings preceding SOX was the need for more communication among audit committees, internal and external auditors, employees, management, and directors.

The audit committee, in the spirit of the law, should always communicate issues that need to be aired rather than sweep such issues under the rug. In particular, the committee should demonstrate a consistent pattern of communication with management regarding the following:

- ✔ The annual audited financial statements and quarterly reports filed by the company
- ✔ Press releases and financial information provided to the public
- ✔ Policies for risk management within the company
- ✔ Problems that occur during an audit and management's response
- ✔ The role and performance of the company's internal auditors
- ✔ Changes in company accounting polices
- ✔ Issues regarding internal controls and audit adjustments
- ✔ Committee policies and procedures

Report Annually

Corporations are required to hold annual meetings, but because shareholders may be located anywhere in the world, not everyone can attend the meetings and exercise their votes directly. Some of the shareholders may need to vote by proxy. (The process of voting by proxy is described in more detail in Chapter 3.)

Therefore, the audit committee is required to make a report in the company's annual proxy statement, which is sent to shareholders just before an annual meeting. The timing is critical because the annual meeting is when members of the board of directors are elected. An unfavorable audit committee report can make it more difficult for directors to hold onto their seats, and because of the timing, directors may have little time to respond to the committee report before they're voted out.

Identify Conflicts . . . and Nonconflicts

Good audit committee members may be hard to come by, so you may not want to disqualify them unnecessarily. Some situations that seem to involve a conflict of interest for a committee member actually may not be a problem, so it's important to be able to draw the line between conflict and nonconflict.

For example, it's *not* a conflict for an audit committee member to also serve on the audit committee of an affiliated company. Both companies benefit from the financial expertise of a single member, and both committees benefit from the added experience the member gains by serving in both positions.

SOX expressly prohibits an executive officer, general partner, manager, or employee who holds any sort of policymaking position in the company or any affiliated company from serving on the audit committee.

Give Notice When Needed

What if an audit committee member ceases to be independent because of a merger or acquisition? What if the sole financial expert on the committee resigns for health reasons? If your company acts promptly and provides the required notice to the exchanges on which its stock is listed, the shortcomings may not be fatal.

Under SOX, stock exchanges must establish procedures for companies to remedy conditions that result in an audit committee's noncompliance. For example, the NYSE and NASDAQ generally allow a committee member who ceases to be independent for reasons outside his or her reasonable control to continue serving until either the next shareholders' meeting or one year passes from the event that caused the member to lose independence. In a case such as this, the company must give prompt notice of the change to the applicable stock exchange.

Chapter 22

Ten Smart Management Moves

A good manager is hard to find, which is why the Sarbanes-Oxley Act (SOX) contains several provisions for those top executives who fail to implement mandated internal controls. Chief executive officers (CEOs) and chief financial officers (CFOs) are expected to keep their companies profitable against an unprecedented backdrop of jittery boards, stringent certification requirements, and threats of personal liability for decisions made in the corporate context.

This chapter contains ten sensible practices that can serve as defensive tactics for management that's caught in the tightly regulated and politically charged post-SOX environment.

Form a Disclosure Committee

Although it isn't required, the SEC recommends that every company form a *disclosure committee* to assist senior management by communicating and reporting material events. Disclosure committees also can be held responsible for evaluating the significance (materiality) of information and deciding how and when to disclose it to the public.

Candidates for your company's disclosure committee may include:

✔ Senior management

✔ Middle management responsible for financial control processes, risk management, information technology, or human resources

✔ Controller

✔ General counsel

✔ Investor relations officer

The committee should review the company's existing practices and make recommendations for providing control in areas of perceived weakness.

Set Reporting Schedules

CEOs and CFOs who establish disclosure committees (see the preceding section) likely will want to work with the committees to schedule and manage the preparation of annual and quarterly reports. SOX's increased reporting, assessment, and certification requirements mean that CEOs must allocate more lead time than ever before for reviewing and communicating report contents.

The disclosure committee can determine a schedule that takes the following into account:

✔ The time needed to collect information about the company's disclosure controls and processes

✔ The time needed to evaluate the effectiveness of the company's disclosure controls and procedures

✔ The time needed for independent auditors to sign off on management's assessment under SOX Section 404 (as discussed in more detail in Chapter 13)

Have More Meetings and Send Less E-mail

One face-to-face meeting may be worth a million memos in the world of corporate compliance. CEOs and CFOs should be sure to schedule regular discussions with the following groups and individuals:

✔ **The disclosure committee:** At least 90 days before the filing of the annual report, the CEO and CFO should meet with the disclosure committee to confirm that company procedures were carefully followed in generating report data and to discuss the results of the committee's evaluation of the effectiveness of disclosure controls and procedures.

✔ **The department heads and senior managers:** The CEO and CFO should meet with senior management in accounting, technology, financial reporting, and other relevant areas to discuss:

- Any problems or issues that have arisen with the company's internal financial controls

- Any changes that have been made to the internal controls

✔ **The independent auditor:** The CEO and CFO should meet with the lead audit partner of the company's independent audit firm to discuss:

- Changes in the accountant-recommended financial statements

- Any alternative treatments that the company should consider in preparing its financial statements

Challenge Outdated and Overly Detailed Policies

Management shouldn't be shy about bringing ambiguous, overly detailed, or outdated financial reporting policies to the attention of the board of directors or the audit committee. Management at all levels should be proactive in promoting policies and internal control procedures that are clearly worded and practical to follow.

Overly detailed policies can be particularly perilous for CEOs and CFOs who are required to personally certify that company financial statements are accurate or provide assessments of internal control (as discussed in Chapter 10). When procedures are outdated or are too detailed, there's an increased risk that the policy can't be followed, and deviations from policies may be red flags to auditors that internal control issues exist.

Review Reports with Their Preparers

Before signing off on and certifying the company's report, the CEO and CFO should thoroughly review specific sections, including the financial statements, with the employees who prepared those sections. It's critical that the CEO and CFO understand how people within the company are making decisions about financial reporting and how these choices impact the report.

To ferret out errors and incorrect assumptions that impact financial reporting, management should directly communicate with those employees who generate key reports.

Keep Up with Current Certification Requirements

SOX Sections 302 and 906 (see Chapter 10) require CEOs and CFOs to personally certify that periodic reports filed with the SEC are accurate. Section 302 imposes civil liability for false certifications, and Section 906 imposes criminal liability under SOX. The fact that two separate certifications are required for essentially the same conduct has caused some confusion among public companies. The form of the certifications is slightly different, as is the liability to which CEOs and CFOs are subject under them.

Section 302 certifications by the CEO and CFO are required for quarterly reports on Form 10-Q and annual reports on Form 10-K. SOX also requires a separate certification under the Section 906 criminal provisions.

On June 5, 2003, the SEC released its final rules interpreting the Section 302 and 906 requirements. The following are a few key points to keep in mind when filing Section 302 and 906 certifications:

- ✔ **All certifications should be included as exhibits.** The final rules issued by the SEC require companies to include the Section 302 and Section 906 certifications as *exhibits* to the reports, which means that they're documents submitted at the end of each report. (Prior to these rules, companies simply added special language to the signature pages of their SEC reports.)

- ✔ **Certifications will soon need to include internal control statements.** The SEC has delayed implementation of the internal control rules under Section 404 for non-accelerated filers for years ending on or after December 15, 2008.

- ✔ **The language of the certifications is different.** Although Section 302 imposing civil penalties and Section 906 imposing criminal penalties under SOX are directed at the same objective, the language required for each type of certification is different. Appendix B contains a sample Section 302 certification and a sample Section 906 certification.

Avoid Animosity with the Audit Committee

Management should never fall into an adversarial relationship with the audit committee and should generally err on the side of overcommunicating events to the committee.

It's important for the CEO and CFO to discuss and fully understand any deficiencies detected by the independent auditors in the company's internal controls. It's also important that they work with the audit committee in developing a plan of action to correct those deficiencies.

In the event that management has a disagreement with the audit committee, it can ask the committee to hire an independent consultant (such as an attorney) to advise the audit committee on how to resolve the issue. If the issue remains unresolved, the CEO and CFO may consider bringing the issue before the company's board of directors.

Don't Confuse Certification with Control

CEOs and CFOs aren't required to certify every form filed with the SEC under SOX Sections 302 and 906 (for the skinny on certifications, flip to Chapter 10). However, every form must be prepared using control procedures and standards that ensure the accuracy of the reporting.

Reports that only cover current events, such as reports on Form 8-K, don't need to be accompanied by Section 302 and 906 certifications.

Consider Getting Subcertifications

It's becoming a trend in corporate America for CEOs and CFOs to ask senior management to provide them with certifications on matters that they (the CEOs and CFOs) must certify. Requiring principal persons within the organization to certify their work can set an important tone for compliance within the organization. However, subcertifications don't have the actual legal effect of shifting any legal liability from the CEO or CFO. (Chapter 10 discusses subcertifications more fully, and you can see a sample subcertification in Appendix B.)

Track All the Timelines

SOX accelerates a number of SEC filing deadlines for standard types of forms. For example, the timelines for filing quarterly report Form 10-Q and annual report Form 10-K are shortened to 35 days and 60 days, respectively, after the end of the related fiscal period. In addition, SOX has increased substantially the number of events that require current reporting on Form 8-K within four days or less. (For more on these forms and the SEC filing requirements check out Chapter 3.)

Chapter 23

Ten Things You Can't Ask an Auditor to Do After SOX

*I*n order to comply with the Sarbanes-Oxley Act (SOX), your company is required to retain several firms simultaneously to do the work that one firm previously performed, and that extra manpower may mean higher accounting costs, both internally and externally. For auditors to maintain the required independence from audit clients, SOX Section 201 as well as SEC and PCAOB regulations tell CPAs what services they can no longer offer to clients to whom they provide audit services.

Prior to passing SOX, Congress concluded that large audit firms and the companies they audited were becoming way too chummy. Auditors who rendered unfavorable opinions risked losing lucrative consulting deals for other services they performed for the company. Also, auditors were sometimes involved in preparing the financial information and statements that they would later audit. To top it all off, management was free to negotiate with auditors about the adjustments the auditors recommended making to the financial statements.

SOX is intended to ensure that auditors remain objective and firm in their commitment to the accuracy of the financial statements on which the investing public relies. This chapter lists ten tasks you can no longer ask a CPA firm to perform if it's auditing your company.

Keep Your Books

During the congressional hearings following the Enron debacle, it came to light that accounting firm Arthur Andersen had received $25 million in audit fees and $27 million in consulting fees from Enron in the years prior to its bankruptcy filing. This revelation led Congress to conclude that auditors shouldn't be auditing their own work. The CPAs who keep the books for a company should be different from those who are auditing the company's books.

SOX Section 201(a) states that it's unlawful for a CPA firm to provide accounting and related services "contemporaneously" with any audit. Specifically, Section 201 forbids firms from performing "bookkeeping or other financial services related to the accounting records or the financial statements of the audit client."

The SEC rule further broadens the prohibition, going beyond simply banning services that are contemporaneously provided. SEC regulations ban CPAs from providing bookkeeping services at any point in time if it's reasonable to conclude that such services will become subject to audit by the same CPA firm at any time in the future. The SEC rule also makes clear that there are no "emergency" exceptions to these regulations.

Fix Your Financial Information Systems

Prior to SOX, most large accounting firms had management information systems departments or similarly designated divisions that helped design and implement software systems for their clients.

However, according to SOX Section 201, your audit firm can no longer help you design or implement financial information systems. Why? The auditors ultimately may be called on to evaluate the same systems they put into place or helped you maintain.

The SEC rules further broaden this SOX prohibition: The SEC directs auditors to steer clear of any system in your company that compiles source data that may end up on your financial statements in one form or another. In some situations, your auditors may not even be able to help you out with software systems *unrelated* to your financial statements.

Subsequent to SOX, many accounting firms, such as PricewaterhouseCoopers, have sold off their computer consulting and information management divisions.

Appraise Company Property

Appraisal and valuation issues directly impact your financial statements, so it isn't surprising that auditors are prohibited from getting involved in them under SOX Section 201. After all, in the course of the audit, your company's auditors may be asked to assess the value of assets reported on your balance sheet. Valuation also involves determinations of fairness and reasonableness of transactions affecting the appraised assets.

Consistent with SOX, auditors can no longer issue opinions as to the fairness of *like-kind exchanges.* Like-kind exchanges are common transactions in which businesses exchange one type of property for another asset of the same type. For example, your company may exchange one factory building for another that meets its current needs. The transaction then qualifies for tax treatment as an exchange rather than a sale, therefore allowing the company to defer some tax liability. But the whole transaction still has to be evaluated from the standpoint of whether it was conducted in an "arms-length" manner, which means that the amounts paid or received should be consistent with similar deals in the marketplace. The overall transaction must be fair to company shareholders.

The SEC rule also prohibits auditors from rendering an opinion on your company's pension liabilities. This service falls within the ambit of appraisal and valuation.

Act as an Actuary

Actuarial services are the kind of number-crunching services many people envision accountants performing. SOX Section 201 now prohibits a company's auditors from providing them because actuarial services involve a determination of amounts recorded in the financial statements. Making this determination can lead to a conflict of interest if the actuarially determined amounts are questioned later in an audit.

Perform Internal Audit Services for Your Company

SOX Section 201 provides a special limitation in the situation where a company hires its auditors to assist its own accounting staff in checking out the company's books. This is known as an *internal audit,* as distinct from the *independent audit* that outside CPA firms are engaged to perform.

Under SOX, the firm that audits your company can't participate in creating or maintaining your company's internal accounting controls because the auditor may ultimately be reviewing and rendering an opinion on the controls.

Internal audits are performed primarily for the purpose of assisting the company's management in running the company profitably. In contrast, the outside audit firm is usually engaged to render opinions on a company's financial statements.

SEC rules don't prohibit your auditor from performing services related to your company's internal audit if those services aren't related to the internal accounting controls, financial systems, or financial statements.

Fill In for Your Management Team

SOX Section 201 says that your auditor can't provide management services to your company. Doing so would be an inherent conflict of interest under SOX because auditors are engaged in large part to evaluate management and to certify management's reports regarding the company's internal controls.

SEC Regulation S-X Rule 210.2-01(c)(4)(vi) explains that auditors are prohibited from "[a]cting, temporarily or permanently, as a director, officer, or employee of an audit client, or performing any decision-making, supervisory, or ongoing monitoring function for the audit client."

Be a Headhunter

SOX seeks to keep auditors from forming the chummy relationships with management that characterized the relationships that Enron, WorldCom, and other large firms developed prior to SOX. Helping a management candidate get a job with the company could lead to a scenario in which the grateful manager recommends a specific audit firm, and, in turn, the audit firm is ingratiated to management. Such events can compromise the objectivity of the audit process.

Auditors can't act as headhunters for your company or recommend a specific candidate for a job under any circumstances. As SEC Regulation S-X Rule 210.2-01 (c)(4)(vii) spells out, they can't help your company find "prospective candidates for managerial, executive, or director positions."

Auditors also can't help your company evaluate prospective management candidates by

- ✔ Performing psychological testing
- ✔ Conducting reference checks
- ✔ Negotiating employment or compensation contracts

Advise You on Investments

Some provisions of SOX simply reiterate what previously has been the law. Such is the case with Section 201's prohibition of auditors from providing "broker or dealer, investment adviser, or investment banking services." Were such a prohibition not in place, auditors would likely tend to uncritically rely on investment performance data they had prepared themselves. Auditors also can't act as promoters or underwriters on behalf of the clients they audit.

Dispense Legal Advice

Attorneys have always carefully guarded their professional turf against accountants and other potentially competing professional service providers, which explains why most states have specific legal prohibitions on practicing law without a law license.

SOX prohibits auditors from providing services to audit clients. However, most CPA firms already are well aware of the restrictions imposed by state statutes prohibiting the unauthorized practice of law and don't have a sense that this particular SOX provision further restricts their activities.

The provision of tax services has always been an area of overlap and controversy between lawyers and accountants. Accountants render tax advice even though it's impossible to do so without interpreting the applicable tax laws and advising clients on the way that the tax laws should be applied.

Give You an Expert Opinion

Auditors can't give their clients expert opinions on specific issues that must be addressed during the course of an audit. For example, your auditor can't write you a memo giving his or her opinion about a regulatory issue, a lawsuit, or an administrative proceeding in which your company may be involved.

The reasoning for this rule is that your auditor may become a witness in such a proceeding or may be subpoenaed to give information in a related investigation in which your company may become embroiled. In a legal proceeding, auditors may be called as witnesses to explain an accounting position your company has taken based on an expert opinion. In that event, you're likely to be thankful for their unimpaired and credible testimony.

Because SOX doesn't define *expert services,* the accounting profession has no real way of knowing how broadly the PCAOB or SEC will define them. CPAs also worry that SOX's limitations in this area could inspire parallel state legislation or rule changes that directly affect both nonpublic companies and CPAs who provide services to them.

Chapter 24

Top Ten Places to Get Smart about SOX

. . . .

In This Chapter

▶ Finding the most prestigious SOX publications

▶ Frequenting the funniest SOX sites

▶ Keeping up with current SOX events and regulatory actions

. . . .

*N*ew Sarbanes-Oxley (SOX) proposals are always popping up, and new standards are spewing forth faster than I can update this book! In the aftermath of the major corporate scandals and trials, the Securities and Exchange Commission (SEC) is still issuing regulations, the Public Company Accounting Oversight Board (PCAOB) is still pumping out standards, and courts continue to make case law. Numerous publications and books (like this one) have been spawned, and Web sites hawk every conceivable SOX service and product from software systems to T-shirts.

Because we've entered the era of information overload, I created this chapter to direct you to the ten best online and print resources for staying in synch with SOX developments.

Sample SOX-online

SOX-online (www.sox-online.com) is definitely the hippest SOX site on the Web. It dubs itself "the vendor-neutral site," and it really is. SOX-online doesn't seem to be selling anything other than advertising. The site is updated daily and links to hundreds of articles on compliance topics and SOX developments. It also has some really fun links, including the following:

✔ **Dear Ms. Sarbox:** An advice column for the SOX-ually frustrated (see the sidebar "Dear Ms. Sarbox" for more details)

✔ **Accountant jokes:** How many accountants *does* it take to screw in a light bulb?

✔ **SOX jokes and games:** Bound to amuse you for hours

✔ **Sing-along with Sarbox:** Features hits like "The Ballad of Kenny-Boy"

Peruse the PCAOB Web Site

The Public Company Accounting Oversight Board (PCAOB) Web site (www.pcaobus.org) is the place to go if you need to access the most current auditing standards or if you want to understand the evolving role of auditors. It's a particularly important site if you're an auditor. The PCAOB is a special board established by SOX to audit the auditors.

After the Enron scandal, the audit profession lost the right to regulate itself, and now it must succumb to the review of the powerful PCAOB. Additionally, the audit profession had to shift its focus from simply adding up the numbers on the financial statements, and testing a few accounts. The auditors are now responsible for certifying every public company's internal controls over their financial reporting. The PCAOB issues the standards that tell the auditors what and how much to test. If you're concerned about preparing for an audit, you'll find the standards very enlightening.

Additionally, the PCAOB Web site contains extensive information about the review process to which audit firms themselves are subject. Audit firms are subject to varying review requirements (once a year or once every three years) depending on the size of the firms that they audit.

Visit the SEC Web Site

In response to popular demand, the Securities and Exchange Commission (SEC) has created a Web site at www.sec.gov/spotlight/sarbanes-oxley.htm with links to press releases, rules, proposed rules, and FAQs about SOX. Unfortunately, there are no good jokes on this site.

Get Inside Sarbanes-Oxley Trenches

The Inside Sarbanes-Oxley Web site (www.insidesarbanesoxley.com) is a comprehensive site with current articles, blogs, discussion groups, and book lists. (Hopefully *Sarbanes-Oxley For Dummies,* 2nd Edition, will get a good review!) Another helpful site is the Candela Solutions Web site located at www.candelasolutions.com. Candela Solutions is an accounting firm that focuses on working directly with boards and management.

Dear Ms. Sarbox

The following is some expert advice from Ms. Sarbox, whose column can be found at www.sox-online.com/ms_sarbox.html. Each letter links you to useful articles about SOX found elsewhere on the SOX-online site. (In the examples below, the links appear in parentheses.)

✔ Dear Ms. Sarbox: Early in my career, the managers of my company actually specified the super extreme (professional) dress code — to the level of "underwear required." I'd like to know if the requirements for SOX are a little less confining.... Or is "al a natural" a little more acceptable in this age? *Becca from Kentucky*

Dear BFK: The key principle behind Sarbanes-Oxley is forced transparency. Now cloaked only in translucent veils of commerce, corporate leaders' little ... inadequacies ... are there for all of Wall Street to see. But a nice girl like you can still take comfort in the modesty provided by proper foundation garments. (Governance Articles)

✔ Dear Ms. Sarbox: The SEC estimates that it will cost $91,000 annually in order to be in compliance with just Sec. 404. Is it really worth it? *Cheap in Charleston*

Dear Cheap: Try looking at it from another angle. Cost of compliance: $91,000. Not being a convicted felon: Priceless. (Costs Articles)

✔ Dear Ms. Sarbox: How will I know if my company practices are ethical? *Clueless in Cleveland*

Dear Clueless: Have you tried changing the batteries twice a year in your ethics detector? (Ethics Articles)

✔ Dear Ms. Sarbox: There is so much advice from vendors about how to prepare. Are they just after my money? *Distrustful in Detroit*

Dear Distrustful: I'm sure they like you for your personality, too. (Press Releases from Vendors)

✔ Dear Ms. Sarbox: The janitor told me that shredders are now illegal. Is this true? *Gullible in Greensboro*

Dear Gullible: Is your janitor a former Arthur Andersen partner? Shredding is now a tricky process, and proper data retention is imperative. (Record Retention Articles)

✔ Dear Ms. Sarbox: I'm having trouble getting my software up. Will this keep me from satisfying Sarbanes-Oxley? *Helpless in Houston*

[Ms. Sarbox to Editor: Are you sure these are all real letters?] (Tools Articles)

✔ Dear Ms. Sarbox: What if I have a small or private company? How does this affect me? *Ignorant in Iowa*

Dear Ignorant: Are you small or private or both? Be honest, we won't judge. (Small/Private/Nonprofit Company Articles)

✔ Dear Ms. Sarbox: Do I need a big tool in order to comply with Sec. 404? *Worried in Wisconsin*

Dear Worried: Why are you readers always worried about the size of your tools? If you know how to use the tool you have, you might not need anything else. (Governance Articles)

✔ Dear Ms. Sarbox: What about the Children? *Concerned in Columbia*

Dear Concerned: If you'd like them to serve as financial experts on Audit Committees, you can sign them up with the Financial Expert Registry at www.fei.org.

Link to the AICPA Web Site

The American Institute of Certified Public Accountants (AICPA) has been a very good sport about sharing its oversight authority with the PCAOB, and it has handled the shift from self-regulation of the accounting profession rather graciously. (See Chapter 7.) The organization has magnanimously added a page to its site, aggregating useful links and resources related to SOX as it pertains to the accounting profession. Visit `http://thecaq.aicpa.org/Resources/Sarbanes+Oxley` for this information.

Frequent the Forum

The Sarbanes-Oxley Act forum at `www.sarbanes-oxley-forum.com` is "an interactive community portal designed to facilitate the exchange of information" about SOX. It has a FAQ section and "fully functional online forum" for visitors to share SOX experiences.

Click On the COSO Web Site

COSO, or the Committee of Sponsoring Organizations of the Treadway Commission, is a voluntary organization that has developed the only set of internal control standards recognized by the SEC (as discussed in Chapter 14). At the COSO Web site, `www.coso.org`, you can download a free set of COSO standards and other resources to help you interpret them.

Find the FEI Web Site

Financial Executives International (FEI) is an organization made up of 15,000 peers — CFOs, vice presidents of finance, treasurers, controllers, tax executives, academics, and audit committee members. Its Web site is located at `www.financialexecutives.org` and contains a copy of the current issue of the organization's magazine, *Financial Executive,* which is heavily loaded with SOX articles.

Spring for a Subscription to Compliance Week

If you're pulling down a six-figure salary in a job that depends on you being smart about SOX, you should invest in a subscription to *Compliance Week*. It's the kind of publication that gives you status just by having a copy on your desk.

For a few thousand dollars a year, your company gets:

- A weekly newsletter written by SOX-perts such as former SEC Chairman Harvey Pitt

- Access to a companion Web site that contains sample documents, databases, and resources

- A glossy print magazine with pictures of all your favorite SOX stars and articles on all sorts of topics, such as reducing compliance costs, cutting-edge governance strategies, perspectives on new rulings, and gossip about turnover and policy changes at the PCAOB and SEC

The publishers of *Compliance Week* boast that the magazine and Web site have more than 4,000 corporate subscribers and are "widely recognized as a critical tool for senior corporate executives to carry out their duties in this heavily regulated business environment."

The single-user price for *Compliance Week* is $999. Firm-wide subscriptions for an unlimited number of users at one company cost $2,999. (It may seem pricey, but it's much cheaper than defending an indictment or weathering an SEC investigation.)

For more information and to get a 30-day trial subscription, visit www. complianceweek.com.

Don't Forget Wikipedia!

For an overview of the evolving impact of SOX legislation, nothing beats Wikipedia (www.wikipedia.com). Wikipedia is a constantly evolving online encyclopedia that's collaboratively written by millions of online readers.

(However, these folks may or may not be experts on a certain topic, so you have to be sure to cross-check your info.) Because Wikipedia is constantly being updated, it's a good place to start examining SOX and all of its many layers.

As the Web site explains, Wikipedia is an ongoing source of information. Changes are made constantly by different users, and these changes are recorded in article histories. Inappropriate changes are omitted when necessary, and if a user continues to make inappropriate changes, he or she can be blocked from editing Wikipedia entries.

Part VII
Appendixes

"Hi, I'm Bob Darrel. I'm here to perform the audit of your books. Don't mind the vultures, they follow me everywhere."

In this part . . .

In the appendixes, I provide sample certifications, a sample audit committee charter, and much more to illustrate real-life applications of SOX and its requirements.

Appendix A

Selected Sections, Auditing Standard No. 5

• •

*T*his appendix contains important information you need to know from Auditing Standard No. 5. The following text is from the *Public Company Accounting Oversight Board Bylaws and Rules – Standards – AS5*, June 12, 2007.

Introduction

1. This standard establishes requirements and provides direction that applies when an auditor is engaged to perform an audit of management's assessment of the effectiveness of internal control over financial reporting ("the audit of internal control over financial reporting") that is integrated with an audit of the financial statements.

2. Effective internal control over financial reporting provides reasonable assurance regarding the reliability of financial reporting and the preparation of financial statements for external purposes. If one or more material weaknesses exist, the company's internal control over financial reporting cannot be considered effective.

3. The auditor's objective in an audit of internal control over financial reporting is to express an opinion on the effectiveness of the company's internal control over financial reporting. Because a company's internal control cannot be considered effective if one or more material weaknesses exist, to form a basis for expressing an opinion, the auditor must plan and perform the audit to obtain competent evidence that is sufficient to obtain reasonable assurance about whether material weaknesses exist as of the date specified in management's assessment. A material weakness in internal control over financial reporting may exist even when financial statements are not materially misstated.

4. The general standards are applicable to an audit of internal control over financial reporting. Those standards require technical training and proficiency as an auditor, independence, and the exercise of due professional care, including professional skepticism. This standard establishes the fieldwork and reporting standards applicable to an audit of internal control over financial reporting.

5. The auditor should use the same suitable, recognized control framework to perform his or her audit of internal control over financial reporting as management uses for its annual evaluation of the effectiveness of the company's internal control over financial reporting.

Integrating the Audits

6. The audit of internal control over financial reporting should be integrated with the audit of the financial statements. The objectives of the audits are not identical, however, and the auditor must plan and perform the work to achieve the objectives of both audits.

7. In an integrated audit of internal control over financial reporting and the financial statements, the auditor should design his or her testing of controls to accomplish the objectives of both audits simultaneously –

   • To obtain sufficient evidence to support the auditor's opinion on internal control over financial reporting as of year-end, and

   • To obtain sufficient evidence to support the auditor's control risk assessments for purposes of the audit of financial statements.

8. Obtaining sufficient evidence to support control risk assessments of low for purposes of the financial statement audit ordinarily allows the auditor to reduce the amount of audit work that otherwise would have been necessary to opine on the financial statements.

   Note: In some circumstances, particularly in some audits of smaller and less complex companies, the auditor might choose not to assess control risk as low for purposes of the audit of the financial statements. In such circumstances, the auditor's tests of the operating effectiveness of controls would be performed principally for the purpose of supporting his or her opinion on whether the company's internal control over financial reporting is effective as of year-end. The results of the auditor's financial statement auditing procedures also should inform his or her assessments in determining the testing necessary to conclude on the effectiveness of a control.

Role of Risk Assessment

Risk assessment underlies the entire audit process described by this standard, including the determination of significant accounts and disclosures and relevant assertions, the selection of controls to test, and the determination of the evidence necessary for a given control.

Scaling the Audit

The size and complexity of the company, its business processes, and business units, may affect the way in which the company achieves many of its control objectives. The size and complexity of the company also might affect the risks of misstatement and the controls necessary to address those risks. Scaling is most effective as a natural extension of the risk-based approach and applicable to the audits of all companies. Accordingly, a smaller, less complex company, or even a larger, less complex company might achieve its control objectives differently than a more complex company.

Addressing the Risk of Fraud

✔ When planning and performing the audit of internal control over financial reporting, the auditor should take into account the results of his or her fraud risk assessment. As part of identifying and testing entity-level control, as discussed beginning at paragraph 22, and selecting other controls to test, as discussed beginning at paragraph 39, the auditor should evaluate whether the company's control sufficiently address identified risks of material misstatement due to fraud and controls intended to address the risk of management override of other controls. Controls that might address these risks include –

  • Controls over significant, unusual transactions, particularly those that result in late or unusual journal entries;

  • Controls over journal entries and adjustments made in the period-end-financial reporting process;

  • Controls over related party transactions;

  • Controls related to significant management estimates; and

  • Controls that mitigate incentives for, and pressures on, management to falsify or inappropriately manage financial results.

✔ If the auditor identifies deficiencies in controls designed to prevent or detect fraud during the audit of internal control over financial reporting, the auditor should take into account those deficiencies when developing his or her response to risks of material misstatement during the financial statement audit, as provided in AU sec. 316.44 and .45.

Using the Work of Others

The auditor should evaluate the extent to which he or she will use the work of others to reduce the work the auditor might otherwise perform himself or herself. AU sec. 322, The Auditor's Consideration of the Internal Audit Function in an Audit of Financial Statements, applies in an integrated audit of the financial statements and internal control over financial reporting.

Using a Top-Down Approach

The auditor should use a top-down approach to the audit of internal control over financial reporting to select the controls to test. A top-down approach begins at the financial statement level and with the auditor's understanding of the overall risks to internal control over financial reporting. The auditor then focuses on entity-level controls and works down to significant accounts and disclosures and their relevant assertions. This approach directs the auditor's attention to accounts, disclosures, and assertions that present a reasonable possibility of material misstatement to the financial statements and related disclosures. The auditor then verifies his or her understanding of the risks in the company's processes and selects for testing those controls that sufficiently address the assessed risk of misstatement to each relevant assertion.

Note: The top-down approach describes the auditor's sequential thought process in identifying risks and the controls to test, not necessarily the order in which the auditor will perform the auditing procedures.

Appendix B

Sample Certifications

• •

SOX Sections 302 and 906 require Chief Executive Officers and Chief Financial Officers to certify the accuracy of their company's financial statements in filings and periodic reports to the Securities and Exchange Commission (SEC). A misleading or inaccurate Section 302 certification may result in civil penalties, and criminal penalties may attach for failure to execute an accurate Section 906 certification (discussed in Chapter 9). The substance of both certifications is somewhat redundant, and experts have questioned whether the requirement of separate certifications was an error.

SOX doesn't require Chief Information Officers and other management to sign Section 302 and 906 certifications, but it's the practice of many companies to require them to sign employee subcertifications. A sample form for an employee subcertification is included at the end of this appendix.

If your company's auditor believes that modifications are necessary to make these certifications accurate, you must include an explanation describing the reasons that the auditor believes management's disclosures should be modified.

Sample General Section 302 Certification

I, [identify the certifying individual], certify that:

1. I have reviewed this [specify report] of [identify registrant];

2. Based on my knowledge, this report does not contain any untrue statement of a material fact or omit to state a material fact necessary to make the statements made, in light of the circumstances under which such statements were made, not misleading with respect to the period covered by this report;

3. Based on my knowledge, the financial statements, and other financial information included in this report, fairly present in all material respects the financial condition, results of operations and cash flows of the registrant as of, and for, the periods presented in this report;

4. The registrant's other certifying officer(s) and I are responsible for establishing and maintaining disclosure controls and procedures (as defined in Exchange Act Rules 13a-15(e) and 15d-15(e)) and internal control over financial reporting (as defined in Exchange Act Rules 13a-15(f) and 15d-15(f)) for the registrant and have:

   (a) Designed such disclosure controls and procedures, or caused such disclosure controls and procedures to be designed under our supervision, to ensure that material information relating to the registrant, including its consolidated subsidiaries, is made known to us by others within those entities, particularly during the period in which this report is being prepared;

   (b) Designed such internal control over financial reporting, or caused such internal control over financial reporting to be designed under our supervision, to provide reasonable assurance regarding the reliability of financial reporting and the preparation of financial statements for external purposes in accordance with Generally Accepted Accounting Principles;

   (c) Evaluated the effectiveness of the registrant's disclosure controls and procedures and presented in this report our conclusions about the effectiveness of the disclosure controls and procedures, as of the end of the period covered by this report based on such evaluation; and

   (d) Disclosed in this report any change in the registrant's internal control over financial reporting that occurred during the registrant's most recent fiscal quarter (the registrant's fourth fiscal quarter in the case of an annual report) that has materially affected, or is reasonably likely to materially affect, the registrant's internal control over financial reporting; and

5. The registrant's other certifying officer(s) and I have disclosed, based on our most recent evaluation of internal control over financial reporting, to the registrant's auditors and the audit committee of the registrant's board of directors (or persons performing the equivalent functions):

   (a) All significant deficiencies and material weaknesses in the design or operation of internal control over financial reporting which are reasonably likely to adversely affect the registrant's ability to record, process, summarize and report financial information; and

   (b) Any fraud, whether or not material, that involves management or other employees who have a significant role in the registrant's internal control over financial reporting.

Date: _____

Signature: _____

Title: _____

Sample Section 906 Certification

The undersigned officer of _____ (the "Company") hereby certifies [to my knowledge][1] that the Company's quarterly report on Form 10-Q for the quarterly period _____ [Modify Name of Report as Appropriate] (the "Report"), as filed with the Securities and Exchange Commission on the date hereof, fully complies with the requirements of Section 13(a) or 15(d), as applicable, of the Securities Exchange Act of 1934, as amended, and that the information contained in the Report fairly presents, in all material respects, the financial condition and results of operations of the Company. This certification is provided solely pursuant to 18 U.S.C. Section 1350, as adopted pursuant to Section 906 of the Sarbanes-Oxley Act of 2002 *[, and shall not be deemed to be a part of the Report or "filed" for any purpose whatsoever][2]*.

Date: _____

Signature: _____

Title: _____

The bracketed language should be used if the certification is delivered as separate correspondence.

Sample Subcertification of Employee

Certificate of Employee Regarding SEC Filings Of _____ Company ("the Company")

I am aware that in connection with _____ Company's (the "Company") quarterly report on Form 10-K for the year ended _____ (as the Chief Executive Officer and Chief Financial Officer of the Company) file certifications with the Securities and Exchange Commission (the "SEC"), as to the best of their knowledge, regarding the accuracy and completeness of the covered filing.

I understand that I have been asked to file this Certificate to help ensure that the Certifications that the Chief Executive Officer and Chief Financial Officer will file with the SEC are complete and accurate. A substantially final draft of the SEC filing accompanies this Certificate.

In executing this Certificate, I have considered information that I believe would be important to a reasonable investor, including (without limitation) significant business developments and trends, the Company's cash flow situation, capital resources, critical accounting policies, executive compensation and related party transactions.

I understand the Chief Executive Office and Chief Financial Office of the Company rely upon these statements, and I hereby certify, represent, and warrant to the Company the following:

1. I have read the portions of the accompanying draft SEC filing that relate directly to the scope of my employment responsibilities, and I am in a position to certify the information relevant to my employment responsibilities (the certified information). Based on my knowledge:

2. The certified information, as of the end of the period covered by such filing, does not contain any untrue statement of a material fact or omit to state a material fact necessary to make the statements accurate and not misleading.

3. The certified information fairly presents, in all material respects, the financial condition, results of operations and cash flows of the Company for the period covered by the accompanying draft filing.

4. Sales transactions have been fully documented and recorded in a manner sufficient to allow accurate representation of such sales in financial documents for the appropriate period.

5. All agreements relating to future periods have been fully documented and recorded in a manner sufficient to allow accurate representation in financial documents.

6. All costs related to production and inventory have been completely incorporated in financial documents.

7. No significant undisclosed expenses or liabilities exist for the covered filing period that have not been invoiced or otherwise communicated to the Finance department.

8. I am not aware of any deficiencies in the effectiveness of the Company's disclosure controls and procedures that could adversely affect the Company's ability to record, process, summarize, and report information required to be disclosed.

9. I am not aware of any significant deficiencies or material weaknesses in the design or operation of the Company's internal controls that could adversely affect the Company's ability to record, process, summarize and report financial data.

10. I am not aware of any fraud, whether or not material, that involves the Company's management or other employees who have a significant role in the company's internal controls.

11. I understand that the Chief Financial Officer and Chief Executive Officer will be filing their certifications with the SEC for the material contained in the attached draft filing. If, at any time before such filing date, if I become aware that this Certificate is incorrect for any reason, I will immediately notify the Chief Financial Office and Chief Executive Officer of the Company.

Dated this _____day of _____, 2007.

Signature: _____

Printed name: _____

Title: _____

Appendix C

Sample Audit Committee Charter

. . . .

*E*ndorsed by the Association of Public Pension Fund Auditors (APPFA)

The following Example Audit Committee Charter is reproduced with permission from the APPFA. Of course, no example charter encompasses all activities that might be appropriate to a particular audit committee, nor will all activities identified in an example charter be relevant to every committee. Accordingly, this example charter may be tailored to each committee's needs and governing rules. Moreover, as applicable laws, rules, and customs change, the audit committee charter should be updated.

This sample charter was developed for use in connection with public pension systems, but it's an excellent example to which you can refer in creating your company's own audit committee charter.

Audit Committee Charter

Purpose

The purpose of this "Example Audit Committee Charter" is to assist the Board of Directors in fulfilling its fiduciary oversight responsibilities for the:

1. Financial Reporting Process
2. System of Risk Management
3. System of Internal Control
4. Internal Audit Process
5. External Audit of the Financial Statements
6. Engagements with Other External Audit Firms

7. Organization's Processes for Monitoring Compliance with Laws and Regulations and the Ethics Policy, Code of Conduct and Fraud Policy

8. Special Investigations and Whistleblower Mechanism

9. Audit Committee Management and Reporting Responsibilities

Authority

The audit committee has authority to conduct or authorize investigations into any matters within its scope of responsibility. It is empowered to perform the following functions, which are numbered according to the purposes listed above:

(1) Financial Reporting Process

✔ Oversee the reporting of all financial information.

✔ Resolve any disagreements between management, the external auditor, and/or the internal auditor regarding financial reporting.

(2) System of Risk Management

✔ Provide the policy and framework for an effective system of risk management, and provide the mechanisms for periodic assessment of the system of risk management, including risks of the information systems, and risks of business relationships with significant vendors and consultants.

✔ Oversee all consultants and experts that make recommendations concerning the risk management structure and internal control structure.

(3) System of Internal Control

✔ Provide the policy and framework for an effective system of internal controls, and provide the mechanisms for periodic assessment of the system of internal controls, including information systems, and internal control over purchases from significant vendors and consultants.

✔ Ensure that contracts with external service providers contain appropriate record-keeping and audit language.

✔ Seek any information it requires from employees — all of whom are directed to cooperate with the committee's requests, or the requests of internal or external parties working for the audit committee. These parties include the internal auditors, all external auditors, consultants, investigators, and any other specialists working for the audit committee.

(4) Internal Audit Process

✔ Appoint, compensate, and oversee the work of the Chief Audit Executive and oversee the work of the internal audit unit.

✔ Serve as the primary liaison and provide the appropriate forum for handling all matters related to audits, examinations, investigations, or inquiries of the State Auditor and other appropriate State or Federal agencies.

(5) External Audit of the Financial Statements

✔ Appoint, compensate, and oversee the work of the certified public accounting firm employed by the organization to audit the financial statements.

✔ Pre-approve all auditing, other attest and non-audit services performed by the external financial statement audit firm.

(6) Engagements with Other External Audit Firms

✔ Appoint, compensate, and oversee the work of any other certified public accounting firm employed by the organization to perform any audits or agreed-upon-procedures other than the audit of the financial statements.

(7) Organization's Processes for Monitoring Compliance with Laws and Regulations and the Ethics Policy, Code of Conduct and Fraud Policy

✔ Provide the policy and framework for compliance with laws and regulations, and provide the mechanisms for periodic assessment of compliance, including compliance by significant vendors and consultants.

✔ Communicate with the Board regarding the organization's policy on ethics, code of conduct and fraud policy as it relates to internal control, financial reporting, and all auditing activities.

(8) Special Investigations and Whistleblower Mechanism

✔ Retain independent counsel, accountants, or other specialists to advise the committee or assist in the conduct of an investigation.

✔ Ensure creation of and maintenance of an appropriate whistleblower mechanism for reporting of financial statement fraud and other fraud and inappropriate activities.

(9) Audit Committee Management and Reporting Responsibilities

✔ Receive and review reports on all public disclosures related to the purpose, authority, and responsibilities of the Audit Committee. Consider having a Disclosure Subcommittee for this purpose.

✔ Report to the Board on the activities, findings, and recommendations of the Audit Committee.

(1 – 9) Comprehensive Communication Responsibility

Meet with the organization's officers, external auditors, internal auditors, outside counsel and/or specialists, as necessary.

Composition

The audit committee will consist of at least three and no more than seven members of the Board of Directors. The Board or its nominating committee will appoint committee members and the committee chair.

Each committee member will be both independent and financially literate. At least one member shall be designated as the "financial expert," as defined by applicable legislation and regulation.

Meetings

The committee will meet at least four times a year, with authority to convene additional meetings, as circumstances require. All committee members are expected to attend each meeting, in person or via tele- or video-conference. Meeting notices will be provided to interested parties in conformance with applicable laws, regulations, customs, and practices. The committee will invite members of management, external auditors, internal auditors and/or others to attend meetings and provide pertinent information, as necessary. It will hold private meetings with auditors {Subject to open meeting laws} and executive sessions as provided by law. Meeting agendas will be prepared and provided in advance to members, along with appropriate briefing materials. Minutes will be prepared.

Responsibilities

The committee will carry out the following responsibilities:

(1) Financial Reporting Process

- ✔ Obtain information and training to enhance the committee members' expertise in financial reporting standards and processes so that the committee may adequately oversee financial reporting.

- ✔ Review significant accounting and reporting issues, including complex or unusual transactions and highly judgmental areas, and recent professional and regulatory pronouncements, and understand their impact on the financial statements.

- ✔ Review with management, the external auditors, and the internal auditors the results of the audit, including any difficulties encountered.

- ✔ Review all significant adjustments proposed by the external financial statement auditor and by the internal auditor.

✔ Review all significant suggestions for improved financial reporting made by the external financial statement auditor and by the internal auditor.

✔ Review with the General Counsel the status of legal matters that may have an effect on the financial statements.

✔ Review the annual financial statements, and consider whether they are complete, consistent with information known to committee members, and reflect appropriate accounting principles.

✔ Review other sections of the annual report and related regulatory filings before release and consider the accuracy and completeness of the information.

✔ Review with management and the external auditors all matters required to be communicated to the committee under Generally Accepted Auditing Standards.

✔ Understand how management develops interim financial information, and the nature and extent of internal and external auditor involvement.

✔ Review interim financial reports with management and the external auditors before filing with regulators, and consider whether they are complete and consistent with the information known to committee members.

✔ Review the statement of management responsibility for and the assessment of the effectiveness of the internal control structure and procedures of the organization for financial reporting. Review the attestation on this management assertion by the financial statement auditor as part of the financial statement audit engagement.

(2) System of Risk Management

✔ Obtain information about, training in and an understanding of risk management in order to acquire the knowledge necessary to adequately oversee the risk management process.

✔ Ensure that the organization has a comprehensive policy on risk management.

✔ Consider the effectiveness of the organization's risk management system, including risks of information technology systems.

✔ Consider the risks of business relationships with significant vendors and consultants.

✔ Reviews management's reports on management's self-assessment of risks and the mitigations of these risks.

✔ Understand the scope of internal auditor's and external auditor's review of risk management over financial reporting.

✔ Understand the scope of internal auditor's review of risk management over all other processes, and obtain reports on significant findings and recommendations, together with management's responses.

✔ Understand the scope of any other external auditor's or consultant's review of risk management.

✔ Hire outside experts and consultants in risk management as necessary.

(3) System of Internal Control

✔ Obtain information about, training in, and an understanding of internal control in order to acquire the knowledge necessary to adequately oversee the internal control process.

✔ Ensure that the organization has a comprehensive policy on internal control and compliance.

✔ Review periodically the policy on ethics, code of conduct, and fraud policy.

✔ Consider the effectiveness of the organization's internal control system, including information technology security and control.

✔ Consider any internal controls required because of business relationships with significant vendors and consultants.

✔ Understand the scope of internal auditor's and external auditor's review of internal control over financial reporting, and obtain reports on significant findings and recommendations, together with management's responses.

✔ Understand the scope of internal auditor's review of internal control over all other processes, and obtain reports on significant findings and recommendations, together with management's responses.

✔ Review the role of the internal auditor's involvement in the corporate governance process, including corporate governance documentation and training.

✔ Ensure that contracts with external service providers contain appropriate record-keeping and audit language.

✔ Direct employees to cooperate with the committee's requests, or the requests of internal or external parties working for the audit committee. These parties include the internal auditors, all external auditors, consultants, investigators, and any other specialists working for the audit committee.

(4) Internal Audit Process

✔ Obtain the information and training needed to enhance the committee members' understanding of the role of internal audits so that the committee may adequately oversee the internal audit function.

✔ Oversee the selection process for the chief audit executive.

✔ Assure and maintain, through the organizational structure of the organization and by other means, the independence of the internal audit process.

✔ Ensure that internal auditors have access to all documents, information, and systems in the organization.

✔ Ensure there are no unjustified restrictions or limitations placed on the Chief Audit Executive and internal audit staff.

✔ Review with management and the Chief Audit Executive the charter, objectives, plans, activities, staffing, budget, qualifications, and organizational structure of the internal audit function.

✔ Receive and review all internal audit reports and management letters.

✔ Review the responsiveness and timeliness of management's follow-up activities pertaining to any reported findings and recommendations.

✔ Receive periodic notices of advisory and consulting activities by internal auditors.

✔ Review and concur in the appointment, replacement, or dismissal of the Chief Audit Executive, if allowed by state law.

✔ Review the performance of the Chief Audit Executive periodically.

✔ Review the effectiveness of the internal audit function, including compliance with The Institute of Internal Auditors' *Standards for the Professional Practice of Internal Auditing.*

✔ On a regular basis, meet separately with the Chief Audit Executive to discuss any matters that the committee or internal audit believes should be discussed privately {Subject to open meeting laws}.

✔ Delegate to the Chief Audit Executive the management of the contract for the external financial statement auditor, and the management of the contracts for any other certified public accountants.

✔ Designate the Chief Audit Executive as the primary point of contact for handling all matters related to audits, examinations, investigations, or inquiries of the State Auditor and other appropriate State or Federal agencies.

(5) External Audit of the Financial Statements

✔ Obtain the information and training needed to enhance the committee members' understanding of the purpose of the financial statements audit and the role of external financial statement auditor so that the committee may adequately oversee the financial statement audit function.

✔ Review the external auditor's proposed audit scope and approach, including coordination of audit effort with internal audit.

✔ Review the performance of the external financial statement audit firm, and exercise final approval on the request for proposal for, and the appointment, retention or discharge of the audit firm. Obtain input from the Chief Audit Executive, management, and other parties as appropriate.

✔ Define the services that the external financial statement auditor is allowed to perform and the services that are prohibited.

✔ Pre-approve all services to be performed by the external financial statement auditor.

✔ Review the independence of the external financial statement audit firm by obtaining statements from the auditors on relationships between the audit firm and the organization, including any non-audit services, and discussing these relationships with the audit firm. Obtain from management a listing of all services provided by the external audit firm. Obtain information from the Chief Audit Executive and other sources as necessary.

✔ Review and approve the audited financial statements, associated management letter, attestation on the effectiveness of the internal control structure, and procedures for financial reporting, other required auditor communications, and all other auditor reports and communications relating to the financial statements.

✔ Review and approve all other reports and communications made by the external financial statement auditor.

✔ Review the responsiveness and timeliness of management's follow-up activities pertaining to any reported findings and recommendations.

✔ On a regular basis, meet separately with the external financial statement audit firm to discuss any matters that the committee or auditors believe should be discussed privately {Subject to open meeting laws}.

✔ Provide guidelines and mechanisms so that no member of the audit committee or organization staff shall improperly influence the auditors or the firm engaged to perform audit services.

✔ Ensure production of a report of all costs of and payments to the external financial statement auditor. The listing should separately disclose the costs of the financial statement audit, other attest projects, agreed-upon-procedures, and any non-audit services provided.

(6) Engagements with Other External Audit Firms

✔ Obtain the information and training needed to enhance the committee members' understanding of the role of the other external audit firm(s) so that the committee may adequately oversee their function(s).

✔ Review the other external audit firm's (firms') proposed audit or agreed-upon-procedures scope and approach, including coordination of effort with internal audit.

✔ Review the performance of the other external audit firm(s), and exercise final approval on the request for proposal for, and the appointment, retention, or discharge of these audit firm(s).

✔ Pre-approve the scope of all services to be performed by the other external auditor.

✔ Review the independence of the other external audit firm(s) by obtaining statements from the audit firm(s) on relationships between these audit firm(s) and the organization, including any non-audit or non-attest services, and discussing the relationships with the audit firm(s). Obtain from management a listing of all services provided by the other external audit firm(s). Obtain information from the Chief Audit Executive and other sources as necessary.

✔ Review and approve the reports of the audits and/or agreed-upon-procedures.

✔ Provide a forum for follow up of findings from the audit reports or agreed-upon-procedures.

✔ Meet separately with the other external audit firm(s) on a regular basis to discuss any matters that the committee or staff of the audit firm(s) believes should be discussed privately {Subject to open meeting laws}.

✔ Ensure production of a report of all costs of and payments to other external audit firm(s). The listing should separately disclose the costs of any audit, other attest projects, agreed-upon-procedures, and any non-audit services provided.

(7) Organization's Processes for Monitoring Compliance

✔ Review the effectiveness of the system for monitoring compliance with laws and regulations and the results of management's investigation and follow-up (including disciplinary action) of any instances of noncompliance.

✔ Review the findings of any examinations by regulatory agencies, and any auditor observations, including investigations of misconduct and fraud.

✔ Review the process for communicating to all affected parties the ethics policy, code of conduct and fraud policy to organization personnel, and for monitoring compliance therewith.

✔ Obtain regular updates from management and organization legal counsel regarding compliance matters.

✔ Monitor changes and proposed changes in laws, regulations, and rules affecting the organization.

(8) Special Investigations and Whistleblower Mechanism

✔ Institute and oversee special investigations as needed.

✔ Provide an appropriate confidential mechanism for whistleblowers to provide information on potentially fraudulent financial reporting or breaches of internal control to the audit committee.

(9) Audit Committee Management and Reporting Responsibilities

✔ Regularly report to the Board of Directors about all committee activities, issues, and related recommendations.

✔ Perform other activities related to this charter as requested by the Board of Directors, and report to the Board.

✔ Provide an open avenue of communication between internal audit, the external financial statement auditors, other external auditors, management, and the Board of Directors.

✔ Review any other reports that the organization issues that relate to audit committee responsibilities.

✔ Confirm annually that all responsibilities outlined in this charter have been carried out. Report annually to the Board, members, retirees, and beneficiaries, describing the committee's composition, responsibilities, and how they were discharged, and any other information required by rule, including approval of non-audit services.

✔ Evaluate the committee's and individual member's performance on a regular basis, and report to the Board.

✔ Review and assess the adequacy of the committee charter annually, requesting Board approval for proposed changes, and ensure appropriate disclosure as may be required by law or regulation.

Appendix D

Sample Code of Ethics

One Sarbanes-Oxley innovation is the requirement that companies adopt a written code of ethics to help managements, boards, and rank-and-file employees from rationalizing themselves over the line when ethical dilemmas arise and tough choices must be made. Here is a sample code adopted by the company that publishes this book, Wiley Publishing, Inc.

Business Conduct and Ethics Policy

Policy

It is the Company's policy to manage and operate worldwide business activities in conformity with applicable laws and high ethical standards. Both the Board of Directors and management are determined to comply fully with the law, and to maintain the Company's reputation for integrity and fairness in business dealings with others.

Scope

This policy applies to all employees, officers and directors at all Company locations.

Responsibility

All employees, officers and directors are expected to adhere to all ethical and legal standards as outlined in this policy and to preserve the Company's integrity and reputation.

Provisions

1. Financial Record-Keeping

It is the policy of the Company to fully and fairly disclose the financial condition of the Company in compliance with the applicable accounting principles, laws, rules and regulations and to make full, fair, accurate, timely and understandable disclosure in our periodic reports filed with the Securities and Exchange Commission ("SEC") and in other communications to securities analysts, rating agencies and investors. Honest and accurate recording and reporting of information is critical to our ability to make responsible business decisions. The Company's accounting records are relied upon to produce reports for the Company's management, rating agencies, investors, creditors, the SEC and other governmental agencies and others. Therefore, our financial statements and the books and records on which they are based must accurately reflect all corporate transactions and conform to all legal and accounting requirements. Our system of internal control is designed to provide this information.

All employees have a responsibility to ensure that the Company's accounting records do not contain any false or intentionally misleading entries. Information on which our accounting records are based is the responsibility of all employees.

We do not permit intentional misclassification of transactions as to accounts, departments or accounting periods. In particular we require that:

- all Company accounting records, as well as reports produced from those records, are kept and presented in accordance with the laws of each applicable jurisdiction;

- all records fairly and accurately reflect the transactions or occurrences to which they relate;

- all records fairly and accurately reflect in reasonable detail the Company's assets, liabilities, revenues and expenses;

- the Company's accounting records do not contain any intentionally false or misleading entries;

- no transactions are misclassified as to accounts, departments or accounting periods;

- all transactions are supported by accurate documentation in reasonable detail and recorded in the proper account and in the proper accounting period;

- all Company accounting financial reports be prepared in accordance with generally accepted accounting principles; and

- the Company's system of internal accounting controls, including compensation controls, to be followed at all times.

2. Improper Payments

No payment or transfer of Company funds or assets shall be made that is not authorized, properly accounted for and clearly identified on the Company's books. Payment or transfer of the Company's funds and assets are to be used only as specified in the supporting documents.

No employee, officer or director may authorize any payment or use any funds or assets for a bribe, "kickback," or similar payment that is directly or indirectly for the benefit of any individual (including any government official, agent or employee anywhere in the world), company or organization in the United States or any foreign country, and which is designed to secure favorable treatment for the Company. Under federal legislation it is a felony to make payments of this kind to foreign government officials.

3. Political Contributions

It is the Company's policy not to contribute any Company funds or assets to any political party, committee, organization, or candidate for any office (federal, state or local) in the United States or any foreign country. Employees may, on their own time, support individual candidates or political committees, all subject to applicable laws, and may make voluntary contributions to such candidates or committees, including any Company-related political action committee.

4. Acceptance of Payments

Employees, officers and directors may not seek or accept either directly or indirectly, any payments, fees, services, or other gratuities (irrespective of size or amount) outside the normal course of the employee's business duties from any other person, company or organization that does or seeks to do business with the Company. Gifts of cash or cash equivalents of any amount are strictly prohibited. The receipt of common courtesies, sales promotion items of nominal value, occasional meals, and reasonable entertainment appropriate to a business relationship and associated with business discussions are permissible.

5. Business Entertainment

All solicitations or dealings with suppliers, customers, or others doing or seeking to do business with the Company shall be conducted solely on a basis that reflects both the Company's best business interests and its high ethical standards. The Company does permit the providing of common courtesies, entertainment, and occasional meals for potential or actual suppliers, customers, or others involved with the Company's business, in a manner appropriate to the Company's relationship and associated with business discussions. Expenses in this connection must be reasonable, customary and properly authorized.

6. Conflicts of Interest

The Company expects all employees, officers and directors to exercise good judgment and the highest ethical standards in private activities outside the Company that in any way can affect the Company. They shall at all times exercise particular care that no detriment to the interest of the Company may result from a conflict between those interests and any personal or business interests which the individual may have. In particular, every employee, officer and director has an obligation to avoid any activity, agreement, business investment or interest or other situation that might, in fact or in appearance, cause an individual to place his or her own interest, or that of any other person or entity, above his or her obligation to the Company. The words "in appearance" should be noted particularly since the appearance of an action might tend to impair confidence even if the individual may not actually do anything wrong.

To this end, employees, officers and directors must avoid any investments, associations or other relationships that could conflict with the staff member's responsibility to make objective decisions in the Company's best interests. Any potential conflicts of interest must be reported immediately to the senior officer of the staff member's division or subsidiary, and the Company's General Counsel. In the case of an officer, conflicts of interest must be reported immediately to a senior officer or the Company's CEO as applicable, and its General Counsel. In the case of a director, conflicts should be reported to the Chairman of the Board, the CEO, and the Company's General Counsel.

7. Corporate Opportunities

No employee, officer or director of the Company shall for personal or any other person's or entity's gain deprive the Company of any business opportunity or benefit which could be construed as related to any existing or reasonably anticipated future activity of the Company. Employees, officers and directors who learn of any such opportunity through their association with the Company may not disclose it to a third party or invest in the opportunity without first offering it to the Company.

8. Confidentiality

All employees, officers and directors are responsible for safeguarding and keeping confidential any information that the Company considers to be of a confidential or sensitive nature. Such information includes, but is not limited to financial records and reports, marketing and strategic planning information, employee-related documents, unpublished manuscripts as well as information relating to potential mergers and acquisitions, stock splits and divestitures, and other materials that the Company would not want disclosed to a competitor or any unauthorized recipient, or that might be harmful to the Company or its customers if disclosed whether or not such information is marked "confidential." Confidential information also includes information concerning possible transactions with other companies or information about the Company's customers, suppliers or joint venture partners, which the Company is under an obligation to maintain as confidential. Employees, officers and directors may not use Confidential Information for their own personal benefit or the benefit of persons or entities outside the Company, and must exercise caution and discretion with respect to any appropriate temporary removal of confidential or sensitive information from the Company's premises, and should safeguard the information from unintended disclosure or loss. Employees must at all times adhere to the Company's policies regarding the transmission and storage of the Company's confidential and sensitive business records.

9. Compliance With Laws and Regulations

The Company requires its employees, officers and directors to comply with all applicable laws and regulations in countries where the Company does business. Violation of domestic or foreign laws and regulations may subject an individual, as well as the Company, to civil and/or criminal penalties. Employees have an obligation to comply with all laws and regulations and policies and procedures and to promptly alert management of any deviation from them.

(a) Antitrust Laws

It is the Company's policy to comply with the letter and spirit of all applicable antitrust laws. If the legality of any contemplated transaction, agreement or arrangement is in doubt, employees, officers and directors must consult with a Company staff attorney.

Discussions with competitors regarding the Company's prices, credit terms, terms and conditions of sale, strategies or other confidential, sensitive or proprietary information are not permissible. This applies both to individual discussions and to participation in trade and professional associations and other business organizations. If a competitor initiates such a discussion, the staff member should refuse to participate or request that counsel be contacted. Staff members should seek guidance from a Company staff attorney when appropriate.

(b) Insider Trading

No employee, officer or director may trade in securities while in possession of material inside information or disclose material inside information to third parties ("tipping"). Material inside information is any information that has not reached the general marketplace through a press release, earnings release or otherwise, and is likely to be considered important by investors deciding whether to trade (e.g., earnings estimates, significant business investments, mergers, acquisitions, dispositions and other developments, expansion or curtailment of operations, and other activity of significance). Using material inside information for trading, or tipping others to trade, is both unethical and illegal. Accordingly, no employee, officer or director of the Company may: (a) trade securities of the Company or any other company while in possession of material inside information with respect to that company; (b) recommend or suggest that anyone else buy, sell, or hold securities of any company while the employee is in possession of material inside information with respect to that company (this includes formal or informal advice given to family, household members and friends); and (c) disclose material inside information to anyone, other than those persons who need to know such information in order for the Company to properly and effectively carry out its business (e.g., to lawyers, advisers and other Company employees working on the matter). Of course, where material inside information is permitted to be disclosed, the recipient should be advised of its non-public nature and the limitations on its use. Any questions as to whether information is material or non-public should be directed to the Company's General Counsel.

10. Fair Dealing

Each employee, officer and director should endeavor to deal fairly with the Company's suppliers, competitors and employees. No one should take unfair advantage of another through manipulation, concealment, abuse of privileged information, misrepresentation of material facts, or any other unfair-dealing practice. Information about the Company's competitors must be used in an ethical manner and in compliance with the law. Under no circumstance should information be obtained through theft, illegal entry, blackmail, or electronic eavesdropping, or through employees misrepresenting their affiliation with the Company or their identity. Any proprietary or non-public information about the Company's competitors should not be used if it is suspected that such information has been obtained improperly.

11. Employment of Relatives

The Company's policy is to require advance approval before a relative of an employee is hired by the Company, or is engaged as a consultant or independent contractor of the Company, if the relative of the employee will be in the same department or chain of command of the Wiley employee. Such approval should be sought from the requisite member of the Wiley Leadership Team (for US locations) or the Managing Director (international locations) and the most senior Human Resources officer at the location. A relative of the Wiley Leadership Team and the Managing Directors of international locations may only be hired or engaged with the advance review and approval of both the CEO of the Company and the Senior Vice President–Human Resources. A "relative" may include a member of the employee's family (spouse, child, parent, sibling, in-law) but may also include, for purposes of this Policy, any individual who is living with or otherwise in a significant relationship with the employee, or a relative of such an individual.

12. Duty to Report Violations

Each employee, officer and director is responsible for promptly reporting to the Company any circumstances that such person believes in good faith may constitute a violation of this policy. Except as provided in the next paragraph, suspected policy violations are to be reported (including confidential and anonymous reports) to the Company's General Counsel and its Chief Audit Executive.

Any complaint regarding accounting, internal accounting controls or auditing matters must be reported (including confidential and anonymous complaints) to the Company's General Counsel and its Vice President, Internal Audit, who will be responsible for reporting as appropriate to the Chairman of the Company's Audit Committee Alternatively, complaints may be mailed directly to the Chairman of the Company's Audit Committee at P.O. Box 1569, Hoboken, NJ 07030-5774.

No retribution against any individual who reports violations of this Policy in good faith will be permitted. However, the reporting of a violation will not excuse the violation itself. The Company will investigate any matter which is reported and will take any appropriate corrective action.

13. Violations of Policy

Violations of any of the foregoing provisions may expose the Company and the individuals involved to lawsuits and possible criminal action. Staff members who violate this policy are subject to appropriate disciplinary action, up to and including termination. Any alleged violations of this Policy will be reviewed by the Company's legal department and other appropriate staff members.

Appendix E

Sample SAS 70 Report

*W*hat follows in this appendix is a sample SAS form used by a company called SAS70 Solutions. To view an online version of the form, you can visit the company's Web site, located at www.sas70solutions.com.

INDEPENDENT SERVICE AUDITOR'S REPORT

To [Service Organization]:

We have examined the accompanying description of the controls related to the [system name(s), application name(s), process name(s), service name(s), etc.] of [Service Organization]. Our examination included procedures to obtain reasonable assurance about whether (1) the accompanying description presents fairly, in all material respects, the aspects of [Service Organization]'s controls that may be relevant to a user organization's internal control as it relates to an audit of financial statements; (2) the controls included in the description were suitably designed to achieve the control objectives specified in the description, if those controls were complied with satisfactorily; [If the application of controls by user organizations is necessary to achieve the stated control objectives, insert the italicized prhase following the words "complied with satisfactorily" in the scope and opinion paragraph: - "and user organizations applied the controls contemplated in the design of [Service Organization]'s controls."] and (3) such controls had been placed in operation as of [last day of review period]. The control objectives were specified by the management of [Service Organization]. Our examination was performed in accordance with standards established by the American Institute of Certified Public Accountants and included those procedures we considered necessary in the circumstances to obtain a reasonable basis for rendering our opinion.

In our opinion, the accompanying description of the aforementioned [system(s), application(s), process(es), service(s), etc.] presents fairly, in all material respects, the relevant aspects of [Service Organization]'s controls that had been placed in operation as of [last date of review period]. Also, in our opinion, the controls, as described, are suitably designed to provide reasonable assurance that the specified control objectives would be achieved if the described controls were complied with satisfactorily. [If the application of controls by user organizations is necessary to achieve the stated control objectives, insert the italicized phase following the words "complied with satisfactorily" in the scope and opinion paragraph: - "and user organizations applied the controls contemplated in the design of [Service Organization]'s controls."].

In addition to the procedures we considered necessary to render our opinion as expressed in the previous paragraph, we applied tests to specific controls, which are presented in Section(s) [Section #'s] (the Matrices) of this report, to obtain evidence about their effectiveness in meeting the related control objectives described in the Matrices, during the period from [first day of review period] to [last day of review period]. The specific controls and the nature, timing, extent, and results of the tests are listed in the Matrices. This information has been provided to user organizations of [Service Organization] and to their auditors to be taken into consideration, along with information about the internal control at user organizations, when making assessments of control risk for user organizations. In our opinion, the controls that were tested, as described in the Matrices, were operating with sufficient effectiveness to provide reasonable, but not absolute, assurance that the control objectives specified in the Matrices were achieved during the period from [first day of review period] to [last day of review period]. [The following sentence should be added when all of the control objectives listed in the description of controls placed in operation are not covered by the tests of operating effectiveness. This sentence would be omitted when all of the control objectives listed in the description of controls placed in operation are included in the tests of operation effectiveness – "However, the scope of our engagement did not include tests to determine whether control objectives not listed in the Matrices were achieved; accordingly, we express no opinion on the achievement of control objectives not included in the Matrices."]

The relative effectiveness and significance of specific controls at [Service Organization] and their effect on assessments of control risk at user organizations are dependent on their interaction with the controls and other factors present at individual user organizations. We have performed no procedures to evaluate the effectiveness of controls at individual user organizations.

The description of controls at [Service Organization] is as of [last day of review period], and information about tests of the operating effectiveness of specific controls covers the period from [first day of review period] to [last day of review period]. Any projection of such information to the future is subject to the risk that, because of change, the description may no longer portray the controls in existence. The potential effectiveness of specific controls at [Service Organization] is subject to inherent limitations and, accordingly, errors or fraud may occur and not be detected. Furthermore, the projection of any conclusions, based on our findings, to future periods is subject to the risk that (1) changes made to the system or controls, (2) changes in processing requirements, (3) changes required because of the passage of time, or (4) the failure to make needed changes to the system or controls may alter the validity of such conclusions.

The information included in Section [Section #] of this report is presented by [Service Organization] to provide additional information to user organizations and is not a part of [Service Organization]'s description of controls placed in operation. The information in [Section #] has not been subjected to the procedures applied in the examination of the description of the controls related to [system name(s), application name(s), process name(s), service name(s), etc.], and accordingly, we express no opinion on it.

This report is intended solely for use by the management of [Service Organization], its user organizations, and the independent auditors of its user organizations.

Sas 70 Solutions

[last day of review period]

Index

and state laws, 113
  Web site, 302
public float, 87
public investors, 35
Public Oversight Board (POB), 107

• Q •

qualified opinion, 96, 189
quality control, 111, 112
questionnaires, 284

• R •

rank-and-file employees, 18
real-time disclosure, 58, 211–213
receivership, 58
reclamation, of bonuses, 38
reconciliations, to controls, 202
recordkeeping, 155, 177
registration(s)
  online viewing of, 61
  pending, 51
  requirements of, 10–11
regulation
  of accounting, 107
  of Certified Public Accountant, 97, 98
  self-regulation, 94–95
Regulation D, 47
Regulation S-K Item 406, 160
Regulation SX Rule 2-1(c) (4), 100, 298
Rehnquist, William, 259
report(s)
  annual, 77–79, 80, 286
  and audit committee, 282, 286
  auditor's, 270
  business description in, 80
  compensation in, 80
  competition in, 80
  drafting, 282
  Form 8-K, 56
  Form 10-K, 55, 80
  Form 10-Q, 55
  internal control report, 40, 225
  legal documents in, 80
  legal proceedings in, 80
  in not-for-profits, 270
  preparers of, 291
  provisions for, 39

review of, 291
  in SarbOxPro, 240, 245
  from small businesses, 84–85
  and SOX, 22–23
reporting
  amendments, 57
  articles, 57
  bylaws, 57
  disclosure, 57
  discussed, 54
  financial, 154–155
  internal control with, 154–155
  issues with, 282
  and management, 145, 290, 291
  PCAOB on, 112
  periodic, 47–48, 147
  in SarbOxPro, 245
  schedules for, 290
  Section 302 on, 147
  under Securities Exchange Act of 1934,
    47–48
  shareholder rights, 57
  significant sales, 57
  stock exchange, 57
research, on software, 233–234
resignation, of management, 29
resources, 301
  AICPA Web site, 304
  Candela Solutions Web site, 302
  Compliance Week, 305
  COSO Web site, 304
  FEI Web site, 304
  forums, 304
  Inside Sarbanes-Oxley Web site, 302
  magazine, 304, 305
  newsletter, 305
  PCAOB Web site, 302
  Sarbanes-Oxley Act forum, 304
  SEC Web site, 302
  SOX-online, 301–302
  Wikipedia, 305–306
responsibility, 26
restatements, 21, 57
retained earnings, 72
retirement plans, 165
revenue, 71
review
  documentation of, 88
  for financial control process, 88

BUSINESS, CAREERS & PERSONAL FINANCE

0-7645-9847-3

0-7645-2431-3

Also available:
- Business Plans Kit For Dummies
  0-7645-9794-9
- Economics For Dummies
  0-7645-5726-2
- Grant Writing For Dummies
  0-7645-8416-2
- Home Buying For Dummies
  0-7645-5331-3
- Managing For Dummies
  0-7645-1771-6
- Marketing For Dummies
  0-7645-5600-2

- Personal Finance For Dummies
  0-7645-2590-5*
- Resumes For Dummies
  0-7645-5471-9
- Selling For Dummies
  0-7645-5363-1
- Six Sigma For Dummies
  0-7645-6798-5
- Small Business Kit For Dummies
  0-7645-5984-2
- Starting an eBay Business For Dummies
  0-7645-6924-4
- Your Dream Career For Dummies
  0-7645-9795-7

HOME & BUSINESS COMPUTER BASICS

0-470-05432-8

0-471-75421-8

Also available:
- Cleaning Windows Vista For Dummies
  0-471-78293-9
- Excel 2007 For Dummies
  0-470-03737-7
- Mac OS X Tiger For Dummies
  0-7645-7675-5
- MacBook For Dummies
  0-470-04859-X
- Macs For Dummies
  0-470-04849-2
- Office 2007 For Dummies
  0-470-00923-3

- Outlook 2007 For Dummies
  0-470-03830-6
- PCs For Dummies
  0-7645-8958-X
- Salesforce.com For Dummies
  0-470-04893-X
- Upgrading & Fixing Laptops For Dummies
  0-7645-8959-8
- Word 2007 For Dummies
  0-470-03658-3
- Quicken 2007 For Dummies
  0-470-04600-7

FOOD, HOME, GARDEN, HOBBIES, MUSIC & PETS

0-7645-8404-9

0-7645-9904-6

Also available:
- Candy Making For Dummies
  0-7645-9734-5
- Card Games For Dummies
  0-7645-9910-0
- Crocheting For Dummies
  0-7645-4151-X
- Dog Training For Dummies
  0-7645-8418-9
- Healthy Carb Cookbook For Dummies
  0-7645-8476-6
- Home Maintenance For Dummies
  0-7645-5215-5

- Horses For Dummies
  0-7645-9797-3
- Jewelry Making & Beading For Dummies
  0-7645-2571-9
- Orchids For Dummies
  0-7645-6759-4
- Puppies For Dummies
  0-7645-5255-4
- Rock Guitar For Dummies
  0-7645-5356-9
- Sewing For Dummies
  0-7645-6847-7
- Singing For Dummies
  0-7645-2475-5

INTERNET & DIGITAL MEDIA

0-470-04529-9

0-470-04894-8

Also available:
- Blogging For Dummies
  0-471-77084-1
- Digital Photography For Dummies
  0-7645-9802-3
- Digital Photography All-in-One Desk Reference For Dummies
  0-470-03743-1
- Digital SLR Cameras and Photography For Dummies
  0-7645-9803-1
- eBay Business All-in-One Desk Reference For Dummies
  0-7645-8438-3
- HDTV For Dummies
  0-470-09673-X

- Home Entertainment PCs For Dummies
  0-470-05523-5
- MySpace For Dummies
  0-470-09529-6
- Search Engine Optimization For Dummies
  0-471-97998-8
- Skype For Dummies
  0-470-04891-3
- The Internet For Dummies
  0-7645-8996-2
- Wiring Your Digital Home For Dummies
  0-471-91830-X

* Separate Canadian edition also available
† Separate U.K. edition also available

SPORTS, FITNESS, PARENTING, RELIGION & SPIRITUALITY

0-471-76871-5

0-7645-7841-3

Also available:
- Catholicism For Dummies
  0-7645-5391-7
- Exercise Balls For Dummies
  0-7645-5623-1
- Fitness For Dummies
  0-7645-7851-0
- Football For Dummies
  0-7645-3936-1
- Judaism For Dummies
  0-7645-5299-6
- Potty Training For Dummies
  0-7645-5417-4
- Buddhism For Dummies
  0-7645-5359-3

- Pregnancy For Dummies
  0-7645-4483-7 †
- Ten Minute Tone-Ups For Dummies
  0-7645-7207-5
- NASCAR For Dummies
  0-7645-7681-X
- Religion For Dummies
  0-7645-5264-3
- Soccer For Dummies
  0-7645-5229-5
- Women in the Bible For Dummies
  0-7645-8475-8

TRAVEL

0-7645-7749-2

0-7645-6945-7

Also available:
- Alaska For Dummies
  0-7645-7746-8
- Cruise Vacations For Dummies
  0-7645-6941-4
- England For Dummies
  0-7645-4276-1
- Europe For Dummies
  0-7645-7529-5
- Germany For Dummies
  0-7645-7823-5
- Hawaii For Dummies
  0-7645-7402-7

- Italy For Dummies
  0-7645-7386-1
- Las Vegas For Dummies
  0-7645-7382-9
- London For Dummies
  0-7645-4277-X
- Paris For Dummies
  0-7645-7630-5
- RV Vacations For Dummies
  0-7645-4442-X
- Walt Disney World & Orlando
  For Dummies
  0-7645-9660-8

GRAPHICS, DESIGN & WEB DEVELOPMENT

0-7645-8815-X

0-7645-9571-7

Also available:
- 3D Game Animation For Dummies
  0-7645-8789-7
- AutoCAD 2006 For Dummies
  0-7645-8925-3
- Building a Web Site For Dummies
  0-7645-7144-3
- Creating Web Pages For Dummies
  0-470-08030-2
- Creating Web Pages All-in-One Desk
  Reference For Dummies
  0-7645-4345-8
- Dreamweaver 8 For Dummies
  0-7645-9649-7

- InDesign CS2 For Dummies
  0-7645-9572-5
- Macromedia Flash 8 For Dummies
  0-7645-9691-8
- Photoshop CS2 and Digital
  Photography For Dummies
  0-7645-9580-6
- Photoshop Elements 4 For Dummies
  0-471-77483-9
- Syndicating Web Sites with RSS Feeds
  For Dummies
  0-7645-8848-6
- Yahoo! SiteBuilder For Dummies
  0-7645-9800-7

NETWORKING, SECURITY, PROGRAMMING & DATABASES

0-7645-7728-X

0-471-74940-0

Also available:
- Access 2007 For Dummies
  0-470-04612-0
- ASP.NET 2 For Dummies
  0-7645-7907-X
- C# 2005 For Dummies
  0-7645-9704-3
- Hacking For Dummies
  0-470-05235-X
- Hacking Wireless Networks
  For Dummies
  0-7645-9730-2
- Java For Dummies
  0-470-08716-1

- Microsoft SQL Server 2005 For Dummies
  0-7645-7755-7
- Networking All-in-One Desk Reference
  For Dummies
  0-7645-9939-9
- Preventing Identity Theft For Dummies
  0-7645-7336-5
- Telecom For Dummies
  0-471-77085-X
- Visual Studio 2005 All-in-One Desk
  Reference For Dummies
  0-7645-9775-2
- XML For Dummies
  0-7645-8845-1

HEALTH & SELF-HELP

0-7645-8450-2   0-7645-4149-8

Also available:

Bipolar Disorder For Dummies
0-7645-8451-0

Chemotherapy and Radiation
For Dummies
0-7645-7832-4

Controlling Cholesterol For Dummies
0-7645-5440-9

Diabetes For Dummies
0-7645-6820-5* †

Divorce For Dummies
0-7645-8417-0 †

Fibromyalgia For Dummies
0-7645-5441-7

Low-Calorie Dieting For Dummies
0-7645-9905-4

Meditation For Dummies
0-471-77774-9

Osteoporosis For Dummies
0-7645-7621-6

Overcoming Anxiety For Dummies
0-7645-5447-6

Reiki For Dummies
0-7645-9907-0

Stress Management For Dummies
0-7645-5144-2

EDUCATION, HISTORY, REFERENCE & TEST PREPARATION

0-7645-8381-6   0-7645-9554-7

Also available:

The ACT For Dummies
0-7645-9652-7

Algebra For Dummies
0-7645-5325-9

Algebra Workbook For Dummies
0-7645-8467-7

Astronomy For Dummies
0-7645-8465-0

Calculus For Dummies
0-7645-2498-4

Chemistry For Dummies
0-7645-5430-1

Forensics For Dummies
0-7645-5580-4

Freemasons For Dummies
0-7645-9796-5

French For Dummies
0-7645-5193-0

Geometry For Dummies
0-7645-5324-0

Organic Chemistry I For Dummies
0-7645-6902-3

The SAT I For Dummies
0-7645-7193-1

Spanish For Dummies
0-7645-5194-9

Statistics For Dummies
0-7645-5423-9

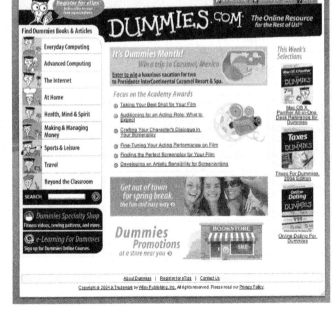

Get smart @ dummies.com®

- **Find a full list of Dummies titles**
- **Look into loads of FREE on-site articles**
- **Sign up for FREE eTips e-mailed to you weekly**
- **See what other products carry the Dummies name**
- **Shop directly from the Dummies bookstore**
- **Enter to win new prizes every month!**

* Separate Canadian edition also available
† Separate U.K. edition also available

Available wherever books are sold. For more information or to order direct: U.S. customers visit www.dummies.com or call 1-877-762-2974.
U.K. customers visit www.wileyeurope.com or call 0800 243407. Canadian customers visit www.wiley.ca or call 1-800-567-4797.